THE ALLEGIANCE PARADOX

Book One of *The Collapse of Trust* series

*Beyond the Law:
How Ethical Erosion and Policy Drift
Undermine American Citizenship*

Sebastian Saviano

STATERA PRESS

2025

The Allegiance Paradox

Beyond the Law: How Ethical Erosion and Policy Drift Undermine American Citizenship

© 2025 Sebastian Saviano

All rights reserved. No part of this book may be reproduced, stored in a retrieval system, or transmitted in any form or by any means—electronic, mechanical, photocopying, recording, or otherwise—without prior written permission from the publisher, except for brief quotations in critical reviews or articles.

This is Book One of The Collapse of Trust series.
(See full series listing on page xi.)

Published by **Statera Press**

ISBNs:
Hardcover: 979-8-9985117-1-4
Paperback: 979-8-9985117-4-5
e-Book: 979-8-9985117-7-6

Library of Congress Control Number (LCCN): 2025940193

For inquiries or permissions, visit:
www.SebastianSaviano.com

Printed in the United States of America and in select international locations.

This book is a work of historical research and informed analysis. While every effort has been made to ensure accuracy, the author and publisher assume no responsibility for errors, omissions, or any consequences arising from its use.

For Lisa Snyder, and for all like her, who loved this country enough to give their lives—
and for the silent majority who sense what has gone wrong, yet still believe citizenship must mean more.

Author's Note

Why I Wrote this Book

This book was born out of discomfort—a growing sense that something fundamental about American citizenship has been quietly unraveling. I see a nation where the meaning of allegiance, once a sacred civic ideal, has become fragmented—split between sacrifice and self-interest, obligation and opportunity.

At one end of the spectrum stand those who give their lives for the republic: young Americans, many of them immigrants, who wear the uniform and swear allegiance not as ceremony but as commitment. These Americans are often the first to serve, and too often the last to be acknowledged. Their loyalty is total. Their burden is real. Their contribution is immeasurable.

At the other end are those who treat American citizenship as a passport of convenience— a hedge, an asset, a transactional tool—securing U.S. birthright through birth tourism, golden visa programs, or legal loopholes. They flaunt their wealth in New York, Miami or Los Angeles, maintain loyalties elsewhere, and treat citizenship as a commodity, not an identity. Their relationship to the country is strategic, not civic. Their contribution, if any, is negligible.

In between are millions of American-born and naturalized dual citizens who must navigate the civic ambiguity and ethical tension of divided allegiance—holding rights in one nation while exercising influence in another. Alongside them stand the institutions that have permitted this drift: federal agencies and courts that have blurred the line between pluralism and divided loyalty. And at the helm are legislators and elected officials who, at times, struggle to define or promote—let alone embody—what allegiance actually means.

We have built a system where some citizens die for the republic—and others merely purchase their way into it. And we have done so without debate, without clarity, and without the honesty this moment demands.

This book is my attempt to confront that silence. It is a call to reclaim what citizenship was always meant to be: not a convenience, but a commitment.

It also marks the beginning of a broader inquiry. *The Allegiance Paradox* is the first book in *The Collapse of Trust* series, a four-part exploration of how public belief in institutions falters—from the erosion of allegiance and the rise of conspiratorial thinking, to the performative nature of legitimacy and the quiet replacement of human judgment by systems and code *(see page xi)*.

Sebastian Saviano
September 17, 2025
Released on Citizenship Day

Table of Contents

Prelude - A Paradoxical Allegiance 1
Introduction - The Meaning of Citizenship in Crisis 3
Chapter 1 - Undivided by Design 7
    I. Citizenship as Allegiance, Not Inheritance 8
    II. Naturalization and the Immigrant Ideal 11
    III. The 19th Century: Migration and Suspicion 14
    IV. Foundations of Exclusive Allegiance 18
    V. Special Spotlight: Citizenship as Commodity 21
    VI. From Civic Duty to Citizenship by Convenience 24
    Conclusion: Reclaiming Allegiance 27
Chapter 2 - Legal Ambiguity and Policy Drift 30
    I. The Genesis of Allegiance: America's Radical Citizenship Principle 31
    II. Key Legal Turning Points and Judicial Drift 33
    III. Bureaucratic Policy vs. Statutory Silence 37
    IV. The Practical Consequences of Legal Ambiguity 40
    V. Case Studies in Dual Allegiance 44
    VI. Toward Clarity: The Case for Reform 48
    Conclusion: Citizenship Without Coherence 51
Chapter 3 - How Other Nations Handle It 53
    I. Citizenship as Policy, Not Accident 54
    II. Models of Citizenship Management 58
    III. Emerging Global Trends 65
    IV. Administrative Systems and Enforcement 70
    V. Special Spotlight: The Rise of Golden Passports 74
    VI. Lessons for American Policy 77
    Conclusion: American Exceptionalism or Evasion? 80
Chapter 4 - The Ethics of Allegiance 81
    I. What Does It Mean to Belong? 83
    II. Philosophical Foundations of Allegiance 85
    III. Civic Erosion in a Dual-Allegiance Regime 90
    IV. The Fragile Fabric of Democratic Trust 94
    V. Ethical Blind Spots in a Globalized World 98
    VI. Rethinking Allegiance in a Pluralist Society 100
    Conclusion: Allegiance as an Ethical Horizon 102
Legal Report - Accountability in the Extradition Era 105
Chapter 5 - The Consequences of Policy Drift 111
    I. Citizenship in Action 112
    II. Military Service and Government Roles 114
    III. Voting and Political Influence 116

    IV. Taxation and Financial Compliance..118
    V. Legal Conflicts and Jurisdictional Tensions 121
    VI. The Case for Clarity...125
    Conclusion: Rebuilding the Civic Frame 128
Chapter 6 - Citizenship for Sale 130
    I. Citizenship at the Crossroads of Law and Loyalty 131
    II. Birth Tourism: Exploiting a Constitutional Guarantee......................133
    III. Industry Profile: The Business of Birthright 135
    IV. Born American, Raised Elsewhere: Two Profiles............................138
    V. Legal and Constitutional Context 140
    VI. Ethical and Philosophical Dimensions...141
    VII. How Others Handle Birthright Citizenship....................................143
    VIII. Civic Implications of Stateless Integration 146
    IX. Fixing the Gaps in Our Citizenship System 148
    Conclusion: Citizenship Must Mean More Than Geography....................151
Chapter 7 - Reclaiming the Civic Contract...153
    I. The Meaning of Allegiance in a Liberal Democracy 153
    II. What's Broken: The Erosion of the Civic Contract 155
    III. Legislative and Policy Solutions 158
    IV. Civic Education and Cultural Renewal..160
    V. Spotlight Case: A Civic Contract for the Next Generation 160
    VI. Tiered Legislative and Reform Strategy 163
    VII. Loyalty and Liberty Can Coexist...165
    Conclusion: Citizenship with Meaning..166
Chapter 8 - Belonging in the Digital Age 168
    I. Citizenship on the Edge of Transformation.......................................169
    II. Digital Nomads, Remote Work, and "Sovereignty Shopping"..............171
    III. Platforms, Networks, and the Illusion of Community 173
    IV. Blockchain Governance and the Mirage of Stateless Freedom............174
    V. Digital Identity in an Age of Geopolitical Contest 178
    VI. Reclaiming Allegiance in a Networked Republic 181
    Conclusion: Citizenship in a Disrupted Age — Adaptive, Not Liquid 183
Chapter 9 - Rebuilding the Civic Contract...184
    I. From Drift to Deliberation 185
    II. Clear Rules for Loyalty in Public Service..186
    III. Reforming Dual Citizenship in Security Roles................................187
    IV. Redefining Birthright Through Parental Jurisdiction......................192
    V. Tracking Dual Citizenship in a Digital Age.......................................192
    VI. Linking Civic Education to Citizenship 194
    VII. Modernizing the Oath of Allegiance and Naturalization.....................196
    VIII. Future Horizons: Citizenship in a Global Age 198
    IX. Summary & Implementation Roadmap 199

Conclusion 199
Conclusion - Reclaiming the Meaning of Citizenship 201
Afterword - To Bind the Nation's Wounds 203
Glossary of Key Terms 205
Appendix A - The Emancipation Proclamation (1863) 209
    A concise chronology of key laws, court rulings, and policy shifts shaping American citizenship from the Fourteenth Amendment to recent reforms and controversies.
Appendix B - Foundational Texts of American Allegiance 211
    An overview of how other democracies manage dual citizenship, allegiance, and civic coherence—featuring models from Germany, France, Canada, India, and more.
Appendix C - Political and Philosophical Sources 213
    An analysis of constitutional precedent, executive orders, and litigation surrounding birthright citizenship—arguing that reform likely requires a constitutional amendment.
Appendix D - Citizenship in Practice and Controversy 215
    A philosophical reflection on citizenship, responsibility, and democratic trust—drawing from key political thinkers to ground allegiance in civic ethics.
Appendix E - Contemporary Debates and Practices 217
    Outlines potential statutory and constitutional pathways to modernize U.S. citizenship law, including short-, medium-, and long-term strategies for policymakers.
Appendix F - Civic Observances & Legal Foundations of Citizenship 219
    Explores how civic education, the naturalization process, and public affirmations of allegiance can reinforce the meaning and responsibilities of citizenship.
Appendix G - Birthright Citizenship and the Future of *Jus Soli* 227
    Synthesizes legal scholarship and recent court rulings to examine whether birthright citizenship can be restricted without a constitutional amendment.
Bibliograhy (by chpater) 232
Index 232
About the Author 247

THE COLLAPSE OF TRUST SERIES

A four-volume investigation into the fracturing of civic allegiance, institutional credibility, and cultural coherence in American democracy. Rather than claiming the collapse of the American republic, the series traces a quieter unraveling—legitimacy strained by ethical drift, symbolic governance, epistemic distortion, and the recursive performance of trust itself. At once diagnostic and synthetic, the series culminates in *The Collapse of Trust*, a capstone work that integrates the foundational arguments of the preceding books:

Book One – *The Allegiance Paradox*
Beyond the Law: How Ethical Erosion and Policy Drift Undermine American Citizenship
(2025)

Book Two – *Legitimate Distrust*
Why Conspiracy Theories Grow When Institutions Fail
(2026)

Book Three – *The Theater of Trust*
The Performance of Legitimacy in a World of Institutional Doubt
(2026)

Book Four – *Overruling Common Sense*
How Rules, Code, and Institutions Are Replacing Human Judgment
(2027)

Learn more at:
www.SebastianSaviano.com

In the humble corners of America, the weight of belonging is still borne quietly—but with unwavering resolve.
— from The Allegiance Paradox

Prelude

A Paradoxical Allegiance

O**ver 1.3 million Americans have given their lives in service** to the republic and the ideals for which it stands.[1] Their service was never transactional. It rested on the belief that citizenship bound people together through shared obligations as well as rights.

Today, the meaning of that bond is less certain. For some, citizenship functions more as a global credential than as a shared civic identity—detached from the mutual duties that once defined it.

> **This is the Allegiance Paradox**:
> The American system demands unity while permitting division.
> It relies on allegiance it no longer ensures.

---

[1] Based on figures compiled by the U.S. Department of Defense, the Congressional Research Service, and the National Archives, more than 1.3 million Americans have died in military service since the founding of the republic. This includes approximately 4,400 in the Revolutionary War; 2,200 in the War of 1812; over 13,000 in the Mexican-American War; between 620,000 and 750,000 in the Civil War; 2,400 in the Spanish-American War; 116,500 in World War I; 405,000 in World War II; 36,500 in Korea; 58,000 in Vietnam; 294 in the Gulf War; over 6,800 in Iraq and Afghanistan; and thousands more in post-9/11 operations. These numbers represent uniformed personnel killed in action or service-related death and do not include civilian contractors or post-service fatalities due to injury or suicide.

From its founding, the United States envisioned itself not as an ethnic nation, but a civic one—bound not by bloodlines, but by shared commitment to a constitutional republic. And for much of its history, that vision included a serious expectation: that citizenship be chosen freely, and that allegiance be exclusive.

From the Naturalization Act of 1790 to the Expatriation Act of 1868, American law insisted that to become a citizen was to renounce former loyalties and commit wholly to the new. This vision of undivided allegiance helped forge a common identity in a pluralistic republic. But a gradual erosion of that expectation has been underway for decades—and it has culminated in the 21st century.

Dual citizenship, legal ambiguity, and commodified paths to nationality have created a system in which individuals may hold multiple allegiances without ever being asked to reconcile them. The state no longer actively safeguards the expectations of citizenship, even as it depends on loyalty, sacrifice, and participation to sustain democratic life.

> If the civic bond of allegiance no longer defines American citizenship, what does?

This book begins with that question. It is not a call for cultural uniformity or political exclusion. It is a reckoning with the civic contradictions we've allowed to fester. It is an argument for restoring clarity, responsibility, and ethical coherence to the meaning of American citizenship.

Introduction

The Meaning of Citizenship in Crisis

> *"The most deadly adversaries of republican government may naturally be expected to spring from the desire in foreign powers to gain an improper ascendant in our councils."*
> — Alexander Hamilton, *Federalist No. 68* (1788)

In 2025, President Trump's proposed "Gold Card" investor visa reignited a long-dormant debate: can U.S. citizenship be bought? Almost simultaneously, indictments of Senators Menendez and Cuellar cast new light on the legal and ethical murk of dual loyalties in public office. And halfway across the world, Estonia's e-governance model and Silicon Valley's experiments with "network states" have begun to redefine what it even means to belong to a nation.

American citizenship, once a sacred bond between the individual and the nation, has quietly become negotiable. Today, it is possible—common, even—to hold two passports, swear allegiance to two sovereigns, vote in multiple elections, and enjoy the full rights and protections of U.S. citizenship while maintaining active loyalty to another state.

This is not a theoretical concern. It is the political and legal reality of our time. And yet, despite its far-reaching implications, the rise of dual citizenship in the United States has gone largely unexamined. There has been no national commission, no sustained debate, no public reckoning with its effects on trust, accountability, or democratic legitimacy.

> *What was once an unthinkable contradiction—divided allegiance—has become a tolerated norm.*

This book begins with a paradox: The United States, a nation founded on the idea of exclusive civic loyalty, now permits—and in many cases promotes—divided allegiance as a matter of routine. While some see this as a sign of openness or cosmopolitan progress, it comes at a cost: the erosion of civic meaning, the weakening of institutional trust, and the unraveling of the democratic contract.

The Civic Fabric, Unraveling

This is not merely a legal problem. It is a moral and cultural one. In a democratic republic, citizenship is not just a legal status—it is a public commitment. It entails both rights and responsibilities. Allegiance is what binds a diverse population into a coherent political community. When that allegiance becomes optional, diluted, or secondary, the democratic fabric begins to fray.

Can a republic function when some of its citizens vote in foreign elections, serve in foreign militaries, or shield themselves from American law with a second passport? Can it survive when others access its benefits without sharing in its burdens? When allegiance is severed from citizenship, democracy does not expand—it fractures.

A Nation That Forgot to Ask

Unlike many peer democracies—Germany, India, France, even Canada—the United States has no coherent dual citizenship policy. It is neither fully authorized nor fully prohibited. It exists in a legal gray zone: permitted by precedent, ignored by statute, and left to drift by courts and bureaucracies. Congress has remained silent. The result is confusion, inconsistency, and civic incoherence.

This silence is not neutrality. It is abandonment.

What This Book Argues

This book makes a simple but urgent claim: that allegiance must be reimagined not as mere loyalty or legal formality, but as ethical infrastructure—the foundational framework that sustains civic trust, institutional integrity, and democratic accountability. In a time of strategic dualism and mobility, restoring allegiance means reconstructing the very terms of political belonging—not to exclude, but to embed responsibility in status, and reciprocity in rights.

The Allegiance Paradox is not a call to wall off America. It is a call to rebuild its civic foundation—through principled reforms to naturalization, diplomatic law, dual allegiance in high-trust roles, and constitutional clarity. Beneath each policy stands a core idea: that citizenship without allegiance is not inclusion. It is dissolution.

How This Book Is Structured

- **Chapter 1** traces the historical foundations of exclusive allegiance in American citizenship law and political culture.
- **Chapter 2** examines how bureaucratic drift and judicial ambiguity allowed dual citizenship to expand unchallenged.
- **Chapter 3** compares how other nations address dual allegiance—and reveals America's lack of clarity as a global outlier.
- **Chapter 4** explores the ethical foundations of allegiance, drawing from political philosophy and democratic theory.
- **Chapter 5** shows how the erosion of allegiance disrupts key institutions: voting, the military, taxation, and public trust.
- **Chapter 6** explores birth tourism, investor visas, and the

commodification of citizenship as forms of civic distortion.
- **Chapter 7** lays out a civic renewal framework—reconnecting status with responsibility through legal and educational reforms.
- **Chapter 8** examines the digital transformation of citizenship and the rise of algorithmic and network-based identities.
- **Chapter 9** concludes with a forward-looking blueprint: restoring the coherence of American citizenship through institutional, constitutional, and cultural renewal.

A Time for Civic Reckoning

In a fragmented world, it is tempting to treat allegiance as outdated—an impediment to global citizenship. But this book contends the opposite: that allegiance is the ethical architecture of democracy. It is what turns paper rights into living obligations. It is what transforms a nation of strangers into a republic of shared fate.

> *We cannot legislate allegiance—but we can restore its place in law, in education, and in civic expectation. The future of American citizenship depends on whether we choose to do so.*

Chapter 1

Undivided by Design
Allegiance in a Nation of Immigrants

America has always been a nation of immigrants. From the Puritans to political refugees, and from laborers to entrepreneurs, the United States was forged not by a singular ethnic identity but by the ambitions and allegiances of those who arrived to build a new life. Yet this openness to newcomers was never unconditional. What made the American experiment unique was not just its welcome, but the nature of the civic bond it demanded in return.

Unlike Old World monarchies and empires, which gave citizenship through bloodlines and bound subjects to lifelong allegiance, the American republic rested on a radical idea: political belonging should be chosen. Citizenship was not inherited by ancestry or imposed by accident of birth. It was to be entered into willingly, through acts of consent, allegiance, and commitment to a shared constitutional project.

This chapter follows the rise of the idea that national allegiance should be exclusive. From the thinkers who influenced the Founders, to the early laws of naturalization, to the public rituals that welcomed new

Americans, the message was consistent: national identity was meant to be singular. To become American was to *be* American—fully, intentionally, and exclusively.

The Founders feared divided loyalties. Their writings reveal deep anxieties about foreign influence, inherited fealty, and the destabilizing effects of dual allegiances. In a diverse and pluralistic republic, what bound citizens together was not language or ancestry, but a shared civic identity anchored in undivided loyalty to the nation and its principles.

This expectation shaped not only immigration policy but the broader political culture. Oaths of allegiance, Americanization campaigns, and public rituals—from flag salutes to naturalization ceremonies—reflected a belief that democratic citizenship required more than legal status. It required emotional, ethical, and political belonging.

Yet in recent decades, this ethic has come under strain. The rise of dual citizenship, birth tourism, investor migration, and strategic naturalization reflects a profound shift in how citizenship is understood and practiced. What was once a solemn act of allegiance is increasingly treated as a convenience, a contingency, or an asset.

To understand how we arrived at this moment—and why it matters—we must begin where the American story of belonging begins: with a bold claim that citizenship is not a birthright of geography, nor an inheritance of blood, but a choice of allegiance.

I. Citizenship as Allegiance, Not Inheritance

The Revolutionary Reimagining of Belonging

In the summer of 1776, the American founders did something radical. They didn't just declare independence from Britain; they reimagined what it meant to belong to a nation. While European societies defined citizenship through bloodlines, aristocratic privilege, and inherited status, the nascent United States proposed a revolutionary alternative: citizenship as a deliberate choice, not an accident of birth.

Hamilton's Paradox: The Foreign-Born Nationalist

Few figures embody the paradox of allegiance and identity in American history more vividly than Alexander Hamilton. Born on the Caribbean island of Nevis, Hamilton was the only major Founding Father not born in the American colonies. Orphaned as a child, he emigrated to New York in his teens and rose—through intellect, ambition, and military service—to become a principal architect of the U.S. Constitution and the nation's first Secretary of the Treasury.

Despite being foreign-born, Hamilton was also one of the most forceful voices for national unity, centralized authority, and unambiguous civic allegiance. He distrusted divided loyalties and believed the survival of the Republic depended on clarity of commitment. Writing in *Federalist No. 68* (1788), Hamilton warned:

"The most deadly adversaries of republican government may naturally be expected to spring from the desire in foreign powers to gain an improper ascendant in our councils." [2]

Five years later, in the *Pacificus* essays (1793), Hamilton returned to this theme while defending Washington's Proclamation of Neutrality. There he stressed the dangers of factional attachments to foreign nations and the need to keep America free from imported rivalries.

This tension—between Hamilton's immigrant background and his fierce insistence on undivided loyalty—mirrors the very debates this book seeks to explore: What does it mean to belong to a nation? Can plural identity coexist with civic obligation? And where, in a republic, must the line be drawn?

Hamilton's story doesn't offer easy answers—but it does remind us that allegiance, while inclusive, must be rooted in responsibility and clarity.

---

[2] **Federalist No. 68**, published in March 1788 under the pseudonym "Publius," was written by Alexander Hamilton as part of the Federalist Papers. In this essay, Hamilton addressed the process of electing the president and the dangers of foreign influence. His warning about foreign powers seeking "an improper ascendant in our councils" reflected a broader concern with divided loyalties and external interference in the new Republic. The Federalist Papers, co-authored with James Madison and John Jay, became foundational arguments for ratifying the Constitution and remain central to American political thought. This theme reappeared five years later in the "Pacificus" essays (1793), where Hamilton, writing under that pseudonym, defended President Washington's Proclamation of Neutrality. In *Pacificus No. 1*, he emphasized executive authority in foreign affairs and cautioned against entanglement in European rivalries, particularly those driven by partisan attachments to foreign nations. Together, *Federalist No. 68* and the Pacificus–Helvidius debates reveal Hamilton's consistent anxiety about divided allegiances, foreign favoritism, and their corrosive effect on republican stability.

Drawing from Enlightenment philosophers like John Locke and Jean-Jacques Rousseau, as we shall see later, they conceived of national belonging as a social contract—a reciprocal relationship built on mutual consent, shared democratic ideals, and collective responsibility.

Against the backdrop of hereditary monarchies in 18th-century Europe, the American experiment offered a radical alternative: national identity based on consent, not birth.

Voices of a New Civic Identity

The writings of the founders reveal the depth of this transformative vision. Thomas Jefferson, in his characteristic intellectual boldness, argued that "the earth belongs in usufruct to the living"—a radical statement suggesting that no generation could bind future generations to perpetual political allegiances. This was more than a legal concept; it was a philosophical declaration of human agency and potential.

James Madison viewed citizenship as a nuanced social contract. In his perspective, allegiance was not a one-sided submission but a dynamic relationship of trust and shared purpose between individuals and their political community. Alexander Hamilton, as pointed out, took an even more pointed stance, warning repeatedly about the dangers of divided loyalties and foreign influences that could undermine the republic's unity.

The Practical Revolution: Consent over Inheritance

The Declaration of Independence's assertion that governments derive "their just powers from the consent of the governed" was revolutionary in its simplicity and profound in its implications. This was a fundamental reimagining of political legitimacy.

For immigrants and newcomers, this model meant citizenship was not a passive reception of status, but an active, intentional transformation. To become American was not a matter of paperwork, but a deliberate act of civic alignment—a choice to adopt shared values, engage in public life, and contribute to the democratic project.

Crucially, this vision of citizenship was exclusive. To become American meant fully embracing a new political identity, which necessitated renouncing previous allegiances. The republic could not sustain itself if citizens maintained competing political loyalties or treated citizenship as a mere convenience.

A Living Legacy

This founding principle—that citizenship is chosen, not inherited—to this day remains a powerful, if contested, ideal. It challenged the old world's hierarchical systems and proposed a radical notion: that political belonging could be based on shared values, mutual commitment, and collective aspiration, rather than accidents of birth.

As we navigate the complexities of 21st-century global mobility and transnational identities, the founders' vision continues to provoke critical questions about nationalism, belonging, and what it truly means to be a citizen.

II. Naturalization and the Immigrant Ideal

A Radical Legal Experiment

In the summer of 1790, the young United States Congress passed a law that would become a cornerstone of American identity—the Naturalization Act. At first glance, the act might seem unremarkable. But beneath its legal language lay a revolutionary concept that would reshape understanding of national belonging.

The law was undeniably flawed by modern standards. It explicitly limited citizenship to "free white persons," reflecting the deeply racist assumptions of its time. This racial exclusivity reveals a tension at the heart of the early republic: a universalist civic ideal constrained by a discriminatory legal framework.[3]

The Oath: A Symbolic Transformation

Imagine standing before a federal judge, raising your hand, and publicly declaring your commitment to a new nation. The Oath of Allegiance was more than a legal formality—it was a ritual of transformation. Immigrants were required to "absolutely and entirely renounce and abjure all allegiance and fidelity to any foreign prince, potentate, state, or sovereignty."

This was radical. In an era dominated by monarchies and imperial powers, the United States proposed a different model of political belonging. Citizenship was not a gift bestowed by a ruler, but a commitment voluntarily undertaken. The oath symbolized a profound personal and political metamorphosis.

Scholars like Rogers Brubaker have since analyzed this process as a unique form of "civic nationalism"—where national identity is defined by shared political values rather than ethnic or racial characteristics. Even as the specific racial limitations were deeply problematic, the underlying principle of voluntary allegiance was transformative.

Integration as Transformation

Early American society viewed naturalization as a holistic process of cultural and political integration. It wasn't enough to simply take an oath. Immigrants were expected to learn English, adopt American customs,

---

[3] **The 1790 Naturalization Act**'s racial limitation to "free white persons" excluded enslaved Africans, free Black Americans, Indigenous peoples, and non-European immigrants. These exclusions persisted in various legal forms until the mid-20th century, with key restrictions remaining in place until the 1940s and 1950s—most notably for Asian and Indigenous populations. This long arc of exclusion reveals how the ideals of civic nationalism were historically circumscribed by prevailing racial hierarchies. See Ian Haney López, *White by Law: The Legal Construction of Race* (New York: NYU Press, 2006), and Mae Ngai, *Impossible Subjects: Illegal Aliens and the Making of Modern America* (Princeton: Princeton University Press, 2004).

participate actively in civic life, and raise children who identified as fully American.

The cultural mantra "One flag, one nation" captured this expectation. It wasn't mere jingoism, but a vision of unity through voluntary commitment. In a republic built on pluralism, allegiance—not ancestry—was the binding force.

Comparative Perspectives

To understand the uniqueness of this approach, consider the global context. While many countries in that era rooted citizenship in lineage, royal authority, or ethnic identity, the United States offered a different vision: citizenship as an earned status and national identity as an act of choice.

This didn't mean erasing one's cultural heritage. Instead, it meant adding a layer of political commitment that transcended previous identities. The naturalized citizen wasn't expected to forget their origins but to embrace a new, additional identity with full conviction.

A Continuing Conversation

The Naturalization Act of 1790 was not an endpoint, but the beginning of an ongoing negotiation about what it means to belong. Its racist limitations would be challenged and gradually dismantled, but its core idea—that citizenship is a deliberate, transformative commitment—remains a powerful ideal.

As global migration increases and national boundaries become more fluid, the questions first posed by this early law remain urgent: What does it mean to truly belong to a nation? How do we balance respect for diverse origins with a shared commitment to collective ideals?

III. The 19th Century: Migration and Suspicion

The Great Demographic Upheaval

Between 1820 and 1900, nearly 19 million immigrants arrived in the United States, transforming its social fabric and reshaping national identity. Irish, German, and later Southern and Eastern European newcomers brought cultural traditions that would challenge—and ultimately redefine—what it meant to be "American."

Contested Belonging: The Immigrant Experience

Each wave of immigration triggered a complex social drama of inclusion and suspicion. The Irish, overwhelmingly Catholic, faced particularly intense scrutiny. Protestant America viewed them with deep suspicion, questioning their ultimate loyalty. Could a Catholic immigrant truly pledge allegiance to the U.S. Constitution when the Vatican was perceived as a foreign power seeking influence in American civic life?

German immigrants encountered similar challenges. Their commitment to preserving language and cultural institutions—maintaining German-language schools and cultural societies—was interpreted not as cultural preservation, but as potential subversion. They were viewed with suspicion for seemingly maintaining Old World identities rather than fully embracing American life.

Italian immigrants, arriving later in the century, faced their own set of challenges. They were often associated with anarchist movements or secret societies like the Black Hand,[4] further fueling nativist anxieties about divided loyalties and potential social disruption.

---

[4] **The Black Hand** was a loosely organized criminal network associated with extortion and violence among Italian immigrant communities in the early 20th century. Its activities—often sensationalized in the press—fueled fears of foreign conspiracies. Simultaneously, anarchist movements, especially after events like the 1901 assassination of President McKinley by anarchist Leon Czolgosz, a 28-year-old American of Polish descent, were often linked in the public imagination to Italian and Eastern European immigrants, despite the political diversity within those communities.

The Anatomy of Nativist Fear

These tensions weren't mere xenophobic panic—they exposed fundamental questions about national identity and civic cohesion. Could a republic built on voluntary allegiance absorb such diverse populations without diluting its core political identity?

The rise of the Know-Nothing Party[5] in the 1850s represented a political manifestation of these anxieties. With a platform focused on restricting immigrant rights and enforcing stricter naturalization requirements, the party captured the deep-seated fears of a changing national landscape. Even Abraham Lincoln, while defending immigration, acknowledged the delicate balance: a diverse republic could only survive through a shared political loyalty.

Despite the nativist backlash, the federal government's response was nuanced. Rather than closing its doors, it sought to reinforce the terms of national membership. The underlying message was clear: allegiance to the United States must be singular, overt, and demonstrable. The price of inclusion was undivided loyalty.

The Expatriation Act of 1868: A Statement of Civic Sovereignty

The Expatriation Act of 1868 emerged as a pivotal moment in this ongoing negotiation of belonging. Passed in the immediate aftermath of the Civil War, the law declared that "the right of expatriation is a natural and inherent right of all people"—a deceptively simple statement with profound implications.

This was a direct challenge to European monarchies—particularly Britain, Prussia, and Austria—that maintained the doctrine of perpetual allegiance. These powers routinely harassed naturalized American citizens, claiming that once a subject, always a subject. In some cases,

---

[5] **The Know-Nothing Party**, a mid-19th century nativist movement, was formally known as the American Party and was characterized by its anti-immigrant and anti-Catholic rhetoric.

U.S. citizens were conscripted or imprisoned abroad, based on the claim that they could not legally renounce their former loyalties.

By declaring expatriation a natural right, the United States sent an unambiguous signal: American citizenship was voluntary and exclusive. The law affirmed that Americans could renounce their citizenship, but more crucially, that new Americans were expected to abandon all prior political allegiances. Citizenship was not a layered identity, but a binary civic condition—one could be American, or something else, but not both.

This principle was soon exported through a series of bilateral agreements—known as the Bancroft Treaties—which secured international recognition of the American view that allegiance could be renounced and citizenship voluntarily chosen.[6]

The Civil War: Allegiance Tested in Practice

No event more forcefully tested the idea of exclusive national loyalty than the Civil War. The conflict exposed the fragility of political allegiance and raised fundamental questions: Who counts as a citizen? What do they owe the nation? Can allegiance be split between competing sovereignties?

The Union's response was unambiguous. Naturalization became a precondition for immigrants wishing to fight, transforming the act of becoming a citizen into a moral and legal imperative. By the war's end, more than 200,000 foreign-born soldiers had served in the Union

---

[6] **The Bancroft Treaties**, negotiated primarily by American diplomat George Bancroft in the late 1860s and 1870s, established mutual recognition between the U.S. and various European powers (including the German Empire, Bavaria, Baden, Württemberg, and others) that citizenship could be voluntarily renounced and was not perpetual. These treaties marked a turning point in transatlantic legal norms surrounding nationality and allegiance. See: Frederick Van Dyne, *Citizenship of the United States* (Washington, D.C.: U.S. Government Printing Office, 1904), 162–178.

Army—many naturalized just prior to or during their military service.

This was far more than a procedural formality. Naturalization and military service became intertwined acts of civic affirmation. To take up arms for the Union was to declare oneself American—and only American.

The Reconstruction Amendments[7] extended the concept of civic allegiance by redefining American citizenship in more inclusive and egalitarian terms. The 14th Amendment, in particular, marked a transformative moment: it granted citizenship to all persons born or naturalized in the United States, thereby overturning *Dred Scott v. Sandford*[8] and affirming the principle of national belonging beyond race or prior servitude. Yet even in this expanded vision, allegiance was conceived as singular and indivisible. The clause "subject to the jurisdiction thereof" underscored that citizenship entailed not just legal recognition, but a binding civic relationship[9]—one rooted in exclusive loyalty to the United States and its constitutional order.

---

[7] **The Reconstruction Amendments** refer to the 13th, 14th, and 15th Amendments to the U.S. Constitution, ratified between 1865 and 1870. Together, they abolished slavery, established birthright citizenship and equal protection under the law, and prohibited racial discrimination in voting rights.

[8] ***Dred Scott v. Sandford***, 60 U.S. (19 How.) 393 (1857), held that African Americans, whether enslaved or free, could not be citizens of the United States and had no standing to sue in federal court. This decision was effectively overturned by the 14th Amendment in 1868, which established birthright citizenship and enshrined equal protection under the law—marking a constitutional repudiation of the racial exclusion embedded in the *Dred Scott* ruling.

[9] **"Subject to the jurisdiction thereof,"** the phrase in the Fourteenth Amendment, originally established exclusive political allegiance, explicitly excluding diplomats, foreign officials, and Native Americans under tribal governance from automatic birthright citizenship. Contemporary debates often reinterpret this clause more broadly or narrowly than its original meaning. For historical context, see Martha S. Jones, *Birthright Citizens: A History of Race and Rights in Antebellum America* (Cambridge: Cambridge University Press, 2018), 11–16; Akhil Reed Amar, *America's Constitution: A Biography* (New York: Random House, 2005), 380–385.

Institutionalizing Allegiance

By the 19th century's end, the legal and cultural architecture of American citizenship was firmly established. The United States welcomed immigrants—but on the condition that they integrate into the civic fabric. Dual allegiance was not merely discouraged; it was seen as incompatible with the principles of a unified democratic society.

The republic had room for many backgrounds, languages, and faiths—but not for multiple political loyalties. This assumption would begin to fray in the 20th century, as global mobility increased and legal precedents softened.

But in the 19th century, the core ideal remained clear: allegiance to America must be singular, total, and real.

IV. Foundations of Exclusive Allegiance

The Unifying Promise of Citizenship

In a nation as vast and pluralistic as the United States, the concept of citizenship has always functioned as a unifying force. While Americans may differ in ancestry, language, faith, and culture, what has historically bound them together is a shared civic identity—an allegiance not to a monarch or ethnicity, but to a Constitution and a set of democratic ideals.

"A firm union will be of the utmost moment to the peace and liberty of the States... against foreign influence and corruption," warned Alexander Hamilton in *Federalist No. 68*. For the Founders, unity of purpose—not sameness of background—was the bedrock of the American project. This model of citizenship sought to transcend division. It did not erase diversity, but demanded that—amidst that diversity—there be one allegiance. The republic they envisioned was held together not by bloodline, but by belief: belief in a common set of rights and responsibilities that apply to all, and in a mutual obligation to the republic that guarantees them.

Immigrant Success Stories as Arguments for Integration

Throughout American history, the assimilation of immigrants into this civic framework was celebrated as a central democratic virtue. Immigrants were not just welcomed; they were invited to transform—to shed old loyalties and adopt a new identity as Americans. This transformation was not expected to erase cultural heritage, but it did require a clear and primary allegiance to the United States.

American identity was thus built on a profound political idea: that one could become American—not by birth alone, but by choice, commitment, and shared allegiance. The great success stories of American immigration—from Andrew Carnegie to Albert Einstein—were framed as allegorical proof that one could arrive as an outsider and become fully American by pledging loyalty to the nation and engaging in its civic life.

This narrative flourished most powerfully under the "melting pot" metaphor, which emphasized integration over pluralism. While critics later advanced the "mosaic" model to emphasize multicultural preservation, even these perspectives acknowledged the central civic expectation: allegiance to the U.S. had to supersede ties to any other nation.

Civic Education and National Symbols

The ideological commitment to singular allegiance was reinforced through education, rituals, and symbols that cultivated a shared civic consciousness. From early 1900s Americanization programs to Cold War-era civics curricula, schools became key arenas for shaping the identity of future citizens—immigrant and native-born alike.

Pledging allegiance to the flag became a daily ritual in public schools not merely as a patriotic exercise, but as an affirmation of undivided national loyalty. The ritual itself originated in 1892, authored by Francis Bellamy as part of a national effort to inculcate civic unity during the 400th anniversary of Columbus's voyage. From its inception, the Pledge of Allegiance was designed not just to express patriotism but to symbolically reinforce the singular, unbreakable bond between citizen and nation.[10] Naturalization ceremonies, conducted under the American flag and accompanied by oaths of exclusive allegiance, were designed to mark a transformative break with the past—one identity left behind, another fully embraced.

During World Wars I and II, civic education intensified. Immigrant loyalty was publicly affirmed through Liberty Bond drives,[11] military enlistment, and community pledges. Those who failed to demonstrate sufficient patriotic engagement often faced suspicion, scrutiny, or worse. While at times excessive, these pressures reflected a widespread belief that citizenship was moral alignment with the republic.

Even popular culture reinforced the ideal of singular allegiance. From wartime posters urging "Remember, you're an American" to schoolbook tales of Ellis Island renunciations, the civic imagination was populated with stories of immigrants becoming Americans in heart, mind, and duty.

The Tension Resurfaces

Today, in an age of global mobility, plural identities, and transnational ties, this foundational model of citizenship is under pressure. The rituals

---

[10] **The Pledge of Allegiance** was originally written in 1892 by Francis Bellamy, a Baptist minister and Christian socialist, for a school ceremony commemorating Columbus Day. Its early adoption was supported by the National Education Association and youth publications like *The Youth's Companion*, aiming to promote national unity amid rising immigration and regional division. See Richard J. Ellis, *To the Flag: The Unlikely History of the Pledge of Allegiance* (Lawrence: University Press of Kansas, 2005).

[11] **Liberty Bond** drives were nationwide campaigns organized by the U.S. Treasury during World War I and II to finance the war through public investment in government bonds. Marketed as a civic duty, the drives used patriotic imagery, celebrity endorsements, and school programs to encourage participation across all demographics. Immigrants were especially encouraged to purchase bonds as a public affirmation of loyalty to the United States. For more, see James J. Kimble, *Mobilizing the Home Front: War Bonds and Domestic Propaganda* (College Station: Texas A&M University Press, 2006).

remain—naturalization oaths, flag salutes, national holidays—but the assumption of exclusive allegiance has weakened. Dual and multiple citizenships are often regarded as pragmatic rather than problematic, and assimilation is increasingly seen as optional rather than essential.

Yet the ideological framework laid down by the Founders remains vital to democratic cohesion. The civic glue of allegiance—once taught, expected, and celebrated—cannot be quietly dissolved without consequence. When citizenship loses its exclusivity, it risks losing its capacity to unify.

V. Special Spotlight: Citizenship as Commodity

From Civic Ideal to Geopolitical Commodity

In the twilight of the 20th century and the dawn of the 21st, a profound metamorphosis occurred in the understanding of American citizenship. What was once conceived as a sacred civic bond—a deliberate commitment to shared democratic ideals—has increasingly been recast as a strategic asset, a geopolitical instrument to be acquired, leveraged, and strategically deployed.

This transformation signals a fundamental reimagining of national belonging. Citizenship is no longer primarily understood through the lens of identity, allegiance, or shared responsibility. Instead, it has become a form of commodification, of global arbitrage—an investment in optionality, a hedge against uncertainty, a passport to potential opportunities.

A Glimpse at Birth Tourism

Birth tourism represents the clearest (and most controversial) example of this commodification. Each year, tens of thousands of foreign nationals travel to the United States specifically to give birth, thus securing U.S. citizenship for their children under the 14th Amendment.

Countries such as China, Russia, and Nigeria are among the top sources, with entire industries catering to this form of passport acquisition.

Birth tourism is not just a legal loophole; it marks a symbolic inflection point in the shifting meaning of citizenship. The very amendment meant to guarantee dignity and equality to formerly enslaved people has, in practice, become a legal mechanism for global mobility engineering.

We return to this topic in Chapter 6, where birth tourism is examined in greater depth—as both a policy challenge and a case study in the broader redefinition of what citizenship means in a globalized age.

The Global Marketplace of Citizenship

Birth tourism is just one expression of a broader, global shift: the growing commodification of citizenship. Around the world, nations have adopted "golden passport" and "citizenship-by-investment" programs that frame national membership as a premium asset—a transactional benefit rather than a civic bond.

The United States has long participated in this trend through the EB-5 Immigrant Investor Program, which offers a pathway to permanent residency—and eventual citizenship—for foreign nationals who invest $800,000 or more in approved U.S. businesses. Though not a direct sale, the EB-5 program allows financial capital to stand in for civic integration, effectively decoupling citizenship from cultural or political commitment.

That logic may soon be taken to new extremes. In 2025, President Donald Trump proposed a bold plan to create a "gold card" visa priced at $5 million, targeting wealthy foreign investors. While specifics remain limited, the program was framed as a revenue-generating tool that could replace the EB-5 system and potentially offer a path to citizenship. Trump suggested that selling even a fraction of these cards could yield trillions in federal revenue. Yet the plan, as articulated, includes no clear civic vetting requirements, no obligation to participate in democratic life, and no clear path for cultural integration.

The proposal echoes similar "golden visa" schemes in places like Malta, Cyprus, and Turkey, where financial elites acquire citizenship with minimal engagement beyond the transaction. What once symbolized a civic allegiance is now marketed as a luxury credential—citizenship not as responsibility, but as portfolio diversification.

Citizenship as Global Insurance Policy

For the global elite, U.S. citizenship has become a sophisticated form of contingency planning. It offers geopolitical shelter, economic opportunities, and legal protections—without demanding emotional or cultural engagement.

The American passport transforms from a symbol of national identity to a diversification strategy. It becomes a hedge against political instability, economic volatility, or personal legal complications. Allegiance is rendered optional, replaced by a purely instrumental calculus of potential utility.

Theoretical and Ethical Implications

This commodification, beyond representing a legal or economic shift, fundamentally challenges the philosophical foundations of democratic citizenship. The consequences extend beyond individual transactions. When citizenship can be purchased rather than earned through trust, participation, and genuine commitment, it loses its capacity to function as a binding social force.

Children born through birth tourism may never reside in the United States. Wealthy investors might hold U.S. passports without ever engaging with American civic life. In both scenarios, citizenship is acquired without the corresponding assumption of duty or moral investment.

A Cultural Warning Sign

This transformation is not merely a technical legal concern but a profound cultural signal. It indicates a loss of confidence in the very idea that citizenship entails responsibilities alongside rights.

The civic glue that has historically held the American republic together cannot be bought, inherited, or arbitraged. It must be consciously chosen, deeply understood, and sincerely lived.

As we move forward, the challenge becomes clear: How can we reclaim the meaning of citizenship in an age of global mobility and transactional belonging? The chapters ahead will explore this critical question, examining how legal ambiguity and cultural drift have allowed this erosion of allegiance—and why recovering a meaningful conception of citizenship is essential to preserving democratic society.

VI. From Civic Duty to Citizenship by Convenience

The erosion of the allegiance norm is not a sudden rupture, but a slow, systemic drift. Global mobility, transnational economic networks, and evolving legal interpretations have conspired to fundamentally reshape the meaning of national belonging. Dual citizenship, once viewed with deep suspicion, has become not just acceptable but increasingly normative.

Theoretical Foundations of the Shift

This transformation is more than a legal technicality. It represents a fundamental reimagining of political identity. Where once citizenship demanded a clear, unambiguous commitment, it now operates more like a portfolio of rights and opportunities—a strategic asset to be managed rather than a moral obligation to be fulfilled.

These theoretical shifts in how citizenship is understood—no longer as an exclusive identity but as a flexible portfolio of entitlements—did not occur in isolation. They were gradually mirrored, reinforced, and codified by the American legal system itself. Beginning in the mid-20th century, a series of landmark court decisions, policy changes, and administrative reinterpretations began to dismantle the legal infrastructure of exclusive allegiance. In effect, the judiciary and executive branch did not just follow cultural shifts—they institutionalized them, embedding this new model of divided loyalty into the very architecture of American citizenship law.

The Legal Landscape of Divided Loyalty

The judicial system played a crucial role in this metamorphosis. Landmark cases gradually chipped away at the principle of exclusive allegiance. The Supreme Court's 1967 decision in *Afroyim v. Rusk* was particularly pivotal, effectively preventing the government from involuntarily stripping citizenship from individuals who acquired foreign nationality.

Just over a decade later, the Court revisited the question of intent in *Vance v. Terrazas* (1980), a case that further complicated the landscape. While reaffirming that U.S. citizenship could not be revoked without evidence of voluntary renunciation, the Court held that dual nationality in itself did not prove disloyalty. The decision introduced a more nuanced interpretation of "intent," making it harder for the government to enforce exclusive allegiance in practice. It signaled a broader cultural and legal shift: allegiance was no longer presumed to be singular.

Subsequent court decisions and administrative policies further normalized dual citizenship. What was once a potential grounds for expatriation became a routine bureaucratic procedure. Naturalization ceremonies began to treat oaths of allegiance as procedural formalities rather than profound moral commitments.[12]

---

[12] See U.S. Immigration and Naturalization Service, *A Guide to Naturalization*, rev. ed. (Washington, D.C.: U.S. Government Printing Office, 1955), 4–6. The guide instructed that "the new citizen owes full allegiance to the United States and must sever ties to all foreign sovereignties." See also Erika Lee, *America for Americans: A History of Xenophobia in the United States* (New York: Basic Books, 2019), 173–175, on Americanization campaigns during the World Wars and mid-century loyalty oaths as tools to enforce ideological unity.

Before the 1960s, the oath of allegiance was not merely symbolic. Immigration officials, consular officers, and even the Department of Justice treated dual allegiance as grounds for denaturalization. Acts such as voting in a foreign election or serving in a foreign military could result in automatic loss of citizenship under the Nationality Acts of 1907 and 1940. Cultural norms reflected this legal stance: immigrants were expected to shed old loyalties, and naturalization was treated as a full and final civic transformation.

These legal and bureaucratic shifts did more than change policy—they laid the foundation for a new cultural logic. As exclusive allegiance lost its legal enforcement and symbolic weight. Over time, the act of acquiring and holding multiple nationalities became less about belonging—and more about leverage. This legal liberalization helped enable the emergence of what we might now call a global marketplace for citizenship, where nationality can be optimized, exchanged, and accumulated.

The Global Citizenship Marketplace

As we will see in detail in later chapters, this shift is not merely theoretical. According to the U.S. State Department, millions of Americans now hold multiple citizenships. The number of dual citizens has grown exponentially, reflecting a broader cultural acceptance of fluid national identities.

The implications for democratic governance are profound. A constitutional democracy relies on more than legal frameworks—it depends on a shared ethical commitment, a sense of mutual obligation that transcends individual interests.

When citizenship becomes transactional, the moral foundations of collective action begin to erode. If individuals can strategically exit or hedge their national commitments, what remains of the social contract? The expectation of sacrifice—whether through military service, jury duty, or civic participation—becomes increasingly tenuous.

Philosophical and Ethical Tensions

Can a democracy sustain itself when some members hold legal ties to multiple sovereigns? What happens to the concept of civic trust when allegiance becomes a matter of convenience rather than conviction?

The risks are not merely hypothetical. In moments of international tension or conflict, dual citizens may find themselves navigating complex, potentially contradictory loyalties. The state loses its ability to demand unambiguous commitment—a fundamental erosion of democratic cohesion.

A Cultural Warning Sign

This transformation reflects a deeper cultural drift—a growing cynicism about collective responsibility, a prioritization of individual opportunity over shared civic duty.

The republic has always depended on citizens who are willing to subordinate personal interests to collective well-being. But in an age of citizenship-as-convenience, that willingness is increasingly rare.

Conclusion: Reclaiming Allegiance

As we move forward, the challenge becomes clear: How can a democratic society sustain its foundational commitments in an era of fluid national identities? The chapters ahead will explore this critical question, examining the legal, cultural, and philosophical dimensions of this profound transformation.

The stakes are nothing less than the future of democratic citizenship itself.

Immigration Is Not the Issue—Allegiance Is

The United States has always been a nation shaped—and reshaped—by immigrants. From the earliest settlers to today's global arrivals, its vitality has come from those who chose to make this country their home. But that choice has historically come with an expectation: that to become American is to enter into a singular and unambiguous civic relationship with the republic.

That expectation is eroding.

In an age of dual citizenship, investor migration, and birth tourism, American citizenship is no longer assumed to signify exclusive loyalty or moral commitment. What was once treated as a civic covenant—a reciprocal bond of duty and belonging—is increasingly seen as a convenience, a contingency plan, or a tradable asset.

From Covenant to Commodity

U.S. citizenship has undergone a quiet transformation—from a solemn act of allegiance into a flexible strategy of personal mobility. That transformation has profound consequences. When allegiance becomes optional and plural, the social contract weakens. When citizenship becomes an investment vehicle or an insurance policy, it loses its moral content.

The central question we now face is not whether to welcome newcomers. It is whether we still believe that citizenship—true, meaningful citizenship—demands exclusive civic commitment. Can we ask, let alone expect, that allegiance to the United States be primary, enduring, and whole?

Preview of What Follows

The chapters ahead trace how this erosion took root—through legal ambiguity, administrative drift, and a cultural redefinition of citizenship itself. Drawing from historical precedent, comparative systems, political theory, and real-world case studies, this book examines how America lost sight of one of its founding principles: that citizenship is not inherited by accident, purchased by capital, or layered across sovereigns, but chosen, earned, and lived with fidelity.

This is not an anti-immigrant argument. It is a pro-citizen argument.

It is a call to restore the civic architecture of allegiance—not as a relic of the past, but as a precondition for a democratic future. In a world of divided loyalties, America must once again ask of its citizens what every republic requires: undivided allegiance.

Chapter 2

Legal Ambiguity and Policy Drift

In modern law and bureaucracy, citizenship has become less a clear threshold than a shifting category—administered without urgency, interpreted without consensus. While the moral stakes of allegiance were outlined in Chapter 1, this chapter traces the legal, administrative, and institutional blurring that has allowed divided loyalties to become normalized, even routine.

Consider the arc of this transformation: In 1868, the Expatriation Act boldly declared that allegiance was a matter of individual choice, not inherited obligation. Citizens could—and should—voluntarily shed old loyalties. By the early 21st century, that same principle of choice has morphed into something unrecognizable. Dual citizenship is no longer an exceptional circumstance, but an administrative footnote. Foreign allegiances that would once have been considered disqualifying are now processed with bureaucratic indifference.

The stakes of this shift extend far beyond legal technicality. This ambiguity now permeates critical domains of national life:

- Military service and security clearances

- Diplomatic representation
- Tax obligations
- Civic education
- National security protocols

With each administrative decision, each court ruling, the fundamental question grows more urgent: Can a republic truly function when its most fundamental membership—citizenship itself—lacks clear definition?

This chapter traces a profound legal mutation. It is a story of how a robust, principled concept of citizenship gradually eroded—not through dramatic conflict, but through a thousand small compromises. From the bold declarations of 19th-century lawmakers to the passive tolerance of 21st-century bureaucracies, we will follow the path of this transformation.

Our journey begins not with today's confusion, but with the crystalline legal clarity that once defined American civic identity.

We will map how a doctrine central to national belonging became an unspoken casualty of judicial caution and administrative convenience.

I. The Genesis of Allegiance: America's Radical Citizenship Principle

In the aftermath of revolution and civil war, the United States constructed a framework that viewed divided loyalty not just as impractical, but fundamentally incompatible with the very idea of national belonging.

Two pivotal legal currents defined this early vision: the Expatriation Act of 1868 and the subsequent legal doctrine that treated certain actions as inherently incompatible with American citizenship. Together, they articulated a bold principle: allegiance could not be shared, compromised, or negotiated.

The Expatriation Act: A Declaration of Civic Freedom

Passed in 1868—just three years after the Civil War's conclusion and amid the tumultuous reconstruction of the national identity—the Expatriation Act was both a diplomatic thunderbolt and a philosophical manifesto. Its language was unequivocal: "the right of expatriation is a natural and inherent right of all people."

This was a direct challenge to European powers which insisted that subjects remained bound to their original homeland regardless of emigration. Naturalized Americans found themselves caught in a legal nightmare—claimed simultaneously by their country of origin and their new home, particularly in moments of military conscription.

The Act declared that in the American system, loyalty was a matter of conscious choice, not inherited obligation. A citizen could—and should—have the right to shed old allegiances, to remake their political self.

The Normalization of Citizenship Loss

In the decades following the Expatriation Act, U.S. law developed an increasingly sophisticated framework for understanding citizenship as a revocable status. The underlying principle was clear: certain actions were fundamentally incompatible with maintaining American citizenship.

During the World Wars, this principle was enforced with particular vigor. Dual allegiance was not seen as a bureaucratic nuance, but as a potential national security threat. The State Department and immigration authorities actively reviewed naturalized citizens' actions, ready to revoke status for what they perceived as betrayals of American loyalty.

The Nationality Act of 1940 made this principle law, listing actions that could cost someone their citizenship — such as voting in foreign elections, serving in another country's military, swearing allegiance to a foreign state, or accepting foreign titles.

The philosophical underpinning was constitutional and pragmatic: No individual could serve two masters. Citizenship was a bond of exclusive commitment, not a flexible administrative status to be negotiated or manipulated.

This view—of citizenship as an uncompromising allegiance—would hold sway until the latter half of the 20th century. Then, a series of judicial decisions would begin to unravel this clear, principled framework, transforming citizenship from an exclusive commitment to a negotiable identity.

II. Key Legal Turning Points and Judicial Drift

Legal transformations are rarely sudden. They emerge like geological shifts—imperceptible at first, then profound in their cumulative impact. The redefinition of American citizenship in the mid-20th century represents such a transformation: not a dramatic overhaul, but a quiet, systematic reinterpretation of constitutional principles. What appeared on the surface as discrete Supreme Court decisions were, in reality, a fundamental recalibration of the relationship between individual and government. These rulings did not simply adjust legal technicalities; they reimagined the very essence of national belonging.

Between 1952 and 1980, the Supreme Court systematically dismantled the long-standing legal framework that had presumed citizenship as an exclusive, reciprocal commitment. This judicial evolution was more than a series of case-by-case decisions. It was a profound philosophical shift—transforming citizenship from a mutual civic obligation to an individual entitlement, increasingly insulated from traditional expectations of loyalty and service. The three Supreme Court cases that follow—*Kawakita* (1952), *Afroyim* (1967) and *Vance* (1980)—reveal how abstract legal reasoning can reshape the most fundamental social contracts, often without public fanfare or explicit legislative mandate.

Kawakita v. United States (1952)

In *Kawakita v. United States* dual nationality meets treason law. The case represents a pivotal moment in the judicial recognition—and moral ambivalence—toward dual citizenship. Tomoya Kawakita was born in California to Japanese parents and held both U.S. and Japanese nationality. During World War II, while in Japan, he served as an interpreter and overseer at a mining company that used American POWs as forced laborers. He was accused of abusing prisoners and subsequently charged with treason upon his return to the United States.

The Supreme Court ruled that Kawakita retained his U.S. citizenship throughout the war, and was therefore subject to prosecution for treason under Article III of the Constitution. At the same time, the Court acknowledged his Japanese citizenship and the possibility that he had "mentally" pledged allegiance to Japan.

Tension and Paradox: The ruling walked a fine line. On one hand, it affirmed that dual citizens still owe allegiance to the United States. On the other, it exposed the legal uncertainty at the heart of dual nationality. Kawakita had actively supported a foreign power against the U.S., yet the Court upheld his citizenship because he had not explicitly renounced it. This decision underscored the growing judicial reluctance to interpret allegiance in behavioral or situational terms.

Legacy: Kawakita's case demonstrated the limits of prosecuting divided loyalty in a legal system that recognizes dual citizenship but lacks a coherent doctrine for managing its contradictions. It planted early seeds of ambiguity: dual nationality was real, but civic responsibility was still presumed singular—an unstable compromise that continues to shape current law.

The Court ultimately upheld Kawakita's conviction for treason in a 4–3 decision, affirming that U.S. citizenship—and the obligations it entails—remained legally intact despite his dual nationality.

Afroyim v. Rusk (1967)

In the landmark *Afroyim v. Rusk*, the Supreme Court delivered a sweeping reinterpretation of citizenship law: citizenship as an individual right. The petitioner, Beys Afroyim, was a naturalized U.S. citizen who voted in an Israeli Knesset election. Under existing law—specifically Section 401(e) of the Nationality Act of 1940—this act constituted voluntary expatriation. The State Department moved to revoke his citizenship. But the Court, in a 5–4 decision, reversed that action.

Justice Hugo Black's majority opinion held that the Fourteenth Amendment protects the "citizenship of the United States" from involuntary revocation. "In our country," Black wrote, "the people are sovereign, and the Government cannot sever its relationship to the people by taking away their citizenship." The ruling enshrined a new doctrine: citizenship is not a privilege to be regulated by the state, but a civil liberty akin to freedom of speech or religion. Unless the citizen voluntarily chooses to relinquish it, the government has no right to interfere.

Impact: This decision reframed the very purpose of citizenship in constitutional terms. The state's ability to enforce allegiance was subordinated to the individual's right to retain citizenship regardless of behavior that would once have been deemed incompatible with national loyalty. The precedent transformed U.S. citizenship from a reciprocal civic status into a protected legal entitlement—effectively severing the historical link between national allegiance and civic identity.

Vance v. Terrazas (1980)

In *Vance v. Terrazas*, the Court moved one step further in dismantling the traditional link between foreign political behavior and citizenship loss. Laurence Terrazas, a dual U.S.-Mexican citizen, had allegedly signed a Mexican government document pledging allegiance to Mexico while studying abroad. The government argued this was grounds for expatriation under the Immigration and Nationality Act.

The Court decided that even a clear act—like swearing allegiance to another country—wasn't enough unless there was proof the person truly meant to give up U.S. citizenship. The Court reaffirmed the principle from *Afroyim* that loss of citizenship must be voluntary and added that intent must be established by "preponderance of the evidence," a relatively high standard.

Shift in Legal Doctrine: This decision decisively rejected the idea that objective behavior—such as swearing a foreign oath—could constitute loss of U.S. citizenship on its own. The decisive factor was not the act, but the individual's internal state of mind. This placed allegiance firmly in the realm of subjective interpretation, complicating the government's ability to enforce civic standards.

Consequences: *Vance v. Terrazas* made it nearly impossible for the U.S. government to revoke citizenship under most circumstances, effectively rendering dual allegiance a permanent and protected status. It cemented the legal drift away from allegiance as a civic obligation and toward allegiance as a discretionary personal identity.

Together, *Afroyim*, *Kawakita*, and *Vance* represent the judiciary's gradual shift from enforcing exclusive allegiance to accommodating plural citizenship under the guise of civil liberties. While each case addressed different issues—voting abroad, wartime treason, and sworn oaths—their cumulative effect was profound: they weakened the state's authority to define or enforce singular loyalty, leaving the concept of national allegiance largely up to the individual. The result is a fragmented civic framework—where citizenship endures as a legal status, but allegiance, once its moral core, has become legally optional.

III. Bureaucratic Policy vs. Statutory Silence

While the courts redefined the constitutional limits of expatriation, the executive branch quietly recalibrated its administrative posture. The shift was subtle but consequential: from active enforcement of allegiance standards to passive accommodation of divided loyalty. At the same time, Congress remained silent. No legislative framework emerged to clarify or constrain this transformation. What resulted was a civic mutation without deliberation—a policy drift guided not by public consent, but by bureaucratic improvisation.

This section explores how U.S. policy on dual citizenship came to be shaped not by statutory design, but by executive discretion and judicial precedent. It examines the State Department's evolving practices, the continued absence of codified law, and the broader implications of permitting such a fundamental shift in civic meaning to unfold without democratic debate.

State Department Practices - From Enforcer to Accommodator

Following the landmark judicial decisions in *Afroyim v. Rusk* (1967) and Vance v. Terrazas (1980), the U.S. Department of State—historically the chief enforcer of expatriation law—quietly reoriented its approach. For much of the 20th century, the Department had actively revoked the citizenship of individuals who demonstrated foreign allegiance through concrete actions: voting in foreign elections, accepting foreign government positions, serving in non-U.S. militaries, or traveling extensively under a foreign passport.

But in the post-*Afroyim* era, that posture changed dramatically. The State Department began requiring a formal written statement of intent before initiating any expatriation procedures. In practical terms, this meant that a U.S. citizen could engage in a wide range of dual-loyalty behavior without consequence—unless they explicitly stated they no longer wished to remain American.

Institutional Implication: This procedural shift was not codified in legislation but emerged from internal policy memos, Foreign Affairs Manuals, and quiet reinterpretation of administrative guidelines.[13] It was bureaucratic drift masquerading as policy reform. In effect, the Department ceased to act as a guardian of singular allegiance and became a passive registrar of evolving global identities.

A Legal Vacuum with National Stakes

Despite the dramatic shift in administrative practice and judicial interpretation, Congress has yet to pass any legislation formally authorizing, regulating, or restricting dual citizenship. The Immigration and Nationality Act (INA) still contains provisions listing actions that may lead to expatriation, but under *Terrazas*, these actions are essentially unenforceable unless accompanied by proof of intent.

The Result: America's policy on dual citizenship exists in a legal gray zone. The courts have weakened enforcement powers. The executive

---

[13] See U.S. Department of State, *7 FAM 1220: Loss and Restoration of U.S. Citizenship*, Foreign Affairs Manual, Bureau of Consular Affairs, updated periodically since 1990. This section formalized the requirement that intent to relinquish U.S. citizenship must be explicitly stated, rather than presumed from actions such as voting in foreign elections or obtaining a foreign passport. The shift began in earnest following the Supreme Court's decision in *Afroyim v. Rusk* (1967) and was institutionalized through FAM revisions in the late 1980s and 1990s. Also see:
- "CA/OCS/PRI Memo on Dual Nationality" (1990, internal circulation) — A key internal policy briefing that clarified that holding or using a foreign passport was no longer sufficient to trigger a loss of U.S. citizenship unless it was accompanied by intent.
- U.S. State Department Legal Adviser Guidance (1989–1993) — Unpublished internal guidance that influenced revised consular training and implementation practices.

branch has ceased to act. And Congress, the one body empowered to clarify the law, has remained silent. This statutory vacuum leaves key questions unanswered:

- What obligations do dual citizens owe to the United States?
- How should dual allegiance be handled in matters of national security or public office?
- Are there any limits to what dual citizens can do in their "other" country without violating civic trust?

Legal Consequence: The lack of a coherent statute means that the operational status of dual citizenship depends largely on institutional tolerance and case-by-case discretion. This creates uneven enforcement, legal unpredictability, and a growing disconnect between traditional civic expectations and administrative reality.

De Facto Acceptance Without Deliberation

The most remarkable feature of America's dual citizenship policy is not that it evolved—but that it evolved without democratic scrutiny. No congressional hearings, no judicial mandates, no public discourse ever truly examined whether divided allegiance can coexist with undivided civic duty.

Instead, the transformation occurred through what might be called *passive normalization*. Courts emphasized rights over responsibilities. Bureaucrats chose leniency over litigation. And the public, largely unaware of the legal shifts, continued to assume that citizenship implied certain exclusive loyalties that the law no longer requires.

Civic Consequence: This unexamined drift carries real implications. The foundational assumption of American democracy—that citizens share a common allegiance—has been diluted by silent administrative evolution. Allegiance, once presumed to be singular and binding, has become negotiable. And because the change occurred without legislative clarity or public consent, the very definition of citizenship has morphed under the radar of democratic accountability.

When citizenship is reshaped by institutional default rather than democratic debate, the civic bond between citizen and state is quietly rewritten. Dual citizenship is now tolerated but poorly examined—less a product of national deliberation than of bureaucratic drift. Allegiance, once a principle of constitutional clarity, has become a matter of administrative omission.[14]

IV. The Practical Consequences of Legal Ambiguity

The erosion of legal clarity around citizenship has not remained a theoretical or abstract matter. Its effects are tangible—reverberating across multiple domains of American governance and civic life. From security and diplomacy to civic participation and digital engagement, the consequences of tolerating divided allegiance without statutory guidance are increasingly difficult to ignore.

This section explores how the normalization of dual citizenship—absent a coherent legal framework—has produced systemic inconsistencies, administrative confusion, and vulnerabilities across institutions. These are not merely policy inconveniences; they strike at the operational heart of what it means to belong to a single democratic polity.

---

[14] While there is no singular study that systematically examines dual citizenship as a case of policy drift in U.S. governance, several works gesture toward this dynamic. Peter J. Spiro identifies the erosion of traditional norms through court rulings and administrative accommodation, noting that dual citizenship has become tolerated more by bureaucratic passivity than legislative intent (*Beyond Citizenship: American Identity After Globalization*, Oxford University Press, 2008). Similarly, T. Alexander Aleinikoff characterizes American nationality law as an increasingly incoherent field shaped more by judicial improvisation than by democratic deliberation (*Semblances of Sovereignty: The Constitution, the State, and American Citizenship*, Harvard University Press, 2002). For the theoretical framing of policy drift more broadly, see Jacob S. Hacker, "Policy Drift: The Hidden Politics of US Welfare State Retrenchment," in *Beyond Continuity: Institutional Change in Advanced Political Economies*, edited by Wolfgang Streeck and Kathleen Thelen (Oxford University Press, 2005), 40–82.

National Security Risks: Loyalty in an Age of Complexity

National security institutions are predicated on trust. At their core lies an assumption that those with access to classified material, critical infrastructure, or strategic decision-making can be counted upon to act in the best interest of the United States—and only the United States.

Dual citizenship disrupts this assumption. Security clearance reviews regularly flag applicants with foreign citizenship, familial ties abroad, or dual property ownership as potential security risks. The logic is straightforward: dual nationals may face conflicting obligations, be vulnerable to coercion by foreign governments, or possess economic and emotional incentives that compromise singular allegiance.

Yet because there is no uniform legal standard for how dual citizenship should factor into eligibility, the review process is marked by inconsistency and institutional discretion. One applicant may be cleared after renouncing foreign ties or submitting extensive documentation; another may be denied clearance based on similar facts, depending on the agency, adjudicator, or prevailing security climate.

Operational Consequence: The ambiguity burdens both individuals and institutions. Dual nationals face opaque and inconsistent barriers to service. Agencies are forced to make judgment calls without a clear legislative or doctrinal foundation. And the resulting patchwork undermines fairness, coherence, and public confidence in the integrity of national security vetting.

Illustrative Case: In 2022, the GAO reported that 4% of all federal security clearance applications were flagged due to concerns over dual citizenship. While not all were disqualified, many required additional vetting or were stalled indefinitely—creating a bottleneck in talent pipelines and eroding morale among qualified applicants.

Consular Protections Weakened by Divided Allegiance

Dual citizenship becomes especially fraught when Americans are detained or prosecuted in countries that refuse to acknowledge the legitimacy of dual nationality. In such cases, the core promise of U.S. citizenship—protection abroad—collides with the sovereignty claims of foreign states.

Regimes in Iran, China, Turkey, and others routinely deny U.S. consular access to dual nationals held within their borders, claiming that individuals with dual nationality are solely their citizens under domestic law. The U.S. Department of State has recorded at least 27 such instances between 2018 and 2023.

Diplomatic Implication: These denials of access aren't just bureaucratic irritants. They render American citizens legally invisible to their own government, stripping them of due process, oversight, and advocacy. The inability to enforce international norms of consular protection for dual nationals weakens the practical utility of U.S. citizenship—and signals to adversarial governments that they may act with impunity.

Notable Example: The case of Siamak Namazi, an Iranian-American businessman detained in Tehran, is illustrative. Despite holding a valid U.S. passport, Namazi was denied American consular access for years, with Iran claiming sole jurisdiction. His detention, like many others, became both a humanitarian crisis and a geopolitical bargaining chip.

Long-Term Cost: These incidents diminish U.S. soft power and credibility. If the U.S. government cannot guarantee basic protections for its citizens abroad, especially in times of crisis, it undermines the moral and practical legitimacy of American citizenship itself.

Erosion of Democratic Clarity: Citizenship Without Coherence

Citizenship is not only a legal status but a moral framework. It binds the individual to the state through reciprocal duties—taxation, jury service, military registration, civic participation. But in the absence of a legal standard governing dual allegiance, these expectations become muddled.

Dual citizens often find themselves caught between conflicting obligations: a jury summons from the U.S., a military conscription order from another country; taxation demands from both sovereigns, each claiming primary jurisdiction. There is little statutory guidance to resolve such conflicts, leaving dual citizens uncertain—and sometimes unintentionally noncompliant.

Civic Consequence: As these ambiguities proliferate, the experience of citizenship becomes fragmented. The sense of mutual responsibility that underpins democratic governance is replaced by a piecemeal relationship to the state, where rights are retained but obligations are evaded.

Cultural Shift: A model of "citizenship as entitlement" has quietly supplanted the traditional "citizenship as commitment." This shift undermines public trust in shared obligation and erodes the legitimacy of collective sacrifice—foundational tenets of republican self-government.

Institutional Impact: Agencies tasked with enforcing civic duties—such as the Internal Revenue Service (IRS), Selective Service, or local jury commissions—must now navigate a landscape of uncertainty. Dual nationals may claim exemption, ambiguity, or ignorance, while the state lacks a firm legal footing to compel compliance or adjudicate conflicts.

Transnational Political Engagement: Dual citizens today can—and often do—vote in multiple elections, campaign for candidates in different countries, and lobby on behalf of foreign interests within the United States. Social media and encrypted communications allow for the formation of transnational advocacy networks that transcend traditional national boundaries.

Ethical and Legal Challenges: These developments call into question foundational civic principles: What does it mean to belong to a political community when one can simultaneously belong to two or more? Can a person faithfully represent two sovereign interests if those interests collide?

The consequences of legal ambiguity in dual citizenship are neither speculative nor isolated. They reverberate through national security, diplomacy, civic duty, and emerging forms of global engagement. Each domain reveals a system unprepared for the reality it now faces: a world where dual allegiance is both common and destabilizing.

The next section examines how this drift plays out in high-stakes geopolitical contexts, where allegiance is tested not in theory, but in war zones, courtrooms, and detention cells abroad.

V. Case Studies in Dual Allegiance

In moments of peace, the contradictions posed by dual citizenship may remain dormant—masked by the bureaucratic routines of modern governance. But in moments of crisis—wartime, detention, or geopolitical tension—these contradictions surface with unmistakable clarity. This section takes a closer look at how dual citizenship plays out in the highest-stakes scenarios: international detentions, intelligence exposure, foreign military service, and transnational governance.

The cases that follow reveal that the tension between legal recognition and civic expectation is not abstract. It has real consequences—legal, diplomatic, and ethical. When dual citizens are imprisoned abroad, serve in foreign militaries, or hold positions of influence in two governments simultaneously, the question of allegiance is no longer philosophical. It is operational.

When Citizenship Collides with Sovereignty

The protections of U.S. citizenship—particularly abroad—are premised on the state's ability to act on behalf of its nationals. This includes the right to consular access, legal assistance, and diplomatic advocacy. However, dual citizenship compromises this capacity in profound ways, particularly when the other sovereign involved is authoritarian, hostile, or uninterested in honoring dual-status recognition.

Case 1: Iran (2019)

In 2019, an Iranian-American businessman, Akbar Lakestani, traveled to Tehran to visit family. Upon arrival, he was detained and imprisoned by Iranian authorities on charges of espionage. Despite his valid U.S. passport, Iran refused to acknowledge his American citizenship, citing its domestic law that does not recognize dual nationality. The U.S. government was denied all consular access.

This was not an isolated case. Over the past decade, multiple Iranian-Americans have been detained under similar conditions, many of them used as bargaining chips in diplomatic negotiations. Their American citizenship, while valid under U.S. law, became irrelevant within Iranian borders.

Case 2: China

China, too, has followed a parallel strategy. Under its expansive national security framework, it has detained dual nationals—particularly Chinese-American academics and businesspeople—without acknowledging their U.S. citizenship. In 2023, Joey Siu, a U.S. citizen born in China was arrested in Hong Kong under suspicion of political subversion. U.S. diplomatic officials were denied access on the grounds that the individual was "only" Chinese.

Strategic Pattern: These incidents expose a clear and dangerous trend: authoritarian states use the ambiguity of dual citizenship to their advantage, asserting unilateral sovereignty when convenient and rejecting international obligations. The protections U.S. citizens presume as guaranteed suddenly vanish when dual nationality is weaponized by foreign powers.

Institutional Cost: The U.S. government is left with diminished leverage and limited recourse. The rights of American citizens abroad become contingent not on treaty obligations or constitutional protections, but on the unilateral discretion of foreign states. In effect, dual citizens become stateless in moments of crisis—trapped between two sovereigns, and protected by neither.

"Dual Service" - Conflicts of Loyalty in Uniform and Office

Even more complicated are cases involving what might be called "dual service"—when individuals hold official roles, either civilian or military, in a foreign government while maintaining U.S. citizenship. These situations challenge the core assumption of exclusive allegiance and expose the fragility of institutional trust when roles of service straddle two sovereign authorities.

Case 3: Andrew Scheer (Canada, first elected 2004)

Andrew Scheer, a dual Canadian–American citizen and longtime Member of Parliament, became leader of Canada's Conservative Party in 2017. During the 2019 federal election, his U.S. citizenship—with associated Selective Service obligations and tax responsibilities—fueled public debate over potential loyalty conflicts. Scheer considered renouncing his U.S. citizenship but ultimately did not. His experience highlights the ambiguity surrounding dual citizens holding office in legislative bodies that engage with national security and intelligence oversight.

While no misconduct was alleged, Scheer's case revealed how even passive dual citizenship can raise questions about eligibility for sensitive roles—especially in areas involving foreign policy, intelligence, or national security.

Case 4: Israeli-Americans in the IDF – Loyalty, Law, and the Limits of Dual Allegiance

Military service has long served as a crucible for national loyalty. But what happens when a citizen wears the uniform of another state—especially one entangled in global conflict?

Israel mandates military service for most of its citizens, including those with dual nationality. This policy has led thousands of Israeli-American dual citizens to serve in the Israel Defense Forces (IDF), some as volunteers known as "lone soldiers." While their service often stems from cultural or familial ties, it introduces profoundND dilemmas when these individuals later return to the United States and pursue roles in government, intelligence, or national security.

The Case of Edan Alexander: In October 2023, Edan Alexander, a dual U.S.–Israeli citizen and IDF soldier, was captured by Hamas during its cross-border attack on southern Israel. For 584 days, he was held hostage in Gaza. His situation triggered a complex diplomatic and symbolic reckoning: Was he a U.S. citizen in distress, a foreign combatant, or both?

Despite the fact that Alexander had been actively serving in a foreign military, the United States assumed responsibility for securing his release, ultimately facilitating a prisoner exchange in May 2025. Throughout the ordeal, U.S. officials publicly emphasized his American citizenship, while Israel viewed him as an enlisted soldier fulfilling mandatory service. Alexander's case spotlighted the strategic ambiguities of dual allegiance:

- Who bears responsibility when a dual citizen is detained while serving a foreign power?
- What obligations, rights, or protections follow from such service—especially when the individual may later seek employment in sensitive U.S. policy domains?
- What standards should apply to dual citizens entering public office after prior foreign military duty?

Legal Gray Zones and Policy Gaps: Currently, U.S. law does not prohibit dual citizens from serving in foreign militaries unless that military is actively engaged in hostilities against the United States. However, this restriction is narrow and largely reactive. It fails to account for broader risks: exposure to classified foreign operations, deep-rooted institutional loyalties, and reputational vulnerabilities in times of crisis.

Moreover, there are no statutory restrictions preventing such individuals from seeking U.S. security clearances, working in intelligence roles, or shaping American foreign policy—despite prior oaths or service commitments to another nation.

A Broader Dilemma of "Dual Service": Alexander's case is not isolated. Across the globe, dual citizens have served in foreign armies, worked in foreign ministries, or held posts that blur the line between cultural identity and civic allegiance. While the law tolerates such dual service, institutions increasingly struggle to interpret and reconcile its implications.

In times of war, diplomacy, or national emergency, the stakes are amplified. Alexander's experience is a cautionary illustration: in the absence of a legal doctrine or standardized protocol, the U.S. government is left to navigate loyalty conflicts on an ad hoc basis—through improvisation, public messaging, and case-by-case diplomacy.

VI. Toward Clarity: The Case for Reform

A functioning democracy is built not only on the rule of law but on a shared ethic of trust and responsibility. Allegiance—while often invoked symbolically—serves as the connective tissue between citizens and the state. It is the basis for national defense, legal protection, taxation, and representation. And yet, as this chapter has shown, the meaning of allegiance in the American civic imagination has grown vague, inconsistently enforced, and legally ambiguous.

Reforming the framework of citizenship does not require the rejection of plural identities or the rollback of civil rights. Rather, it demands a reaffirmation: that allegiance entails responsibility, not just entitlement. In its current legal posture, the United States allows dual allegiance by default—without codifying its boundaries, addressing its risks, or even acknowledging its implications.

Reform must begin with clarity. The goal is not punitive exclusion but principled coherence. It is to ensure that citizenship—especially in roles of trust and authority—signifies more than a passport. It must reflect a meaningful, exclusive civic commitment in contexts where national interest and public duty are non-negotiable.

This effort would not entail sweeping restrictions, but modest, focused reforms to restore coherence to a system drifting into contradiction.

Proposing a Legal Doctrine of Singular Citizenship

Rather than banning dual citizenship outright—a measure that would likely be unworkable and overly punitive—the United States should adopt a clear, codified doctrine that defines where and when exclusive allegiance is required. This would reflect the principle that while plural identity may be accepted in ordinary civic life, there are *thresholds* where shared allegiance is incompatible with national responsibility.

Three key domains where exclusive allegiance is warranted:

1. **Defense and Intelligence Roles:** In roles involving national defense, intelligence, or homeland security, ambiguity in allegiance is not a theoretical concern—it is a functional risk. Individuals with foreign citizenship may face divided loyalties in crisis scenarios, be vulnerable to coercion, or hold residual ties that conflict with operational integrity. A legal requirement for exclusive U.S. citizenship in these roles would reinforce trust, accountability, and national cohesion at the highest levels of service.

2. **Elected Federal Office:** Those who serve in Congress or the executive branch are stewards of the national interest and architects of public policy. Their actions shape immigration, diplomacy, and national security. Requiring exclusive allegiance from elected federal officials would restore public confidence that representation is rooted in undivided civic duty. It would also resolve growing concerns about foreign influence, conflicting obligations, and symbolic ambiguity at the highest levels of democratic governance.
3. **Diplomacy and Treaty Negotiation:** Diplomats are tasked with representing the United States abroad—not just administratively, but morally and symbolically. Negotiators must embody undivided loyalty to the American state and people. Holding dual citizenship in this context raises valid concerns about conflicting priorities or compromised credibility. A formal requirement of exclusive allegiance for diplomatic appointments would align practice with the core assumptions of international representation.

Practical Implementation: A Balanced Framework

A legal doctrine of singular citizenship does not necessitate broad prohibition. It could be operationalized through a tiered system:

- **Disclosure Requirements**: Candidates for sensitive positions would be required to disclose all foreign citizenships, past and present. This promotes transparency without immediate disqualification.
- **Conditional Eligibility**: For defined high-trust roles, dual citizenship could disqualify candidates unless renunciation is completed prior to service.
- **Due Process Protections**: Individuals could contest decisions through an administrative or judicial review process, ensuring fairness and constitutional safeguards.

This framework would avoid the excesses of punitive nationalism while restoring ethical clarity to the concept of allegiance. It would recognize plural identity without normalizing divided loyalty in the corridors of state power.

Preview of what follows

The themes outlined in this section—particularly the restoration of reciprocal civic responsibility and the development of practical policy tools—will be examined in greater detail in later chapters. Discussions on bipartisan policy design, international consular agreements, and reforms to the naturalization process will be fully expanded in Chapters 6 through 9, where the legal, ethical, and strategic dimensions of reform are addressed comprehensively.

For now, it is enough to establish that the principle of allegiance—as both a legal requirement and a civic ethic—must be reaffirmed. The goal is not to foreclose inclusion, but to restore clarity.

Conclusion: Citizenship Without Coherence

Chapter 2 has traced the legal evolution of American citizenship from an explicit commitment to exclusive allegiance to a murky tolerance of divided loyalties. What began as a bold assertion of voluntary belonging—the Expatriation Act of 1868—has, over time, devolved into policy drift and statutory silence. Supreme Court decisions like *Afroyim v. Rusk* and *Vance v. Terrazas* elevated citizenship to a near-inalienable right, severing it from the expectation of singular loyalty. Bureaucratic practice followed suit, normalizing dual citizenship through passive enforcement rather than public debate or legislative clarity.

This drift has not been costless. The legal and institutional ambiguity surrounding dual citizenship now touches nearly every domain of American governance—from national security to diplomacy, taxation, and civic education. Institutions are left to navigate competing claims of allegiance without clear doctrine, while citizens encounter a landscape where civic responsibility is uneven, negotiable, or undefined.

The stakes are not merely procedural—they are philosophical. Can a democracy that requires shared trust, common purpose, and mutual accountability sustain itself if the meaning of citizenship becomes fragmented? What happens when the civic bond meant to unite a nation can be held in duplicate, without consequence or coherence?

And yet, the answer cannot be a retreat into rigidity or exclusion. In a world shaped by mobility, migration, and complex identity, pluralism must be preserved. But pluralism is not the same as ambiguity. A functioning republic must be able to say where lines are drawn—when allegiance is optional, and when it is essential.

That is the task ahead.

In Chapter 3, we turn to the global context. How do other democratic societies manage dual citizenship? Where have they drawn boundaries—successfully or not—between plural identity and national cohesion? And what lessons can the United States learn from these comparative models as it reconsiders what citizenship should mean in the 21st century?

Chapter 3

How Other Nations Handle It

In today's world of constant movement, dual citizenship is more common than ever—but not everywhere is it welcomed. As people live, work, and raise families across borders, governments face a basic question: Can one person truly be loyal to more than one nation—and if so, under what rules?

This chapter explores how other nations—large and small, liberal and nationalist, integrated and insular—have answered that question. Some have responded with openness, others with prohibition, and many with carefully managed compromise. What unites these countries is not their uniformity, but their intentionality. Whether they impose strict renunciation clauses, mandate civic service, or extend dual status to their diasporas, these states have treated citizenship as a matter of *policy*—not drift.

Drawing on comparative examples from Germany, India, Israel, Mexico, France, the UK, and others, this chapter demonstrates that clarity—not permissiveness—is the norm in serious citizenship regimes. It also highlights how newer trends—like biometric enforcement, citizenship-by-investment, and digital identity—are shaping the next frontier of national belonging.

The lesson is clear: in the twenty-first century, citizenship must be governed with foresight. Other nations have made their choices. The United States has not.

I. Citizenship as Policy, Not Accident

Across the globe, nations have increasingly recognized the complexity of identity in a mobile, interconnected world. As of 2024, over 60% of countries permit some form of dual or multiple citizenship. Yet crucially, this recognition is rarely passive. Whether through explicit legislation, constitutional safeguards, or administrative enforcement, most governments treat the management of citizenship as an active instrument of national policy—closely linked to questions of sovereignty, security, and civic responsibility.

What varies is not the awareness of dual citizenship, but the seriousness with which it is governed. Some states allow it only under narrow conditions. Others integrate it into broader strategies of diaspora engagement or national defense. And in many cases, governments have imposed clear limitations on the rights and obligations of dual nationals, especially in sensitive roles such as military service, elected office, or diplomatic representation.

The sections that follow examine how other nations have approached this issue—with clarity, constraint, or conditional tolerance. Their examples offer a crucial mirror for the American case, and a pressing question: why has the United States, almost uniquely, allowed such a foundational question of political belonging to go unaddressed?

Global Trends in Dual Citizenship Policy

As a 2023 comparative analysis of 70 countries reveals, dual citizenship is not inherently controversial—rather, it is institutionally managed. Seventy-five percent of EU member states now include explicit legal provisions defining the terms, conditions, and consequences of holding multiple nationalities. Nearly 40% of countries restrict dual citizens from holding public office, working in defense or intelligence sectors, or voting in certain national elections. And approximately 30% require dual nationals to formally register their foreign citizenship with domestic authorities as a condition for maintaining specific public rights or access to government services.

How Other Democracies Manage Dual Citizenship

Key Global Patterns
A 2023 comparative analysis of citizenship regimes—including 70 countries across the EU, OECD, and major immigration destinations—found that dual nationality is not simply permitted or banned, but institutionally governed.[15]

Legal Clarity
- 75% of EU member states have explicit laws outlining the rights, limits, and consequences of dual citizenship.
- Countries like Germany and Austria require special approval for dual citizenship—often limited to hardship exceptions or diaspora ties.

Civic Restrictions
- 40% of countries restrict dual citizens from:
    - Holding elected office
    - Voting in national elections
    - Serving in intelligence, diplomacy, or military roles
    (Examples: India, Israel, Lithuania)

Mandatory Disclosure
- 30% of countries require dual nationals to:
    - Register their foreign citizenship with domestic authorities
    - Update authorities on foreign passport use
    (Examples: Norway, Japan, Singapore)

Key Insight
Across political systems—liberal and conservative, old and new—dual citizenship is treated as a managed exception, not a default status. The American system remains an outlier in its near-total policy silence.

These findings highlight a crucial insight: *dual citizenship is not inherently problematic*, but it is actively governed. Across legal traditions and political

---

[15] European University Institute, *Global Database on Modes of Acquisition of Citizenship (GLOBALCIT)*, 2023; and Migration Policy Institute, *Global Trends in Dual Citizenship: Comparative Overview and Country-Level Analysis*, 2023.

systems, democratic states tend to manage divided allegiance through coherent frameworks—not through passive tolerance or institutional neglect. While policies differ in form, they share a common premise: that civic integrity requires structure, not silence.

Dual Citizenship as an Instrument of Policy

Whether permissive or restrictive, most nations approach citizenship through the lens of statecraft. They weigh competing priorities—diaspora engagement, national unity, cultural integration, and security risk—and calibrate their legal frameworks accordingly. This allows them to:

- Enforce obligations such as military service or taxation
- Regulate eligibility for public office or sensitive government roles
- Establish protocols for consular protection in cases of detention abroad
- Preserve symbolic coherence in the meaning of citizenship.

Why Comparative Policy Matters

Understanding how other countries handle dual citizenship sharpens our lens on America's approach. While the U.S. drifts in legal ambiguity—as seen in Chapter 2—many peer nations have made deliberate choices. From India's outright bans to France's integrative model, these policies reflect a conscious balancing of allegiance, security, and civic coherence.

Framing the Comparative Inquiry Ahead

The goal of this chapter is to investigate how peer nations have handled the question of dual allegiance—not to suggest direct transplantation of foreign models, but to surface lessons, contrasts, and cautionary tales. The cases that follow—Germany, India, Israel, Mexico, the United Kingdom, France, and others—highlight a central principle: *where citizenship is taken seriously, dual citizenship is clearly defined.*

The Invisible Millions: Charting America's Dual Citizenship Landscape

Dual citizenship, once uncommon and actively discouraged, has become a normalized feature of American civic life. While precise figures are hard to come by—since neither the U.S. Census nor other federal surveys systematically track dual nationality—reliable estimates indicate the phenomenon is far from marginal.

According to the U.S. State Department, an estimated 1 to 3 million Americans held dual citizenship as of the mid-2010s. More recent estimates from the Migration Policy Institute place the figure above 10 million, accounting for both naturalized citizens who retain their original nationality and U.S.-born individuals eligible through descent. The gap reflects both data limitations and the expanding scope of global mobility.

Today, dual citizens broadly fall into two major categories:
- **Naturalized Americans retaining original nationality:** Of the 23 to 25 million naturalized U.S. citizens, many retain citizenship from their country of origin—especially those from nations like Mexico, the Philippines, South Korea, and several in Europe and Latin America that now permit or encourage dual nationality.
- **U.S.-born citizens with foreign nationality:** Millions of Americans acquire a second citizenship at birth through foreign-born parents or later through ancestry or marriage. Countries such as Ireland, Italy, Israel, and Canada grant citizenship by descent, making many U.S.-born individuals eligible.

The shift toward widespread dual nationality has unfolded over the past five decades due to three interconnected factors:
1. **Legal Acceptance**: Supreme Court rulings such as *Afroyim v. Rusk* (1967) affirmed that Americans could not lose citizenship without voluntary renunciation, opening the door to legal acceptance of dual status.
2. **Global Liberalization**: Since the 1990s, many countries have reversed restrictions on dual citizenship to maintain ties with emigrants and attract talent and investment.
3. **Immigration Growth**: High immigration levels and record naturalization rates further expanded the dual citizen population, embedding it into America's demographic fabric.

A small number of Americans hold three or more citizenships—typically through multinational parentage or successive naturalizations—though such cases remain rare, likely in the tens of thousands.

Dual citizenship in the U.S. now mirrors global shifts in citizenship law and identity. Once regarded with suspicion, dual allegiance has become a normalized, if largely unexamined, feature of contemporary American civic life.

Sources: U.S. State Department; Migration Policy Institute; Pew Research Center; Center for Immigration Studies; Michael A. Olivas, "The Changing Face of Citizenship," Los Angeles Times, 2014.

II. Models of Citizenship Management

Nations do not treat dual citizenship uniformly. Some restrict it outright, others tolerate it selectively, while a few incorporate it as part of broader civic strategy. These divergent models reflect not only legal doctrine, but distinct national judgments about identity, loyalty, and state responsibility.

This section explores five representative models—Germany, India, Israel, Mexico, and the United Kingdom and France—each offering a distinctive logic of citizenship management. In addition, we examine the more coercive approaches of China and Russia, whose restrictive and punitive policies treat dual nationality as a threat to state sovereignty. Together, these comparative cases illuminate the wide spectrum of global norms and raise important questions about how the United States might better define, disclose, or regulate allegiance in a complex world.

A. Germany: Conditional Tolerance through Integration

Germany has long approached dual citizenship with caution, historically viewing exclusive allegiance as essential to national unity. For decades, the German naturalization process required applicants to renounce their previous citizenships, a reflection of the country's postwar commitment to integration and civic coherence. This policy was rooted in the belief that true membership in the German polity required a singular national identity—linguistically, culturally, and politically.

However, this strict stance began to soften in the early 2000s with limited exceptions for EU citizens and Swiss nationals, recognizing the practical and diplomatic realities of European integration. The most significant shift came in 2023, when Germany enacted sweeping reforms to its citizenship law. These changes allowed broader retention of original citizenships during naturalization, provided applicants demonstrated clear integration into German society.

The results were immediate. Naturalization applications increased by 28% in the following year, and of those who gained German citizenship, 85% retained their previous nationality. At the same time, however, the Interior Ministry reported a 15% rise in security clearance denials for applicants with dual citizenship—an indicator of the persistent institutional concern about divided loyalties in sensitive roles.

Germany shows that dual citizenship doesn't have to weaken national unity—if it's tied to a strong system of integration. By demanding cultural and linguistic fluency, civic education, and demonstrated loyalty, Germany pairs openness with accountability.

B. India: A Model of Zero Tolerance

India represents one of the world's clearest cases of dual citizenship prohibition. Enshrined in its Constitution and reinforced through domestic law, Indian citizenship is automatically terminated if a citizen voluntarily acquires citizenship in another country. The legal reasoning is unequivocal: citizenship and allegiance are indivisible.

This position reflects not only a deep-rooted nationalist ethos but also the practical challenges of governing a vast and diverse population. In India's view, dual loyalty presents not only a constitutional contradiction but a strategic risk to democratic governance, national unity, and internal security.

To balance this strict policy with its desire to engage the global Indian diaspora, India introduced the Overseas Citizen of India (OCI) card—a legal innovation that confers significant rights without granting full political membership. OCI holders can live, work, and own property in India, but they may not vote, run for office, or serve in the military. In effect, India offers a long-term visa to its diaspora, not a second passport.

This model affirms that even in a globalized world, a large and complex democracy can maintain an unambiguous civic boundary. By providing legal and economic privileges through OCI status without extending sovereign rights, India preserves the principle that citizenship must rest on undivided allegiance.

C. Israel: Identity, Obligation, and Existential Citizenship

Israel presents a unique fusion of identity-based inclusion and compulsory civic obligation. Under the Law of Return, any Jewish person in the world is eligible to claim Israeli citizenship. This provision—rooted in the memory of diaspora and persecution—reflects a global conception of peoplehood rather than a purely territorial or bureaucratic model of nationality.

Yet despite its broad openness to Jewish identity, Israel does not treat citizenship as symbolic alone. For those residing in Israel, citizenship entails real obligations—most notably, mandatory service in the Israel Defense Forces (IDF). Dual nationals are not exempt. From 2022 to 2024, over 12,000 dual citizens were conscripted into military service. Of those called up, 89% completed their service, a figure that underscores the degree to which civic duty remains non-negotiable, even in an era of global mobility.

Israel occasionally grants deferrals for exceptional cases—such as business leaders or prominent academics—but these are scrutinized on a case-by-case basis and remain rare. The underlying message is clear: national belonging entails shared sacrifice. Citizenship, in the Israeli model, is both a right and a burden. It is not just about identity; it is about responsibility.

D. Mexico: Diaspora Democracy and Strategic Inclusion

In the 1990s, Mexico underwent a dramatic reorientation of its citizenship policy. For decades, the country adhered to a rigid principle of exclusive nationality. But by 1998, in response to changing migration patterns and the growing importance of remittances, Mexico legalized dual citizenship for its emigrant population.

This policy shift was not only legal—it was strategic. By embracing its diaspora as part of its extended national fabric, Mexico aimed to strengthen cultural ties, encourage investment, and extend its influence abroad. Mexican nationals living in the United States and elsewhere were granted the right to vote in Mexican elections, participate in civic life, and pass on their Mexican citizenship to their children.

In short, Mexico turned its emigrants into political assets. This model of "diaspora democracy" exemplifies how dual citizenship can serve a nation's geopolitical interests—if it is acknowledged and managed transparently. While Mexico's approach is inclusive, it is not accidental. Civic identity is still cultivated, and participation remains institutionally anchored in formal structures.

E. France and the UK: Liberal Models Anchored in Tradition

France and the United Kingdom are often cited as exemplars of permissive dual citizenship regimes, but their tolerance is grounded in distinct political traditions.

France formally allows dual citizenship and does not require individuals to renounce prior nationalities upon naturalization. However, this legal flexibility is anchored in a firm expectation of loyalty to the French Republic—particularly among public servants, military personnel, and elected officials. The French republican model emphasizes *laïcité* (secularism), civic integration, and indivisible national sovereignty. As such, dual nationals may enjoy full rights, but they are also expected to demonstrate unequivocal allegiance to the Republic's values. For sensitive posts—such as roles in national defense, foreign service, or intelligence—dual nationality may be a disqualifying factor unless the second citizenship is renounced. This approach balances plural identity with institutional loyalty, showing that multiple passports need not mean divided allegiance.

The United Kingdom broadly permits dual citizenship and imposes no general restrictions on holding multiple nationalities. However, this permissive framework exists within a historically complex and legally stratified system. Rooted in its post-imperial legacy, British nationality includes a hierarchy of statuses—such as British Overseas Territories Citizen (BOTC) and British National (Overseas) [BN(O)]—many of which do not carry full political rights or the right of abode in the UK. Moreover, while legal dual nationality is accepted, practical limitations still apply in specific contexts: individuals with dual citizenship may be ineligible for certain sensitive roles in national security, such as positions within MI5, MI6, or GCHQ (a signals intelligence and cybersecurity agency), unless they renounce their other nationality. Thus, the UK model remains legally flexible but not without important distinctions and institutional boundaries.

Together, France and the UK demonstrate that liberal approaches to dual citizenship can coexist with clear legal boundaries. These are not cases of neglect, but of structured permissiveness. Both countries treat citizenship as a legal construct that evolves alongside national interest—but always within a defined institutional framework.

F. China and Russia's Citizenship Enforcement Regimes

While liberal democracies grapple with the legal ambiguities and civic tensions of dual citizenship, authoritarian states like China and Russia offer an entirely different paradigm—one where dual nationality is either legally denied or tightly manipulated as a tool of state control. These regimes do not merely reject the liberal assumption that citizenship is a matter of personal identity and civic participation; they repurpose it as an instrument of surveillance, coercion, and political leverage, both at home and abroad.

China: Denial in Law, Exploitation in Practice

China's official line is simple: dual citizenship doesn't exist. The law says anyone who becomes a citizen of another country automatically loses

Chinese citizenship—but in practice, the state applies that rule when it serves its interests.

For individuals born in China who later naturalize elsewhere—including thousands of Chinese-American dual nationals—China continues to assert jurisdiction and identity claims. Dual nationals traveling to China are routinely treated exclusively as Chinese citizens, regardless of what passport they enter with. This policy renders them ineligible for U.S. consular protection and places them at greater risk of detention, surveillance, or political retaliation.

The case of Kai Li, a Chinese-American businessman imprisoned in China from 2016 to 2024 on espionage charges, remains illustrative. Despite his U.S. citizenship, Li was denied American consular access, with Chinese authorities insisting he was solely a Chinese national under their law. His eight-year detention—widely condemned as arbitrary—underscored a broader pattern in which dual or disputed nationality is used as a tool for diplomatic leverage and political hostage-taking. Though now released, his case reveals how states can manipulate citizenship status to defy international norms.

China's approach to citizenship reflects a deep fusion of national identity with state control. There is no space for divided loyalty in the Chinese conception of sovereignty—yet that rigidity paradoxically creates space for manipulative ambiguity, especially when dealing with dual nationals from democratic states.

While China rigidly denies dual citizenship and asserts exclusive claims over its nationals abroad, it offers almost no pathway for foreigners to become Chinese citizens. Naturalization is legally permitted but exceedingly rare—reserved for tightly controlled exceptions. In effect, the state grants itself maximal discretion: rejecting foreign allegiances while refusing to extend its own citizenship outward. This asymmetry reinforces a model of citizenship as sovereign instrument, not mutual contract.

Russia: Legal Recognition, Strategic Instrumentalization

Russia occupies a more ambiguous middle ground. Legally, Russia recognizes dual citizenship but demands registration of foreign nationalities with the Interior Ministry. Failure to report a second citizenship can result in fines or legal penalties. More critically, Russia reserves the right to treat any person it deems a Russian citizen as exclusively Russian within its territory, regardless of any other citizenship they hold.

This policy has enabled the Russian government to deny U.S. consular access in numerous high-profile cases involving Russian-American dual nationals detained in Russia on vague or politically charged grounds. In such instances, the Kremlin has invoked its domestic citizenship laws to assert unilateral jurisdiction—and to exclude foreign governments from intervening.

Beyond individual cases, Russia's broader "compatriot policy" extends the logic of dual citizenship into a geopolitical doctrine. Under this policy, Russia asserts a special obligation to "protect" ethnic Russians and Russian-speaking populations abroad—whether or not they are actual citizens. This policy was central to the justification for the annexation of Crimea in 2014 and continues to underlie Russian actions in eastern Ukraine and elsewhere. Citizenship, in this context, becomes a tool of extraterritorial influence and a pretext for intervention.

Russia also maintains broad discretion over revoking or restricting citizenship for political dissenters, particularly dual nationals involved in protest movements or international activism. As in China, the legal framework provides a veneer of legitimacy to what are often coercive and unpredictable exercises of power.

Unlike China, Russia does grant citizenship to a wider range of foreign nationals—including through simplified procedures for those with Russian ancestry or residence ties. Yet this openness is not grounded in liberal inclusion; it serves strategic ends. Naturalization can extend the state's extraterritorial reach, while citizenship revocation remains a tool of domestic control. As with dual nationals inside Russia, the boundaries of belonging are drawn less by law than by loyalty

Lesson: The Authoritarian Use of Ambiguity

China and Russia show how dual citizenship ambiguity can become a tool of coercion—not just a legal gray zone. In both regimes, the state manipulates nationality to assert power over individuals and project influence beyond borders. These are not lapses in enforcement—they are deliberate strategies, cloaked in law.

For the United States, the lesson is not to mirror authoritarian rigidity, but to confront the costs of strategic silence. Without clear doctrine or legal boundaries, dual citizenship remains a vulnerability—one that authoritarian states are already exploiting.

III. Emerging Global Trends

As the global landscape of citizenship evolves, national approaches to dual nationality reflect not only historical legacies and political philosophies, but also strategic calculations. From restrictive prohibitions to liberal openness, the range of citizenship models reveals a complex matrix of civic inclusion, security prioritization, and statecraft.

The comparative table of global citizenship models that follows is more than a static inventory—it is a dynamic map of how nations navigate the complex terrain of identity, belonging, and allegiance in the 21st century. Beyond mere policy classifications, these entries reveal a profound global dialogue about citizenship's evolving meaning. While the rows and columns suggest categorical distinctions—restrictive, conditional, liberal—the real story lies in the nuanced strategies nations employ to manage an increasingly mobile, interconnected world. The data points are not just legal classifications, but signals of how states perceive their relationship with citizens in an era where national boundaries have become simultaneously more porous and more strategically significant.

Global Citizenship Models: A Comparative View

Model Type	Country	Policy Summary	Key Feature
Restrictive	India	Prohibits dual citizenship; automatic loss upon acquiring another nationality	Zero tolerance; loyalty framed as exclusive
Restrictive	China	Does not recognize dual nationality	No legal recognition; asserts sole claim
Restrictive	Japan	Dual citizens must choose one nationality by age 22	Time-limited tolerance; enforced choice
Conditional	Germany	Allows dual citizenship only in limited cases (e.g., EU nationals, refugees)	Integration-first; renunciation expected
Conditional	Israel	Accepts dual citizenship; mandates military service for residents	Shared obligation through conscription
Conditional	Singapore	Grants citizenship selectively; dual status discouraged	Economic and residency criteria
Conditional	South Korea	Permits dual nationality in limited cases (e.g., talent visas, marriage); others must renounce	Conditional tolerance; merit-based exemptions
Conditional	Mexico	Allows dual nationality; requires civic participation and tax compliance	Emphasis on diaspora ties and national obligation
Conditional	Nigeria	Accepts dual citizenship if Nigerian by birth; prohibits dual status for naturalized citizens	Birth-based duality; restricted for naturalized persons
Liberal	United Kingdom	Broadly permits dual nationality; limited restrictions in sensitive roles	Permissive framework; tiered rights and exceptions
Liberal	France	Accepts dual citizenship; no renunciation required	Strong civic identity; minimal restrictions
Liberal	Canada	Accepts dual nationality with few restrictions; public roles may require sole allegiance	Inclusive legal model; rare limits in security roles
U.S. Position	United States	No formal statutory policy; de facto dual citizenship	Administrative ambiguity; legal silence

While these approaches differ by context, culture, and constitution, several global patterns have begun to crystallize across the spectrum of state responses. These emerging trends—rooted in security, technology, and economics—point to a future in which citizenship is increasingly defined not by inheritance or ideology alone, but by strategic function.

A. Security-First Framework

Across political systems, a growing number of nations have moved to reassert the security dimensions of citizenship. While once primarily a legal or cultural identity, citizenship is now viewed as a national security asset, one that must be protected from dilution, abuse, or weaponization:

- **Germany**, traditionally cautious about dual citizenship, now permits it in more cases—but maintains strict enforcement policies. Since 2019, Germany has had the legal authority to revoke citizenship from dual nationals who join foreign terrorist organizations, even without a criminal conviction.
- **India** has operationalized this logic through its Overseas Citizen of India (OCI) program. Though OCI cardholders enjoy many benefits, the government has exercised broad discretion in revoking OCI status for individuals deemed to have engaged in "anti-national activities," including critical speech and participation in protests.
- **Israel**'s conscription policy similarly reflects this principle. Even dual nationals who acquired Israeli citizenship under the Law of Return are subject to mandatory service in the Israel Defense Forces (IDF) if they reside in Israel. The state's message is clear: citizenship, even when extended broadly, entails a reciprocal obligation of defense.

These examples show that states increasingly treat allegiance as a security-relevant category, not merely a cultural one. Even in liberal democracies, tolerance of dual citizenship does not preclude expectations of undivided loyalty—especially when it comes to matters of war, espionage, or terrorism.

B. Digital Administration

In an era of global mobility and technological surveillance, many countries are turning to digital infrastructure to manage and enforce their citizenship regimes. The 21st-century citizen is now not only documented by paper, but tracked by algorithm:

- **Biometric passports** and identity cards are now standard across the European Union and much of Asia. These tools allow governments to link citizenship status with physical identity in a seamless, globally recognized format.
- **Cross-border information sharing** agreements—like the EU's Schengen Information System or the Five Eyes intelligence alliance—enable states to access real-time data on dual nationals, visa holders, and suspected threats across borders.
- **AI-driven immigration analytics** are being used in Canada, Singapore, and the UK to flag anomalies in travel patterns, financial activity, and allegiance declarations, potentially alerting agencies to dual-national behavior that could indicate risk or noncompliance.

This digital turn raises critical new questions—questions the U.S. has yet to fully grapple with. If citizenship can be documented, tracked, and cross-referenced by machine, what becomes of the subjective, moral dimension of allegiance? And who controls the definitions encoded into those systems?

C. Economic Integration

A third global trend is the increasing use of citizenship as an economic lever. For some countries, especially small states or those with fragile economies, the commodification of citizenship through investment-based programs has become a strategy for attracting capital.

- The rise of "golden passport" programs—explored in greater depth later in this chapter and again in Chapter 6—illustrates a profound shift: from citizenship as a social contract to citizenship as a transactional good.

- Countries such as Malta, Cyprus, and several Caribbean nations openly sell citizenship to foreign investors, typically in exchange for large financial contributions, real estate investments, or business development promises.
- Even countries with stricter frameworks, like Portugal and Greece, have offered "golden visas" that provide long-term residency and a pathway to citizenship through wealth and property acquisition.

These programs have redefined what it means to belong to a nation, transforming a historically identity-laden legal status into a portable, purchasable asset. The security risks are non-trivial: wealthy individuals from authoritarian regimes have used such programs to evade sanctions, launder money, or shield themselves from legal accountability.

The United States is not immune to these trends. While it does not formally sell citizenship, its tolerance of dual status—paired with weak enforcement and a lucrative pathway from green card to naturalization—makes it an attractive endpoint for global elites seeking legal and financial insulation. At the same time, wealthy Americans have taken advantage of foreign citizenship-by-investment programs to secure tax advantages, global mobility, or exit options. In this dual posture, the U.S. becomes both exporter and importer of transactional allegiance—without ever acknowledging the shift. The question is not whether American citizenship is for sale, but whether its silence allows others to set the price

Together, these emerging trends—security-based restrictions, digital surveillance systems, and economic monetization of citizenship—point toward a new global reality: Citizenship is no longer merely about belonging. It is about managing allegiance in a world where mobility, technology, and capital know no borders.

Whether nations resist, regulate, or commodify that allegiance may determine how coherent their civic identity remains in the decades to come.

IV. Administrative Systems and Enforcement

In matters of citizenship, policy without enforcement is performance. Rhetoric alone cannot secure civic coherence, nor can symbolic gestures safeguard national interest. What separates aspirational policy from functional governance is the presence of robust administrative systems—institutions capable not only of recognizing allegiance, but also of monitoring, verifying, and, when necessary, enforcing its obligations.

Among the world's most serious citizenship regimes, enforcement is not an afterthought. It is an integrated component of statecraft, institutionalizing allegiance as a reciprocal relationship between individual and state. These systems do not simply record nationality; they operationalize it.

If registration systems are the foundational infrastructure of citizenship management, verification mechanisms represent the nervous system—constantly monitoring, sensing, and responding to potential disruptions. These layers are not isolated; they form an integrated ecosystem of civic accountability. Where registration documents the baseline of citizenship status, verification tools validate the ongoing integrity of that status. And where both fail, enforcement actions stand as the final arbiter of national belonging, transforming abstract policy into consequential practice. This progression from documentation to validation to potential sanction reveals how serious citizenship regimes transform legal status from a passive designation into an active, monitored relationship between state and citizen.

A. Registration Systems

The first layer of enforcement begins with registration infrastructure—systems that formally document, categorize, and track the legal status of nationals, residents, and dual citizens.

- **Germany** operates the Ausländerzentralregister (AZR), or Central Register of Foreign Nationals, which is one of the most comprehensive systems of its kind in Europe. It logs not only residency status but also dual citizenship where applicable. This database is linked across federal, state, and municipal authorities, ensuring that policy enforcement is consistent and data-driven. When Germany reformed its dual citizenship laws in 2023, the AZR became the cornerstone for managing new entrants and monitoring compliance with integration criteria.
- **India** mandates a self-reporting requirement for any Indian citizen who acquires foreign nationality. Under its Foreigners Act and Citizenship Rules, individuals must notify the Indian government within 90 days of such acquisition. Failure to comply can result in administrative penalties, including the denial of consular services or travel restrictions. While not flawless in execution, the system reflects a legal expectation: citizenship changes are not private matters; they are civic disclosures.
- **Israel** maintains an integrated record system that links civil registration with military obligation. From the moment a dual citizen resides in Israel, their eligibility for service in the Israel Defense Forces (IDF) is tracked alongside their legal and tax status. This intertwining of civic and military databases underscores Israel's belief that citizenship includes existential obligation, particularly in a nation defined by its security environment.

These registration systems do more than identify citizens—they codify accountability. They ensure that allegiance is not diffuse, but tethered to formal systems of recognition and responsibility.

B. Verification Mechanisms

Registration alone is insufficient without mechanisms for ongoing verification. In an era of digital mobility, economic complexity, and transnational identity, states must actively confirm that citizenship status aligns with behavior, benefit, and legal responsibility. Across the globe, nations are investing in tools that allow real-time validation of allegiance:

- **Biometric tracking**—including fingerprint scans, facial recognition, and iris scanning—is now standard in most passport systems. Countries like Singapore, Germany, and Canada use these tools not only for immigration screening but for cross-referencing dual citizenship status during naturalization, border crossings, and background checks.
- **Tax authority coordination** plays a crucial role. Under initiatives like the OECD's Common Reporting Standard (CRS), participating nations share financial data on foreign nationals. This allows governments to identify undeclared assets, tax evasion, or conflicting national obligations—areas where dual citizenship can conceal financial duality.
- **Interpol and EUROPOL** data exchanges further enhance verification efforts. Law enforcement agencies across Europe and the Five Eyes alliance routinely consult shared databases to assess whether dual nationals are subject to foreign criminal warrants, sanctions, or extremist affiliations. In Germany and France, such checks are now routine for naturalization applicants and those seeking security-sensitive roles.

Verification mechanisms signal a shift from passive documentation to active oversight. Allegiance, in this model, is not presumed—it is validated.

C. Enforcement Actions

Ultimately, the legitimacy of any citizenship policy rests on the credibility of its enforcement. Around the world, states have adopted varying levels of disciplinary response to violations of allegiance norms or breaches of civic trust.

- In **Germany**, enforcement includes revocation of citizenship for dual nationals who engage in activities that threaten national security. Since 2019, German law permits the stripping of citizenship from individuals who join foreign terrorist groups, provided they hold a second nationality and do not become stateless. This is more than symbolism—it is a legal articulation of the belief that citizenship can be forfeited through betrayal.
- **India**, while constitutionally prohibiting dual citizenship, enforces allegiance through the Overseas Citizen of India (OCI) regime. If OCI holders are found participating in political activity deemed "anti-national," or convicted of serious crimes, their status can be unilaterally canceled by the Ministry of Home Affairs. Revocation removes residency rights, travel access, and economic privileges. While some have criticized the opaque nature of enforcement, it remains a clear signal of boundary enforcement in a system that distinguishes between civic participation and symbolic affiliation.
- In **Israel**, enforcement is more obligation-focused. Dual citizens who fail to fulfill their IDF service requirements may face deferments of benefits, restrictions on employment in state institutions, or loss of eligibility for certain state-funded programs. Here, enforcement does not operate solely through punishment—it functions through institutional incentives, reinforcing the expectation that allegiance demands shared sacrifice.

Lesson: Administrative Seriousness Reflects Civic Seriousness

Across these varied examples, a consistent theme emerges: serious citizenship regimes do not treat allegiance as merely symbolic. Through registration systems, digital verification, and enforceable sanctions, they treat it as a structured, monitored, and actionable bond between state and citizen.

By contrast, the United States currently lacks any comparable framework for tracking or enforcing the implications of dual citizenship. Its administrative stance remains passive, reliant on individual disclosure and institutional discretion. This stands in stark contrast to peer democracies, which have learned that in a world of layered loyalties and transnational actors, allegiance must be managed—not merely assumed.

V. Special Spotlight: The Rise of Golden Passports

In an era where citizenship is increasingly treated as both an identity and a commodity, a new frontier has emerged in the global landscape of nationality: citizenship-by-investment programs, often referred to as "golden passport" schemes. These arrangements allow individuals to acquire full legal citizenship in exchange for substantial economic contributions—typically through direct investment, real estate purchases, or donations to state development funds. While marketed as strategic tools for economic growth, they raise urgent questions about the moral, legal, and civic meaning of citizenship in the 21st century.

The administrative mechanisms explored in the previous section—registration, verification, and enforcement—represent the structured approach nations take to managing citizenship. Yet, the global landscape reveals a more complex and sometimes contradictory reality. Enter the phenomenon of "golden passports": a radical market-driven transformation of citizenship that challenges every administrative assumption we've just examined. Where careful national systems seek to monitor and validate civic allegiance, citizenship-by-investment programs propose an entirely different logic—one where national belonging becomes a transaction, and loyalty is measured not in service or integration, but in dollars and euros. This section explores how the commodification of citizenship represents the ultimate test of administrative systems: What happens when nationality itself becomes a global commodity to be bought and sold?

Case Study: Malta's Individual Investor Program

One of the most prominent—and controversial—experiments in citizenship-for-sale was Malta's Individual Investor Programme (IIP), a state-run scheme that attracted global elites and provoked intense scrutiny from European institutions.

- **Investment Requirement**: €1.15 million, comprising donations, government bonds, and real estate;
- **Processing Timeline**: 12 to 14 months, with optional fast-track paths;
- **Benefits**: Full EU citizenship, including the right to live, work, and vote in any European Union member state;
- **Criticism**: EU authorities argued the program violated the principle of a "genuine link" between citizen and state, undermining the integrity of Union-wide citizenship.

Though Malta introduced modest reforms and rebranded the scheme in response to EU pressure, the core model remained intact until April 2025, when the European Court of Justice ruled the program unlawful. The ruling forced Malta to halt new applications and initiate legal revisions to align its policies with EU norms.

While existing beneficiaries retain their citizenship, the ruling effectively ended Malta's role as a gateway for transactional access to the European Union. What remains is a more restrictive framework based on longer residency, enhanced due diligence, and credible ties to the state—a marked retreat from the era of passport-for-cash.

Beyond Malta: The Global Marketplace for Citizenship

Similar programs still operate today in Caribbean nations such as Dominica, Antigua & Barbuda, Grenada, St. Kitts & Nevis, and St. Lucia, and in countries like Turkey and Vanuatu—offering rapid access to citizenship through substantial financial investment. In contrast,

European schemes such as Cyprus' and Malta's are now closed—or ending—with major revocations underway. These programs typically compete on price, speed, and visa access—not integration or civic virtue.

While small island nations argue that such programs are vital sources of revenue, the global consequences are harder to dismiss.

Impact on Global Citizenship Norms

The rise of citizenship-by-investment programs has not only redefined how some states commodify legal belonging—it has also triggered mounting concerns about the erosion of democratic norms, global security risks, and the integrity of the international citizenship regime.

1. **Civic Erosion**: Citizenship-by-investment severs the connection between belonging and contribution, reducing a historically civic status to a transactional good. Integration, language, history, or shared experience—hallmarks of most naturalization systems—are replaced by financial capital. This undermines the moral architecture of democratic citizenship, which presumes that legal status arises from lived commitment, not just liquidity.
2. **Security Vulnerabilities**: These programs are vulnerable to abuse by politically exposed persons, sanctioned individuals, and those seeking tax evasion or geopolitical cover. In 2022, INTERPOL flagged dozens of "golden passport" holders as individuals of concern. Lax due diligence in some jurisdictions has enabled money laundering, arms dealing, and illicit finance networks.
3. **Regulatory Backlash**: Major international organizations—OECD, EU, IMF, and the Financial Action Task Force (FATF)—have launched reviews and warnings. The European Commission has threatened legal action against member states whose programs "jeopardize the collective trust of the Union." The OECD has released guidelines for distinguishing genuine residence from tax arbitrage citizenship.

Is Citizenship Still Sacred?

The rise of golden passports presents a profound challenge to the very idea that citizenship is a moral and political relationship. If citizenship can be bought with no expectation of civic duty, allegiance, or democratic participation, can it still claim any binding meaning? Or is it now merely another global asset—alongside yachts, real estate, and offshore accounts?

This question reverberates beyond Malta or the Caribbean. It implicates all democracies, including the United States, which—though not formally operating such programs—grants green cards through investment and lacks coherent limits on dual allegiance tied to financial privilege.

VI. Lessons for American Policy

The comparative landscape of global citizenship reveals a striking truth: while other nations may differ in how they handle dual nationality, they rarely do so passively. Each framework—whether restrictive, conditional, or permissive—reflects deliberate choices about what citizenship means and what it demands. Against this backdrop of intentional policymaking, the United States stands as a conspicuous outlier—not through principled exception, but through institutional silence. The preceding sections have mapped a global terrain of citizenship management, revealing sophisticated approaches from Germany's integration-focused model to India's strict exclusivity. Now, the critical question emerges: How does America's undefined approach measure against these deliberate international strategies? What are the consequences of a citizenship policy defined more by absence than by design?

The United States, by contrast, has drifted into a state of quiet ambiguity. This ambiguity is not benign. It has consequences—for security, civic trust, institutional clarity, and national identity.

From this comparative review, several lessons emerge:

A. Silence Is Not Neutrality

While the United States has avoided codifying a formal policy on dual citizenship, this silence is not a position of neutrality. It is a vacuum—one that allows policy to be defined by court decisions, bureaucratic discretion, and administrative drift rather than democratic deliberation.

Other countries have taken clear positions. India enshrines exclusivity in its constitution. Germany, after decades of restriction, has reformed—but still requires integration and imposes limits. Even flexible systems like those in the UK and France are undergirded by legal definitions and expectations.

Lesson: Citizenship policy is not something a serious democracy can afford to leave unspoken. Where there is no clarity, confusion rushes in—and with it, unequal enforcement and diminished legitimacy.

B. Dual Citizenship Needs Definition

The core issue is not whether dual citizenship should be banned or embraced—it is whether it should be defined. Without clear parameters, contradictions multiply. Can a dual national hold a top-secret clearance? Serve in Congress? Participate in the military of another country? Vote in two national elections?

These are not theoretical questions. They are practical, pressing, and already occurring. For example, a coherent policy must address disclosure requirements and legal boundaries for public officials, security clearance standards for dual citizens, and expectations for civic obligations, including jury duty and tax compliance.

Lesson: Permissiveness without policy is not tolerance—it is abdication. Dual citizenship, if permitted, must come with transparent rules and consistent norms.

C. Administrative Modernization Is Essential

The U.S. lags behind in the administrative infrastructure needed to manage a dual citizenship landscape. Countries like Germany and Israel have developed integrated databases, registration protocols, and cross-agency enforcement mechanisms. India has instituted biometric verification and regular reporting requirements for its diaspora.

By contrast, the United States has no national registry of dual citizens, no standardized vetting procedures, and no dedicated consular framework for handling dual nationality cases. This gap is more than logistical—it reflects a failure to take the implications of dual citizenship seriously.

Lesson: Modern citizenship is a system that must be managed. In the absence of administrative modernization, even the best intentions become unenforceable.

D. The U.S. Can Learn from Its Peers

Each of the countries examined in this chapter offers a potential model—or at least a cautionary tale:

- **Germany** demonstrates how conditional acceptance can be paired with civic integration and institutional seriousness.
- **India** shows that even a vast democracy can maintain exclusivity without alienating its diaspora.
- **Israel** affirms that shared obligations—like military service—can reinforce the meaning of citizenship, even in dual arrangements.
- **France and the UK**, while permissive, do not operate in a vacuum; their approaches are rooted in legal tradition, national narrative, and post-imperial pragmatism.

Lesson: The lesson is not that the United States must copy any one model. It is that it must stop pretending the issue does not require one.

The key takeaway is that serious citizenship regimes are not necessarily strict—but they are always deliberate. Clarity, not coercion, is what preserves the moral and legal coherence of national belonging.

Conclusion: American Exceptionalism or Evasion?

This chapter has not aimed to identify a perfect model of citizenship, but to reveal a central pattern: nations that take citizenship seriously define it seriously. Whether through Germany's integration mandates, India's exclusivity, or Malta's transactional pivot, each approach reflects a deliberate stance on what citizenship should confer—and require.

What emerges across these cases is that ambiguity is rarely neutral. In most systems, dual citizenship is not merely permitted or prohibited—it is *governed*, often through registries, legal conditions, and formal acknowledgment of its implications. Even where motives differ—security, diaspora leverage, or economic gain—the common denominator is intentional design.

By contrast, the U.S. approach stands out not for its permissiveness, but for its lack of engagement. This abdication has consequences, but they are not the only story. The global landscape offers examples—some cautionary, some instructive—of how allegiance can be defined in law without denying plural identity, and enforced without authoritarian overreach.

As the following chapters explore the civic, diplomatic, and institutional consequences of neglecting these questions, this comparative foundation offers more than contrast. It offers possibility.

Chapter 4

The Ethics of Allegiance

What does it mean to be a citizen—not just on paper, but in principle? In an age of global migration, instant communication, and overlapping identities, this question has taken on new urgency. Once assumed to be singular, allegiance is now frequently split across borders, layered across passports, and softened into symbolism. But democracy runs on more than legal paperwork—it runs on trust, sacrifice, and a shared commitment. Without allegiance, citizenship is just a hollow title.

In 2024, several American athletes holding dual citizenship elected to represent other nations at the Paris Olympics.[16] While permitted under international competition rules, their decisions sparked public debate in the U.S. about national loyalty, civic identity, and the meaning of belonging in a globalized world. Were these acts simply expressions of personal heritage and opportunity—or did they reflect a shifting conception of allegiance itself? Such symbolic moments surface deeper

---

[16] For examples of U.S.-born athletes representing other countries in the 2024 Paris Olympics, see "Yes, Some Olympic Athletes Are Allowed to Compete for a Country Other Than the One They Live In," *KGW News*, July 2024; and Susan Warmbier, "Dualing Dreams: Dual Citizenship Fulfills Long-Awaited Olympic Dreams," *Inside Gymnastics*, July 2024.

ethical questions: Can one individual simultaneously owe equal civic duty to multiple sovereigns? And can a democratic polity sustain cohesion when its members divide political loyalties across nations—some of them ideologically aligned, others not?

This chapter argues that allegiance is not obsolete—it is foundational. Drawing from both classical social contract theory and contemporary political thought, it explores how dual citizenship disrupts the moral coherence of civic life. Thinkers such as Hobbes, Locke, and Rousseau envisioned political obligation as singular and reciprocal. More recent theorists—from John Rawls to Michael Walzer, Michael Sandel, Seyla Benhabib, and Kwame Anthony Appiah—remind us that democratic societies are sustained not by laws alone but by civic virtue and ethical commitment.

The chapter proceeds in six sections. It begins by clarifying the concept of allegiance as a form of moral belonging, then turns to the philosophical traditions that shaped our understanding of loyalty and duty in liberal democracies. From there, it examines the civic erosion caused by ambiguous or divided loyalties—declining participation, compromised public service, and fragmented cultural identity. Illustrative ethical dilemmas reveal the real-world stakes: the diplomat torn between two national interests, the voter participating in conflicting elections across borders, and the scientist navigating competing obligations between sovereign states.

Finally, Chapter 4 considers what a renewed ethic of allegiance might look like in a pluralist society. Can we sustain shared democratic life without shared civic bonds? If so, how? And if not, what must be rethought about how we define, teach, and enforce the obligations of citizenship?

The stakes are high. Allegiance may seem like an old-fashioned term—but its absence leaves a vacuum at the heart of democratic belonging. The sections that follow are an argument for reclaiming it, not as coercion, but as an ethical horizon that makes freedom and pluralism possible.

I. What Does It Mean to Belong?

Citizenship is not merely a legal status. It is a moral identity, a civic bond, and a public commitment to a political community. To be a citizen, in a democracy, is to participate in a shared project of law, liberty, and mutual responsibility. It is to say, in effect: *I belong to this people, to this place, and to this promise.*

But what does it mean to *belong* in a world where identity is increasingly fluid, where borders are porous, and where individuals often maintain multiple passports, multiple political obligations, and sometimes conflicting loyalties?

The Crisis of Coherent Allegiance

Dual citizenship hasn't just made travel easier—it's reshaped the moral foundations of what citizenship means. Can an individual owe equal allegiance to two states with different laws, policies, and national interests—especially in times of war, diplomatic conflict, or ideological division?

Michael Sandel, in his work *Justice: What's the Right Thing to Do?*, reminds us that citizenship is not just about autonomy or rights—it is about belonging to a moral community that binds individuals together in mutual obligation. In this sense, dual citizenship—when unmanaged—undermines the possibility of shared sacrifice and reciprocal trust that citizenship traditionally requires.

The Displacement of Civic Identity

Legal pluralism, economic globalization, and cultural hybridity have produced many benefits. But they have also displaced the core idea of national belonging. As philosopher Kwame Anthony Appiah argues in

The Ethics of Identity, identity is always partially constructed—but it also requires boundaries to be meaningful. Citizenship without civic boundaries becomes identity without civic consequence.

Similarly, Seyla Benhabib, in *The Rights of Others*, explores the tensions between universal human rights and bounded democratic obligations. She recognizes the moral claims of global mobility, but also insists on the legitimacy of democratic communities to preserve their civic integrity. If everyone can belong anywhere, then belonging becomes weightless—lacking the substance of commitment, reciprocity, and trust.

The Diminishing Meaning of Allegiance

Allegiance has been dismissively labeled as obsolete—a relic of bygone nationalism. But this perspective fundamentally misunderstands democracy's moral infrastructure: citizenship is not about uniformity, but about a shared commitment to collective self-governance.

Citizenship must mean more than residency. It must mean standing with others in times of peace and crisis, voting not just for oneself but for the community, paying taxes not as a transaction but as a contribution, and obeying laws not only because they constrain but because they express collective self-rule.

Without allegiance—clear, accountable, and meaningful—democratic citizenship risks becoming a shell: a status with rights but no duties, protections but no participation.

Public Attitudes: Belonging and Loyalty

Polling data suggests the American public still values allegiance, even amid increasing pluralism:

- According to a 2023 Gallup survey, 71% of Americans believe that "citizens should prioritize loyalty to the United States

above other countries."[17]
- A 2024 Pew Research Center study found that 53% of respondents were "concerned" or "very concerned" about the implications of dual citizenship for national security and democratic trust.
- At the same time, 41% agreed that "dual citizenship reflects modern identity," signaling a growing—but divided—conscience on the issue.[18]

These numbers reflect not just demographic shifts, but a philosophical crossroads: Should citizenship be redefined to accommodate personal pluralism—or should it be reinvigorated to reinforce civic coherence?

Understanding allegiance requires more than abstract philosophy. It demands we examine how divided loyalties manifest in real-world scenarios—from diplomatic negotiations to electoral politics, from scientific collaboration to personal identity.

The next section explores these complex terrains where allegiance is tested, challenged, and potentially transformed.

II. Philosophical Foundations of Allegiance

What does it mean to owe loyalty to a political community? This question is not only legal but profoundly ethical, and it lies at the heart of Western political thought. Allegiance, in its deepest sense, is not merely a form of obedience or legal affiliation. It is a reciprocal moral bond—an agreement between individual and state, undergirded by expectations of trust, protection, sacrifice, and shared purpose. From the early social contract theorists to contemporary political philosophers, allegiance has

---

[17] Gallup, *Patriotism and Dual Allegiance*, Gallup Poll Social Series, July 2023.
[18] Pew Research Center, *Public Opinion on Dual Citizenship and National Belonging*, February 2024.

been understood as the moral infrastructure that sustains democratic society.

A. The Social Contract Tradition

The idea that allegiance should be singular and binding has deep roots in Western political thought. At the core of this tradition is the social contract—the idea that individuals agree, either implicitly or explicitly, to form a political community in exchange for protection, law, and mutual benefit. This contract is not merely legal but moral. It is the basis for why citizens owe loyalty to the state—and why the state, in turn, must uphold its duties to them.

Three of the most influential political thinkers in this tradition—Thomas Hobbes, John Locke, and Jean-Jacques Rousseau—each presented a distinct vision of political life. But they all shared a critical assumption: that the social contract binds individuals to a single political authority. None of them imagined a citizen splitting loyalty between two countries. In their view, that would break the very contract holding society together.

Thomas Hobbes, writing in 17th-century England during a period of civil war and political instability, argued that the natural condition of humanity—life without government—was one of chaos, violence, and fear. In his major work, *Leviathan*, Hobbes proposed that to escape this state of nature, individuals must submit to a central authority—what he called a "sovereign"—who would enforce laws and guarantee peace. But this submission had to be complete. There could be no divided loyalty, no partial allegiance to another ruler or state. For Hobbes, the legitimacy of political order depended on each person pledging full and undivided allegiance to one sovereign. Dual citizenship, in this framework, would be unintelligible—it would unravel the very peace the contract was meant to produce.

John Locke, writing a generation later, offered a more liberal version of the social contract. He believed that individuals have natural rights—life, liberty, and property—and that governments exist to protect those rights. Unlike Hobbes, Locke held that if a government violates the trust of its citizens, they have the right to withdraw their consent and form a new government. Yet Locke still assumed a one-to-one relationship between individual and state. Consent was granted to a single polity. To withdraw it was to start anew—not to maintain simultaneous commitments to multiple governments. For Locke, as for Hobbes, the idea of owing allegiance to two sovereign powers at once was not just unlikely—it was incompatible with the contract itself.

Finally, Jean-Jacques Rousseau, writing in 18th-century France, brought a more democratic and participatory vision. In his influential book *The Social Contract*, Rousseau described citizenship as not just a legal status, but a moral vocation. Citizens, in his view, were active participants in shaping the "general will"—the collective good of the community. To be a citizen was to belong wholly to that civic body. Partial or divided membership would fracture the general will and destroy the unity needed for a just society. Rousseau believed that the republic could not survive if its members were torn between competing loyalties. For him, allegiance was not merely legal—it was ethical, emotional, and indivisible.

These three thinkers disagreed on many points, from the nature of rights to the scope of state power. But they converged on one principle: political allegiance was meant to be singular. It was the glue that held the social contract together. If individuals could pick and choose among multiple allegiances—especially ones that might conflict—the stability and legitimacy of the political community would be at risk.

These foundational thinkers could not have anticipated the complexities of 21st-century global citizenship. Yet their core insight remains profound: political allegiance is not a casual affiliation, but a deep moral commitment that sustains the very possibility of collective self-governance.

In the following subsections, we turn to how modern democratic theorists have built on—or departed from—this tradition, and how dual citizenship complicates the fragile trust that democracy requires.

B. Allegiance and Democratic Trust

The twentieth-century philosopher John Rawls offers a more pluralistic, yet still demanding, vision of political community. In *A Theory of Justice*, Rawls introduced the idea of an "overlapping consensus": a model in which individuals from diverse moral, religious, or philosophical backgrounds converge on a shared commitment to certain core political principles. But this convergence assumes a common political framework—a shared commitment to the norms, rights, and institutions of one constitutional order.

Dual citizenship, however, challenges this assumption. When individuals are legal members of multiple polities—each with its own set of obligations, laws, and priorities—the mutual trust that undergirds democratic life becomes fragile. For example, if one citizen can vote in both U.S. and foreign elections, or benefit from U.S. protections while serving in another nation's military, then the presumption of shared civic responsibility erodes. The very concept of democratic reciprocity—*that your vote affects my future and my taxes support your rights*—becomes compromised.

Political trust is not just about confidence in leaders; it is about believing that one's fellow citizens are playing by the same rules and committed to the same outcomes. Divided allegiance renders that belief uncertain.

C. Allegiance as a Public Good

Building on this, political theorist Michael Walzer has emphasized that citizenship is not merely a gateway to rights—it is a bearer of moral obligations. In his influential work *Spheres of Justice*, Walzer argued that political membership carries with it an ethic of shared fate. Allegiance, in this view, is not a symbolic loyalty but a lived commitment to a common civic enterprise.

Yet like all public goods, allegiance is vulnerable to erosion. If too many individuals begin to treat allegiance as optional, symbolic, or secondary—if they vote in one country and live in another, serve one state while enjoying protections from another—the social contract begins to fray. This is a classic free-rider problem: those who bear the burdens of citizenship (e.g., jury duty, taxation, national service) do so alongside others who enjoy the benefits without fully sharing in the obligations. The result is a weakening of solidarity and an increase in democratic cynicism.

Next, Kwame Anthony Appiah, in his work on identity and cosmopolitanism, has argued for a flexible and inclusive understanding of belonging. But even Appiah recognizes the importance of civic grounding—a meaningful connection to one's political community, not simply legal paperwork or cultural nostalgia. Without this grounding, citizenship becomes a hollow credential rather than a moral tie.

Similarly, Seyla Benhabib has championed the idea of democratic iterations—flexible forms of belonging that adapt over time. Yet she warns that without institutional clarity and shared norms, pluralistic societies risk fragmentation. Citizenship must be capacious enough to accommodate difference, but coherent enough to sustain collective action.

Together, these perspectives form a strong philosophical basis for treating allegiance not as a relic of nationalism, but as a moral necessity for democratic life. Citizenship, in this light, cannot function if it becomes an interchangeable token or a secondary identity. It must rest on an unambiguous foundation—one that supports political trust, shared sacrifice, and civic equality. In the sections that follow, we examine what happens when that foundation begins to erode.

III. Civic Erosion in a Dual-Allegiance Regime

Beyond legal recognition, citizenship in a democracy is an invitation to active participation. It is through voting, jury service, local engagement, and public deliberation that citizens co-create their political future. Yet dual citizenship, when left unregulated and ethically unexamined, introduces a corrosive ambiguity into this equation. The result is not merely a legal anomaly, but a slow erosion of civic cohesion.

A. Declining Civic Participation

A healthy democracy depends on broad-based participation—not only at the ballot box, but in the daily work of governance: serving on juries, attending public meetings, contributing to civic organizations, and investing in the local social fabric. These are the activities that turn passive residents into active citizens, and private individuals into public stewards.

Yet a growing body of empirical research suggests that dual citizens—particularly those who reside primarily abroad—are significantly less likely to engage in these practices. This is not simply a logistical issue of geographic distance; it is often an attitudinal one. When political membership is distributed across multiple nations, the sense of exclusive responsibility to any single polity is weakened. The obligations of civic life come to feel optional rather than essential.

Even for dual citizens who reside within the United States, the existence of an alternate passport or fallback nationality may create what political theorist David Miller has called an "exit illusion."[19] When civic burdens such as taxation, jury service, or military registration arise, the dual citizen may feel less compelled to comply—not out of disloyalty per se, but because the psychological anchor of political obligation is diluted. There

---

[19] David Miller, *Citizenship and National Identity* (Cambridge: Polity Press, 2000), 86–89.

is always somewhere else to go, another identity to lean on, another flag to wave.

This phenomenon has consequences. When civic participation declines among a segment of the population, the principle of democratic equality is undermined. The voices that shape collective decisions become narrower, and the legitimacy of public institutions suffers. More troubling still, the burden of civic maintenance becomes unevenly distributed. Some citizens carry the full weight of democratic responsibility, while others drift in and out of obligation as circumstances permit.

If disengagement represents the quiet erosion of civic responsibility, the challenges of public service reveal a more acute vulnerability. When allegiance becomes negotiable, the very institutions designed to protect democratic life become susceptible to structural compromise.

B. Ambiguous Loyalty in Public Service

While all citizens are expected to act in good faith, certain roles in public life demand unambiguous allegiance: diplomatic service, national defense, intelligence operations, and positions of elected leadership. These domains are not morally neutral; they operate on the premise of exclusive loyalty to the nation-state. In these contexts, even the appearance of divided allegiance can compromise institutional trust.

Consider the following real-world-inspired ethical dilemma:

Hypothetical: The Diplomat's Dilemma

A U.S. citizen of Chinese descent working in the State Department is approached by officials from the Chinese government. The interaction is framed as friendly outreach—but it includes subtle pressure to shape internal policy debates in Beijing's favor. The employee has no intention of betraying American interests. But they carry deep cultural, familial, and ancestral ties—connections that foreign powers increasingly exploit to generate influence. In a moment of high-stakes diplomacy or rising geopolitical tension, whose interests prevail?

This scenario is not hypothetical. Intelligence agencies in the U.S. and allied countries have raised growing concerns about foreign influence through diasporic networks—even when formal dual citizenship is not legally recognized. Governments such as China, which does not permit dual nationality, may still treat foreign-born individuals as de facto nationals or kin by descent, blurring the lines between cultural identity and political allegiance.

Congress and Dual Allegiance – Who Do They Serve?

Recent Legislative Developments

In 2024, Representative Thomas Massie introduced the *Dual Loyalty Disclosure Act*, which would require all Members of Congress to:
- Disclose any foreign nationality held at the time of assuming office
- File a signed statement with the House or Senate ethics committee
- Face potential fines up to $2,500 for non-disclosure

Congressional Citizenship Requirements (Current Law):
- **Representatives**: Must be U.S. citizens for at least 7 years
- **Senators**: Must be U.S. citizens for at least 9 years
- No explicit prohibition on dual citizenship

Statistical Context:
- At least 76 members of the 117th Congress were foreign-born or had at least one parent born abroad
- No official count exists of how many hold dual citizenship

Emerging Political Debate:
- Heightened concerns about dual loyalty, especially in foreign affairs and national security
- Growing calls for transparency, ethics disclosure, and possible future restrictions
- Proposed renunciation requirement for federal elected officials

Key Quote: "Dual citizens elected to the United States Congress should renounce citizenship in all other countries."
— Rep. Thomas Massie (R-KY), 2024

Sources: see page 110.

The problem is not personal—it is structural. Without a clear framework for how allegiance intersects with public service—especially under conditions of global interdependence—both the individual and the institution remain vulnerable. In such roles, allegiance must be more than assumed. It must be demonstrable, affirmed, and exclusive.

C. Cultural Fragmentation and the Retreat from Shared Identity

Democratic societies do not require uniformity—but they do require cohesion. What binds a diverse citizenry is not heritage, but a shared sense of belonging: common institutions, civic rituals, and a mutual investment in the future. When allegiance becomes diffuse, that connective tissue begins to fray.

Unregulated dual citizenship risks accelerating this erosion. In the absence of clear legal or educational frameworks for navigating divided loyalties, individuals may become socially embedded in one country, politically active in another, and civically disengaged from both.

This fragmentation is already evident. In some communities, disputes have emerged over school curricula perceived to elevate foreign narratives over national ones. Legal battles over oath-taking ceremonies and symbolic renunciation of prior allegiances reflect deeper questions about identity. And the growing trend of non-resident dual nationals voting in foreign elections while participating in U.S. politics has further blurred the lines of civic responsibility.

Pluralism without a shared civic core turns into factionalism—and factionalism without allegiance breaks into fragments. When people identify more strongly with foreign governments than with the democratic institutions of their country of citizenship, the capacity for collective self-governance is impaired. A democracy cannot thrive when its members lack clarity about what it means to belong—and to whom they are ultimately accountable.

IV. The Fragile Fabric of Democratic Trust

Democracy is not merely a structure of institutions or a collection of rules—it is a moral ecosystem held together by trust. Citizens must trust that others will follow the law, accept election outcomes, and contribute fairly to the collective good. This trust, while often invisible, is foundational. It allows societies to govern without coercion, to deliberate without fear, and to disagree without collapse.

But this trust is not automatic. It is built upon a shared sense of civic belonging and mutual obligation. When the boundaries of allegiance become unclear—when the notion of "we the people" loses coherence—the invisible threads of democratic trust begin to fray.

Dual citizenship, when unmanaged and undefined, accelerates this unraveling. It introduces not only legal ambiguity but ethical uncertainty. In a pluralist society, where people may hold multiple cultural, religious, or ideological identities, citizenship is the one civic identity that must remain grounded and non-negotiable. Without clarity on where a citizen's primary obligations lie, democratic accountability weakens.

Recent discussions and debates reveal complex public attitudes toward dual citizenship and national loyalty. While many Americans support the general concept of dual citizenship, concerns typically increase when it comes to sensitive government positions and national security roles. The question of divided loyalties becomes particularly salient in positions requiring security clearances or handling classified information.

According to federal guidelines, dual citizenship itself does not automatically disqualify individuals from obtaining security clearances, but it requires additional scrutiny and may present complications for certain sensitive compartmented information (SCI) or special access program (SAP) clearances. This policy reflects broader societal tensions between embracing global identity and protecting national interests.

Divided Loyalties in Office

"No man can serve two masters." — Matthew 6:24

The Civic Dilemma: In an age of global wealth, dual loyalties, and transnational influence, even those entrusted with safeguarding the republic sometimes forget to whom they owe their first and only civic allegiance.

The U.S. Constitution demands that elected officials swear an oath to "support and defend the Constitution of the United States against all enemies, foreign and domestic." Yet in recent years, that promise has been blurred by private financial ties, undisclosed foreign holdings, and political entanglements with foreign governments.

Case in Point
- In 2024, the Department of Justice pursued high-profile prosecutions revealing systemic vulnerabilities. Congressman Henry Cuellar faced charges of unlawful foreign influence, representing a broader pattern of potential compromise.
- OpenSecrets documented an unprecedented surge in "dark money" from undisclosed sources, creating complex webs of international financial entanglement that threaten legislative independence.
- A comprehensive investigation revealed that multiple members of Congress held substantial foreign assets or dual nationality, raising critical questions about divided governmental loyalties.

Emerging Investigations: Foreign Influence and Legislative Compromise
1. **High-Profile Foreign Influence Cases**
   - Congressman Henry Cuellar was indicted in May 2024 on charges of accepting bribes from Azerbaijan, allegedly using his office to influence U.S. policy. The charges include bribery, money laundering, and working on behalf of a foreign government.
   - Senator Bob Menendez: in July 2024, a federal jury convicted him on 16 counts, including bribery, fraud, and acting as a foreign agent for Egypt and Qatar. In January 2025, he was sentenced to 11 years in prison.
2. **Systemic Financial Risks**
   - The 2024 election cycle experienced an unprecedented surge in political spending, exceeding $20 billion, with over $4.5 billion coming from outside groups — including a record infusion of dark money from organizations that do not fully disclose their donors.
3. **Regulatory Enforcement**
   - The Department of Justice pursued multiple high-profile prosecutions under the Foreign Agents Registration Act (FARA) throughout 2024.
   - Potential penalties for FARA violations can include up to five years in prison.

Potential Consequences:
- Erosion of legislative independence
- Compromised national security decision-making
- Undermining public trust in democratic institutions

The investigations reveal a complex landscape where divided national loyalties can create real or apparent conflicts of interest, challenging the fundamental principles of singular national commitment.

Sources: see page 110.

But this trust is not automatic. It is built upon a shared sense of civic belonging and mutual obligation. When the boundaries of allegiance become unclear—when the notion of "we the people" loses coherence—the invisible threads of democratic trust begin to fray.

Dual citizenship, when unmanaged and undefined, accelerates this unraveling. It introduces not only legal ambiguity but ethical uncertainty. In a pluralist society, where people may hold multiple cultural, religious, or ideological identities, citizenship is the one civic identity that must remain grounded and non-negotiable. Without clarity on where a citizen's primary obligations lie, democratic accountability weakens.

Recent discussions and debates reveal complex public attitudes toward dual citizenship and national loyalty. While many Americans support the general concept of dual citizenship, concerns typically increase when it comes to sensitive government positions and national security roles. The question of divided loyalties becomes particularly salient in positions requiring security clearances or handling classified information.

According to federal guidelines, dual citizenship itself does not automatically disqualify individuals from obtaining security clearances, but it requires additional scrutiny and may present complications for certain sensitive compartmented information (SCI) or special access program (SAP) clearances. This policy reflects broader societal tensions between embracing global identity and protecting national interests.

Ballots Across Borders

Consider a real-world ethical dilemma that emerged in the 2024 election cycle. Reports surfaced of dual citizens voting in both U.S. federal elections and in the national elections of their other country of citizenship. In one instance, a dual U.S.–Turkish citizen voted in the U.S. midterms for candidates supporting NATO expansion—while also voting in Turkey for a party that explicitly condemned Western military alliances. In another case, a dual U.S.–Venezuelan citizen supported democratic reforms in the U.S., while casting a vote in Venezuela for a regime facing international sanctions.

Legally, many of these actions are permissible. There is no federal prohibition on dual citizens voting in foreign elections. But the ethical dilemma is deeper than the legal technicalities. Can a democratic polity maintain legitimacy when its members participate in the politics of competing nations—particularly when those nations hold opposing values, interests, or geopolitical objectives?

Democratic accountability rests on the assumption that votes are cast in the shared interest of a single polity. When individuals are empowered to vote in multiple systems—systems that may be ideologically or strategically at odds—the meaning of the vote itself becomes unstable. Is the citizen casting a ballot as a participant in a common civic project, or as a consumer navigating two political marketplaces?

This instability undermines not just institutional legitimacy but interpersonal trust. Fellow citizens may begin to question whether their neighbors are fully committed to the same civic enterprise. Elected leaders may hesitate to appoint dual nationals to sensitive roles, fearing divided loyalties. Public discourse becomes tinged with suspicion, and the presumption of shared purpose erodes.

Philosopher Seyla Benhabib has warned that democratic life requires not only legal frameworks but moral boundaries of inclusion. If those boundaries become too porous—if citizenship is treated as an interchangeable asset rather than a stable identity—the moral claims of democratic authority lose their force.

In this context, trust becomes conditional, fragile, and ultimately endangered.

As democratic trust becomes increasingly fragile, we must confront the ethical blind spots created by our current understanding of citizenship. The next section explores these hidden vulnerabilities—the unexamined assumptions that allow divided loyalties to erode our collective civic commitment.

V. Ethical Blind Spots in a Globalized World

The global spread of dual citizenship has outpaced not only legal coherence—but moral clarity. While earlier sections traced how nations define and regulate allegiance through law, this section turns to the ethical vacuum left behind when law alone is insufficient.

In high-stakes sectors—from diplomacy to defense, elections to science—dual allegiance can create quiet conflicts of interest that are not always visible, let alone illegal. These are not dilemmas of treason, but of trust: tensions between personal identity and public responsibility, private advantage and shared obligation.

This is where the deeper challenge lies. In a world where citizenship can be held in multiples, leveraged economically, or downplayed bureaucratically, the question becomes not simply *what rights a citizen holds*—but *what duties they recognize*. And when those duties are undefined, democracy inherits the risk.

The Security Question

Consider the case of a dual-national scientist employed in a U.S. defense research laboratory. They are a U.S. citizen, cleared to work on highly sensitive technologies with national security applications. Unbeknownst to their employer, they are also a citizen of another nation with geopolitical tensions against the United States.

One day, they are contacted by a foreign science ministry and asked to "collaborate" on an overlapping research initiative. There is no legal requirement for them to disclose this dual allegiance—not to the institution, not to their colleagues, and not even during the security clearance process unless specifically asked. No formal law has been violated. But a fundamental ethical question emerges: To whom are they ultimately accountable?

In a regime where allegiance is left undefined, institutional safeguards are undermined not by criminal intent but by moral ambiguity. Loyalty becomes a gray zone. The scientist, though perhaps acting in good faith, now straddles two sovereign obligations that may eventually come into conflict. The public trust that supports national security infrastructure becomes precarious.

This is not an isolated scenario. The rise of dual citizens in high-stakes sectors—defense, cyber, biotechnology, diplomacy—has created a new class of ethical dilemmas. These are not about overt betrayal or espionage; they are about the erosion of clarity in contexts that demand it most.

As Michael Sandel warns, when citizenship is treated as a market commodity rather than a moral commitment, its civic meaning is hollowed out. Similarly, Kwame Anthony Appiah emphasizes that identity must be anchored as well as autonomous. But dual allegiance, when unbounded, privileges individual flexibility at the expense of shared civic purpose. The result is a fragmented sense of belonging—where the duties of citizenship are easily eclipsed by its conveniences.

In this vacuum, ethical responsibility is offloaded onto individuals, institutions, or bureaucracies unequipped to adjudicate it. We rely on good judgment where we once relied on clear standards. The result is not global harmony—but structural vulnerability.

As this chapter has thus far argued, allegiance is not about nostalgia for a monolithic past. It is about moral structure. Without that structure, citizenship becomes untethered from the public good—and democracy becomes a house built on sand.

If the ethical blind spots of dual citizenship reveal the fragility of our current frameworks, they also demand a more constructive response. The challenge is not to retreat into narrow nationalism, but to develop a more sophisticated understanding of allegiance that can accommodate global complexity while preserving democratic integrity.

VI. Rethinking Allegiance in a Pluralist Society

Pluralism is one of the great virtues of liberal democracy. It affirms that people of different origins, beliefs, languages, and customs can live together under a shared political system, bound not by blood or tribe, but by law and mutual respect. The United States, perhaps more than any other nation, has prided itself on this pluralistic ideal.

But pluralism is not the same as relativism. It cannot mean anything goes. For a democratic society to function, it must possess a common civic grammar—a shared understanding of rights, responsibilities, and reciprocal allegiance. It must be capacious enough to welcome difference, yet structured enough to require commitment.

This is where the current practice of dual citizenship reveals its limits. Without ethical guardrails, pluralism risks becoming fragmentation. When citizenship is unmoored from allegiance—when legal status no longer requires loyalty or civic contribution—the very coherence of the political community begins to fray.

As philosopher Seyla Benhabib has argued, democratic inclusion must always be "bounded by the principle of reciprocity." Welcoming others does not negate the need for mutual obligation. A truly pluralist society affirms diversity within a framework of shared civic norms—not above or beyond them.

To preserve both pluralism and civic coherence, we must rethink the ethical architecture of allegiance. This does not mean returning to ethnonationalist models of exclusion. It means recovering the idea that belonging entails responsibility—that the rights of citizenship are inseparable from its duties.

Ethical and Policy Pathways

Allegiance need not be rigid to be meaningful. It can evolve alongside global realities—but it must also be clear. The following proposals are not final answers, but preliminary outlines—each of which will be developed more fully in later chapters. Together, they gesture toward a more deliberate civic framework, one in which allegiance regains moral and institutional relevance:

- **Reinstating Conditional Renunciation -** For certain roles—such as elected federal office, intelligence work, military command, or treaty negotiation—exclusive allegiance should be a prerequisite. These are not ordinary jobs; they involve the exercise of sovereign power or access to the nation's most sensitive information. Requiring singular citizenship for such roles is not punitive—it is prudential.
- **Transparency and Disclosure Requirements -** Transparency in matters of allegiance is essential to public trust. While dual citizenship need not bar public service, it can raise legitimate concerns in security-sensitive, judicial, or policymaking roles if left undisclosed. A consistent system for tracking dual nationality across federal agencies would help prevent conflicts of interest, strengthen vetting, and uphold institutional credibility. This book returns to this issue in Chapter 9, Section V *("Digital Citizenship Disclosure and Accountability")*, where a full proposal for a national dual-citizenship disclosure and registry system is outlined, including key civic touchpoints, interagency coordination, and safeguards for plural identity.

- **Civic Education for the 21st Century -** In schools and universities, civic education should be revitalized—not as rote nationalism, but as a moral framework that links rights to responsibilities. Students should be taught that citizenship involves more than entitlements—it entails participation, sacrifice, and allegiance to shared constitutional principles.

These proposals are not about exclusion. They are about ethical clarity—about drawing a distinction between pluralism as diversity of origin, and pluralism as diversity of allegiance. The former can be inclusive. The latter, if unbounded, can be destabilizing.

Allegiance, rightly understood, is not blind loyalty but fidelity to the democratic conditions that make pluralism possible. It is what turns citizenship from a transactional convenience into a moral and civic commitment.

If allegiance is the ethical infrastructure of democratic life, the chapters that follow take up the task of building that structure for a fragmented and interdependent age.

Conclusion: Allegiance as an Ethical Horizon

Allegiance, rightly understood, is an ethical orientation—a posture of commitment toward one's political community and its shared life. It is the bridge between freedom and responsibility, between identity and obligation. Without it, democratic society becomes a marketplace of preferences, not a covenant of citizens.

This chapter has traced the moral dimensions of allegiance from its roots in classical political theory to its present-day erosion in the face of dual citizenship. The argument is not that plural identities are wrong, or that modern mobility should be resisted. Rather, the concern is that when citizenship becomes fragmented—when it is treated as transferable, divisible, or primarily instrumental—its ethical substance is hollowed out.

When allegiance is optional, civic trust becomes fragile. When obligations can be evaded, reciprocity breaks down. When citizens serve two or more sovereigns without acknowledgment or consequence, the very concept of democratic accountability is called into question.

This erosion does not arise from bad intentions. Most dual citizens are committed, law-abiding, and engaged. The problem is not personal—it is structural. In the absence of legal clarity and ethical discourse, citizenship becomes an increasingly symbolic possession rather than a lived civic practice. It becomes something one has, rather than something one does.

And yet, allegiance remains indispensable. It is what sustains the trust that neighbors will follow the law, that jurors will deliberate fairly, that votes will be cast with the nation's welfare in mind. It is what allows a citizen to say not only "I live here" or "I benefit from this system," but also "I belong to this polity—and I am responsible for it."

If we are to reclaim the full meaning of citizenship in the 21st century, we must be willing to speak of allegiance not as a historical relic, but as a normative horizon. It is what binds diverse individuals into a political "we." Without it, pluralism turns to partition. With it, difference can become a source of strength rather than division.

This chapter has argued that allegiance is not a nostalgic ideal, but a civic necessity. In a time of global mobility and plural identities, the challenge is not to deny the complexity of modern belonging—but to preserve the integrity of democratic citizenship within it.

Citizenship is not a matter of convenience, nor is it merely a passport or legal status. It is a promise: to care for the common good, to stand accountable to a political community, and to participate in the shared life of a democracy. When allegiance becomes divided, optional, or invisible, this promise erodes—not through ill will, but through structural incoherence.

The risks are not abstract. As this chapter has shown, the moral consequences of dual allegiance surface in moments of crisis, conflict, and contested loyalty. Civic trust frays when fellow citizens appear to belong only partially. Responsibility weakens when the burdens of citizenship are unevenly distributed. And democratic institutions suffer when allegiance is treated as a matter of personal preference rather than public responsibility.

To meet this challenge, we need ethical clarity. We need to recover the language of allegiance as a shared horizon—one that can anchor plural identities in common responsibility.

This is the moral work of democratic life: to ensure that citizenship is not just a right, but a relationship. Not merely something we hold, but something we uphold.

> For further analysis of how dual citizenship complicates extradition and legal accountability across jurisdictions—including case studies and policy recommendations—see the Legal Report that follows: *Accountability in the Extradition Era.*

Legal Report

Accountability in the Extradition Era

I. The Complex Landscape of Dual Citizenship and Justice

Extradition—the legal process by which one nation surrenders an individual to another for prosecution or punishment—is a cornerstone of international legal cooperation. But in practice, it is anything but simple. As explored in the preceding chapter's analysis of allegiance, even among close allies, treaties vary significantly in scope, procedure, and exemptions. When dual citizenship enters the equation, extradition becomes even more fraught—raising complex questions of sovereignty, loyalty, and legal obligation that challenge our fundamental understanding of civic commitment.

II. Statistical Context and Global Perspectives

Dual Citizenship Extradition Landscape:
- Approximately 18% of U.S. extradition requests are complicated by dual citizenship status
- An estimated 5-7% of potential extraditions are ultimately blocked due to dual nationality protections
- Countries like Israel, France, and Germany reject over 60% of U.S. extradition requests involving their citizens

Global Extradition Policies: A Comparative View

Countries with Strict No-Extradition Policies:
- Israel: Refuses extradition of citizens under almost all circumstances
- France: Constitutional protections limit citizen extradition
- Germany: Requires extensive legal review for citizen extradition

Countries with Conditional Extradition:
- United Kingdom: More flexible, but still protects citizen rights
- Canada: Cooperative with U.S. extradition requests
- Australia: Negotiates case-by-case extradition agreements

III. Legal Complexities of Dual Citizenship

According to the U.S. Department of Justice's Criminal Resource Manual, extradition decisions must specifically consider "the citizenship of the fugitive, including in particular whether he or she is a dual citizen." This creates several key complications:

1. **Treaty Limitations**
   Many countries' extradition treaties explicitly permit them to refuse extradition of their own citizens, even in cases of dual citizenship. This can create safe havens for individuals seeking to evade justice while claiming protection under their second nationality.
2. **Jurisdictional Conflicts**
   When dual citizens face criminal charges, competing jurisdictional claims can arise between nations. Civil law countries, in particular, often prioritize their nationals' rights over extradition requests, viewing them as "compatriots first, criminals second."
3. **Enforcement Challenges**
   The lack of extradition treaties with certain nations, combined with dual citizenship protections, can create significant obstacles for law enforcement and national security agencies trying to prosecute crimes or enforce judgments.

IV. Potential Policy Solutions

1. Enhanced Bilateral Treaties
   - Develop more comprehensive extradition agreements
   - Create clearer protocols for dual national prosecutions
2. Diplomatic Pressure Mechanisms
   - Implement targeted sanctions for non-cooperative nations
   - Create international legal frameworks for handling dual citizen cases
3. Citizenship Accountability Provisions
   - Require dual citizens to acknowledge potential legal obligations

- 4. Enhanced Bilateral Treaties
    - Develop more comprehensive extradition agreements
    - Create clearer protocols for dual national prosecutions
- 5. Diplomatic Pressure Mechanisms
    - Implement targeted sanctions for non-cooperative nations
    - Create international legal frameworks for handling dual citizen cases
- 6. Citizenship Accountability Provisions
    - Require dual citizens to acknowledge potential legal obligations
    - Create more transparent reporting mechanisms for dual nationals

V. Fundamental Challenge

The core issue remains: dual citizenship can create legal "safe zones" where individuals can potentially evade justice by leveraging their multiple national identities. This challenges fundamental principles of legal accountability and raises critical questions about the nature of citizenship in a globalized world.

Conclusion: Balancing Rights and Responsibilities

As global mobility increases and national boundaries become more porous, the legal community must develop more sophisticated approaches to managing dual citizenship. The goal is not to punish or restrict, but to create a system that ensures accountability while respecting individual rights and the complexities of modern identity.

The future of international justice depends on our ability to navigate these nuanced legal and ethical landscapes—recognizing that citizenship is both a privilege and a responsibility.

The following sidebar, *When Allegiance Becomes an Escape Clause*, examines how dual citizenship can be exploited to evade justice. From Claudia

Hoerig's flight to Brazil after committing murder, to dozens of child abuse suspects fleeing to Israel under the Law of Return, these cases expose how second passports can shield individuals from prosecution—highlighting the legal loopholes and extradition barriers that undermine civic accountability.

When Allegiance Becomes an Escape Clause

In today's globalized world, dual citizenship is often seen as a symbol of cosmopolitan identity. But beneath this appealing veneer lies a hidden vulnerability: for some, a second passport becomes a shield—not of belonging, but of evasion.

Unlike most privileges, citizenship entails obligations—to laws, institutions, and civic responsibility. Yet in case after case, individuals holding dual nationality have used that second citizenship to flee U.S. jurisdiction, avoiding prosecution for serious crimes. Whether in matters of violent assault, financial fraud, or child abuse, some dual nationals have found safe haven in countries that refuse to extradite their own citizens.

Extradition Gaps and Legal Asymmetries

The U.S., unlike many countries, places no formal limits on dual citizenship and does not track dual nationals. Meanwhile, nations such as France, Brazil, and Israel (until recent reforms) maintain policies that block the extradition of their own citizens. This creates legal gray zones where justice can be indefinitely delayed—or denied.

Case Snapshot: Claudia Hoerig

Claudia Hoerig fled to Brazil after murdering her U.S. Air Force pilot husband in Ohio. For years, Brazil's constitutional ban on extraditing nationals protected her. In 2018, after intense pressure, Brazil's Supreme Court ruled that by becoming a U.S. citizen, Hoerig had implicitly renounced her Brazilian citizenship—clearing the path for extradition. She was returned, tried, and convicted.

Widespread Pattern?

Investigations suggest that the problem is far more widespread than commonly recognized:

- A CBS News investigation, citing research from Jewish Community Watch, documented more than 60 U.S. citizens accused of child sexual abuse who fled to Israel and used the Law of Return to obtain instant citizenship and avoid prosecution, with no penalty imposed on their U.S. citizenship status—let alone being extradited.
- DOJ and FBI lists include hundreds of fugitives believed to be overseas, many of whom likely hold dual or multiple nationalities.

Sources: CBS News, "Fleeing Justice: American Pedophiles Found Refuge in Israel," 2018; U.S. Department of Justice, DOJ Press Releases, 2023–2025; Library of Congress, "Israel's Extradition Law Reform after the Sheinbein Case," 2005; U.S. v. Claudia Hoerig, Northern District of Ohio, 2018; Jewish Community Watch, "Project Emet: Tracking Child Sexual Abuse Fugitives."; Washington Institute, "Lebanon's Extradition Practices," 2019.

References: Legal Report

Government and Legal Documents

U.S. Department of Justice. *Criminal Resource Manual: Extradition Guidelines*. Washington, DC: DOJ, most recently updated 2023.

U.S. Department of State. *Foreign Affairs Manual*, Volume 7 (7 FAM 1610): Extradition Procedures. Washington, DC: U.S. Government Publishing Office, 2022.

Congressional Research Service. *U.S. Extradition Treaties and Enforcement Trends*. Washington, DC: Library of Congress, 2023.

Academic and Legal Journals

"Dual Nationality and Jurisdictional Conflicts." *Wisconsin International Law Journal* 41, no. 2 (2023): 155–182.

"The Rule Against Extradition of Nationals." *International Bar Association Legal Briefs*, May 2019.

"Extradition and Citizenship Perspectives." *Harvard International Law Journal* 64, no. 1 (2022): 87–114.

Specific Case Studies and Reporting

International Bar Association. "Ali Salameh and the Limits of Dual National Extradition." Case commentary, IBA Reports, 2019.

Southern District of New York. *United States v. Meir Lahav*, Case No. 1:22-cr-119, U.S. District Court Records, 2022.

Statistical Sources

U.S. Department of Justice. *Extradition and Rendition Annual Statistics, 2022–2024*. Washington, DC: DOJ, 2024.

Congressional Research Service. *Dual Citizenship and Extradition Risk Assessment*. Washington, DC: Library of Congress, March 2024.

Comparative International Law Sources

"Extradition Policies in Democratic Nations." *Comparative Law Review* 15, no. 1 (2023): 42–68.

International Criminal Court. *Rome Statute and Member-State Extradition Protocols*. The Hague: ICC, 2020.

U.S. Senate Committee on Foreign Relations. *Bilateral Extradition Treaty Compendium*. Washington, DC: Government Publishing Office, 2023.

References: Congress and Dual Allegiance – Who Do They Serve?

Foreign Influence and Lobbying

Mayer Brown. "FARA: Key Issues to Watch in 2025." *Legal Insights*, December 2024.

Bresnahan, John. "Cuellar Foreign Agent Charges Put Him in Rare Company." *Politico*, May 3, 2024.

Goldman, Adam. "Azerbaijan, Cuellar, and Lobbying: A Complex Web." *New York Times*, May 4, 2024.

The Economist. "What the Menendez and Cuellar Cases Have in Common." May 23, 2024.

McCullough, Jolie. "Henry Cuellar, Texas Democrat, Indicted by DOJ." *Texas Tribune*, May 3, 2024.

"When Dual Citizenship Becomes a Conflict of Interest." *The Hill*, April 2024.

Campaign Finance and Transparency

OpenSecrets. "Big Money, Big Stakes: Money in 2024 Elections." November 2024.

OpenSecrets. "Outside Spending Shatters Records." November 2024.

OpenSecrets. "Political Spending Projections for 2024." Accessed May 2024.

OpenSecrets. "Dark Money Surge in 2024 Elections." March 2024.

Responsible Statecraft. "Congress, Bribery, and Foreign Influence." Policy Brief, 2024.

References: Divided Loyalties in Office

Security Clearance and Dual Allegiance Risks

U.S. Department of State. "Dual Citizenship and Security Clearance Considerations." *Careers at State*, 2024.

U.S. Department of Justice. "FARA Enforcement and Prosecutions." Departmental Bulletin, 2024.

Burnham & Gorokhov, PLLC. "FARA Violation Penalties and Enforcement." Legal Brief, 2024.

Brookings Institution. *Loyalty, Secrecy, and National Security in a Divided Age*. Policy Memo. Washington, DC: Brookings, January 2024.

Chapter 5

The Consequences of Policy Drift

Citizenship used to mean something clear: one nation, one set of obligations, one political home. This assumption shaped everything from our military protocols to our ballots, our tax laws to our extradition treaties. Allegiance was singular, exclusive, and foundational.

But that clarity has unraveled.

In today's globalized reality, individuals increasingly belong to more than one sovereign—legally, strategically, sometimes by birth, and often by design. What began as rare exception has become structural norm. And yet, the United States' civic institutions—designed for a different era—remain stubbornly anchored to outdated assumptions. The result isn't just complicated—it's contradictory.

This chapter confronts a central dilemma: What happens when the machinery of democracy continues to operate on assumptions of exclusive loyalty, even as millions of citizens legally hold dual or multiple allegiances? From military service and diplomatic security to taxation, voting rights, and legal protection, each domain exposes a widening fault line between legal reality and institutional design.

The stakes are no longer theoretical. Today, more than 10 million Americans may hold dual citizenship—a quiet but consequential shift that challenges long-standing assumptions about civic identity, legal obligation, and national belonging. And as this reality expands, so too does the tension between the plural self and the singular state.

Here, we examine six pressure points: military service, political representation, taxation, legal accountability, civic trust, and institutional legitimacy. In each case, the pattern is the same—policy stayed frozen while practice changed, leaving a dangerous gap between law and lived reality. That gap now threatens the coherence of the democratic project itself.

As the chapter closes, we will not only have mapped these fractures— we will have surfaced the urgent need for reform. Because if allegiance can no longer be assumed, it must be ethically and structurally reimagined. That is the task of Chapter 6.

I. Citizenship in Action

From the ballot box to military service, from tax obligations to diplomatic representation, citizenship defines not just what benefits an individual receives, but what they fundamentally owe to the collective.

But what happens when that foundational identity becomes multiplicative? When a citizen can simultaneously pledge allegiance not to one sovereign, but to multiple political communities?

This is no longer a theoretical abstraction. Dual citizenship has transformed from a rare legal anomaly to a normalized feature of contemporary civic experience. What might once have appeared as an administrative curiosity—a second passport, an inherited cultural identity, a pragmatic solution for transnational families—now represents a profound challenge to institutional assumptions.

The scale is significant. As of 2024, an estimated 5.5 million U.S. citizens live outside the country, according to data from the Association of Americans Resident Overseas and the Federal Voting Assistance Program.[20] These are not fringe populations—they are active participants in global economies, dual legal systems, and, in some cases, foreign political processes. Their very existence complicates traditional assumptions about the territorial nature of citizenship and challenges the idea that national belonging must be rooted in physical presence or exclusive civic commitment.

The implications cascade across multiple institutional domains. In military recruitment, dual citizens may face conflicting service obligations. Electoral systems must now contemplate voting rights that transcend single jurisdictions. Taxation becomes a labyrinthine challenge, with individuals potentially owing civic and financial allegiances to multiple states. Diplomacy itself is transformed, as authoritarian regimes increasingly weaponize dual nationality to undermine consular protections.

These are not isolated complications, but symptoms of a deeper transformation: the gap between citizenship's traditional meaning and its emerging, fluid contemporary practice. As national identities become increasingly mobile and negotiable, our institutional frameworks struggle to adapt.

The fundamental question emerging is not administrative, but philosophical and civic: In an era of intentional, multiplied belonging, what continues to bind a political community together? How can democratic self-governance persist when allegiance itself becomes flexible, layered, and strategically calibrated?

---

[20] Association of Americans Resident Overseas (AARO) and Federal Voting Assistance Program (FVAP), Statistics on Americans Abroad, 2024. See www.aaro.org and www.fvap.gov for population estimates and reports on overseas U.S. citizens.

II. Military Service and Government Roles

Military service represents the most profound expression of civic commitment. Traditionally, it has been understood as an ultimate test of national belonging, a moment when citizens transcend individual interests to defend a collective political identity. Yet the emergence of dual citizenship fundamentally disrupts this foundational understanding.

When an individual can legally pledge allegiance to multiple sovereigns, the philosophical and practical foundations of military service become radically destabilized. Which nation can legitimately call upon a citizen in moments of conflict? When geopolitical interests diverge, how does a dual citizen navigate the moral and legal imperative of service?

These are not merely academic questions. They represent critical challenges to the operational integrity of national defense institutions.

Theoretical Foundations of Divided Loyalty

Political philosopher Michael Walzer has argued that collective defense represents the most sacred social contract—a shared obligation that transforms individual citizens into a unified political community. Dual citizenship introduces a fundamental rupture in this contract. If a citizen can be legally obligated to multiple military services, the very notion of collective security becomes conceptually fragile.

The problem extends beyond legal technicalities. It touches the moral core of national identity: Can true allegiance be divisible? Can a citizen's willingness to sacrifice be meaningfully distributed across multiple political communities?

Institutional Vulnerabilities

The United States occupies a unique and problematic position. While dual citizenship is not an automatic disqualification for military service, it introduces layers of institutional uncertainty.

A growing body of evidence shows that dual citizenship can raise red flags in the security clearance process—not as a presumption of disloyalty, but as a matter of institutional risk management. U.S. government guidelines acknowledge that dual allegiance, foreign military service, or the use of a foreign passport may trigger heightened scrutiny in evaluating eligibility for sensitive roles.

Consider a recent case: In a 2022 decision by the Defense Office of Hearings and Appeals (DOHA), an American-Israeli dual citizen faced challenges in obtaining a security clearance. The applicant, born in the U.S. to American parents, held dual citizenship with Israel and had familial ties to the country. Despite a strong professional background, concerns were raised under the guidelines of foreign influence and foreign preference. Ultimately, the clearance was granted, but the case underscores how dual nationality can complicate the clearance process, especially when involving countries with close yet complex relationships with the United States.[21]

The Deeper Institutional Risk

The challenge transcends individual cases. When national security institutions cannot confidently assert the unambiguous allegiance of their personnel, the entire operational framework becomes vulnerable. In an era of sophisticated geopolitical competition, where adversaries like China and Russia actively exploit diaspora populations, such ambiguity is not a theoretical concern—it is a strategic liability.

Dual citizenship does not inherently suggest disloyalty. But it fundamentally challenges the traditional understanding of military service as a singular, unequivocal commitment to collective defense.

---

[21] See *Defense Office of Hearings and Appeals (DOHA), ISCR Case No. 19-01592* (March 8, 2022); and Eugene Volokh, "An Interesting Decision from Last Year on a Security Clearance for an American-Israeli Joint Citizen," *The Volokh Conspiracy*, December 11, 2023.

The core question emerges: In a world of increasingly fluid national identities, how do we preserve the moral and operational integrity of national service?

III. Voting and Political Influence

Dual Voting Rights and Representation

Voting is a cornerstone of democratic participation and national identity. Yet in an increasingly interconnected world, dual citizens often hold the right to vote in more than one country. According to the International Institute for Democracy and Electoral Assistance (IDEA), approximately 44 countries permit external voting by citizens residing abroad. Of these, at least 12—including France, Italy, Mexico, and Turkey—allow dual nationals to vote in both home and host country elections.[22]

This raises foundational questions about democratic equity and loyalty. Can an individual faithfully represent the interests of two separate political communities—especially when their strategic or moral objectives diverge? For instance, an American-Turkish dual citizen may cast a vote in a U.S. presidential election while simultaneously voting in Turkish parliamentary elections, where positions on NATO, Israel, or press freedom might conflict with U.S. policy. The tension is not merely theoretical; it touches the core of representative legitimacy.

Diaspora Lobbying and Foreign State Strategy

Beyond voting, dual citizens often play an active role in diaspora lobbying. Governments such as Turkey, Israel, India, and Russia have invested in engaging their expatriates—not just as cultural emissaries, but as political actors. These states encourage dual nationals to advocate for their interests within U.S. political structures. This practice, termed

---

[22] International Institute for Democracy and Electoral Assistance (IDEA), *Global Overview of Voting from Abroad Policies*, 2024.

"external nationalization" by political theorist Rogers Brubaker, blurs the line between civic participation and geopolitical leverage.

For example, Turkey's Directorate for Turks Abroad openly encourages Turkish-Americans to maintain political activism aligned with Ankara's policies.[23] Russia has similarly supported media and lobbying networks that echo Kremlin priorities under the rubric of diaspora engagement.[24] In the U.S., organizations such as AIPAC and other pro-Israel advocacy groups have long mobilized American citizens—some of whom hold dual Israeli citizenship—to promote strategic alignment between the United States and Israel.[25]

While such engagement can reflect shared democratic values and legitimate policy interests, it also raises difficult questions about dual allegiance, influence, and national prioritization, particularly when citizens maintain legal or emotional ties to another sovereign. These dynamics are not limited to one community or ideology; rather, they show a deeper challenge: how to balance multiple loyalties with the demands of a representative democracy.

---

[23] Turkey's dual citizenship policy and diaspora strategy are administered by the Presidency for Turks Abroad and Related Communities (YTB), which promotes active civic engagement abroad. While precise U.S. dual citizen figures are unknown, Turkish officials estimate 500,000 individuals of Turkish descent reside in the U.S. See "YTB Mission and Vision," Republic of Turkey; and Carlotta Gall, "How Turkey's Leader Got 99% of the Vote in a Turkish City in Germany," *New York Times*, May 21, 2023.

[24] Russia's "compatriots abroad" policy aims to maintain loyalty and influence through language, culture, and sometimes political alignment. Though U.S. data on dual nationals is limited, Russian-speaking populations exceed 400,000. See Elizabeth Cullen Dunn and Michael S. Gorham, "Diaspora and the Kremlin: Russia's Compatriot Policy," in *Russian Nationalism and the Russian-Ukrainian War* (Routledge, 2022); and U.S. Census Bureau, "Selected Population Profile in the United States," 2019 American Community Survey.

[25] Estimates of U.S. citizens holding Israeli dual nationality range from several hundred thousand to over 500,000, though exact figures are elusive due to the lack of mandatory reporting. See Ruth Levush, *Israel: Dual Nationality* (Library of Congress, 2020). AIPAC (American Israel Public Affairs Committee), a 501(c)(4) organization, does not disclose individual citizenship data but has long operated as one of the most influential lobbying groups in the U.S., with a stated mission to "strengthen, protect and promote the U.S.-Israel relationship."

Symbolism, Perception, and Allegiance

In a democracy, legitimacy is as much about perception as policy. Public confidence in political institutions depends on the assumption of undivided loyalty. When elected officials or civil servants possess dual nationality, they may face scrutiny—not necessarily for misconduct, but for what their status symbolizes. In moments of crisis or international conflict, the presence of dual citizens in sensitive roles can provoke suspicion: Whose side are they on?

This perception gap matters. Political scientist Yascha Mounk has warned that democracies suffer not only from bad governance but from the loss of shared narratives. Allegiance is not just a legal concept; it is a story of belonging. When that story is fractured by competing loyalties, the civic imagination is strained.

The Challenge Ahead

Voting and political participation by dual citizens is not inherently subversive. But it introduces complexity—both in governance and in democratic trust—that U.S. institutions have not fully reckoned with. In a globalized age where foreign governments increasingly act through diasporic channels, the boundary between domestic representation and external influence requires clearer ethical and legal scrutiny. The next sections explore how this blurring of civic lines plays out not only in politics, but in financial and diplomatic domains as well.

IV. Taxation and Financial Compliance

While military service or voting rights may evoke symbolic allegiance, taxation is where the obligations of citizenship are most materially enforced. Nowhere is this more acutely felt than among dual citizens subject to America's uniquely extraterritorial tax regime.

Citizenship-Based Taxation: An International Anomaly

The United States is one of only two countries in the world—alongside Eritrea—that imposes taxation based on citizenship rather than residency. This means that American citizens, regardless of where they live or work, are required to file annual tax returns with the IRS and report foreign assets.

For dual nationals who reside outside the U.S., this creates overlapping and often contradictory obligations. They may be legal residents and taxpayers in one nation, but are still bound by U.S. tax law—including complex rules on income thresholds, retirement accounts, and foreign-held assets.

FATCA and the Consequences of Financial Surveillance

The 2010 Foreign Account Tax Compliance Act (FATCA) intensified this burden. Under FATCA, foreign financial institutions must report account holdings of U.S. citizens or face stiff penalties. While the law aims to prevent tax evasion, its implementation has sparked unintended collateral damage for dual citizens. Key impacts include:

- Numerous European and Asian banks have closed or denied accounts to U.S. dual nationals, citing the administrative complexity and liability risks of FATCA compliance.
- According to a 2021 survey by American Citizens Abroad (ACA), over 85% of dual nationals reported serious disruptions to their banking access and financial services abroad.[26]
- Many are unable to open mortgages, retirement plans, or even basic checking accounts in their country of residence because of their U.S. status.

---

[26] See *The 2021 Survey of American Citizens Living Abroad: Banking and Financial Access*, American Citizens Abroad (2021). For broader context, see U.S. Government Accountability Office, *Foreign Asset Reporting: Actions Needed to Enhance Compliance Efforts, Eliminate Duplication, and Improve Use of Data*, GAO-19-180 (2019).

These financial exclusions make dual citizenship not a benefit—but a bureaucratic liability.

The "Accidental American" Crisis

Tens of thousands of individuals born in the U.S. to foreign parents—or who left the country in infancy—are discovering they are subject to U.S. tax laws despite no economic ties or emotional allegiance to the United States. Labeled "accidental Americans," many of these individuals only realize their U.S. status when they encounter FATCA barriers abroad or receive IRS notices.

In 2023, over 3,200 individuals formally renounced their U.S. citizenship, according to IRS data—part of a continuing pattern driven less by political dissent than by regulatory and financial exhaustion.[27]

> *"I didn't feel American—I felt criminalized for having a bank account."*
> — Anonymous respondent in ACA survey, 2021

Renunciation has become the only way out for many, but even this comes at a price:

- A $2,350 renunciation fee (the highest in the world)
- Possible "exit taxes" on accrued assets
- Lengthy and invasive compliance checks.

What This Reveals About Allegiance

When citizens sever ties not out of betrayal, but to escape disproportionate bureaucratic burdens, it signals a breakdown in the civic contract. Citizenship, once framed as a privilege and moral commitment, becomes a paper trap—one that penalizes those who cannot afford professional compliance support or who live ordinary lives outside U.S. borders.

---

[27] See U.S. Internal Revenue Service, *Quarterly Publication of Individuals Who Have Chosen to Expatriate*, 2023. While the number has declined slightly from its 2020 peak of 6,705, the long-term trend reflects persistent concerns over tax complexity and reporting obligations under FATCA.

The broader question emerges: *What does it say about a nation when its citizens renounce not to defect—but to disengage from administrative overreach they never knowingly agreed to?*

V. Legal Conflicts and Jurisdictional Tensions

Sovereignty Collides: The Fragile Position of Dual Nationals

At the heart of the dual citizenship dilemma lies a contradiction: each state claims full authority over its citizens, but dual nationals are claimed by more than one sovereign. This becomes most perilous in moments of legal crisis—detention, prosecution, consular protection—when citizenship must function as a shield.

Under international law, particularly the Vienna Convention on Consular Relations, arrested individuals are entitled to contact their consulate. Yet many countries—especially authoritarian regimes—refuse this right to dual nationals, asserting that within their borders, those individuals are solely their citizens.

According to U.S. State Department data, between 2018 and 2023, o fewer than 27 publicly documented cases involved U.S. consular officials being denied access to detained dual nationals. One emblematic case—previously noted—is that of Siamak Namazi, an Iranian-American businessman arrested in 2015 and sentenced to ten years in Tehran on charges of espionage. Throughout his detention, Iranian authorities rejected U.S. requests for consular access, citing Namazi's Iranian citizenship under domestic law. His case remains a stark illustration of how dual nationality can nullify the very protections most citizens assume will apply abroad.

Other troubling cases include:
- An American-Chinese dual national, detained in 2023 under Hong Kong's national security law, for whom U.S. embassy

access was blocked by Beijing;[28]
- Turkish-American dual citizens arrested during political crackdowns, with Turkish courts claiming sole jurisdiction and refusing U.S. diplomatic involvement.

These patterns reflect a growing trend of "hostage diplomacy"—the use of dual nationals as strategic leverage in international disputes.

Jurisdictional Ambiguity and Legal No-Man's-Land

Beyond detention, dual citizenship creates legal ambiguity in enforcement, extradition, and civil disputes. Dual nationals may:

- Be prosecuted in one country for conduct legal in another;
- Face overlapping legal claims from both governments;
- Be subject to conflicting duties—such as military service, asset disclosure, or censorship laws.

Such individuals can find themselves trapped in legal limbo. Consider a hypothetical: an Iranian-American academic publishes criticism of Tehran's regime from the U.S.—speech protected by the First Amendment. But on visiting family in Iran, they risk arrest for "propaganda against the state," a charge that applies to all Iranian nationals, including duals.

Strategic Erosion: When Citizenship Cannot Protect

The inability of the U.S. to protect dual citizens undermines the symbolic and strategic value of American citizenship. Those who believe the U.S. passport ensures protection may find that assumption unraveling the moment another state asserts primary claim.

---

[28] U.S. Department of State, *2023 Country Reports on Human Rights Practices: China (Includes Hong Kong, Macau, and Tibet)* (Washington, D.C.: Bureau of Democracy, Human Rights and Labor, March 2024).

This dynamic carries broader implications:

- Authoritarian regimes can detain dual nationals to pressure the U.S. diplomatically;
- The U.S. response is often constrained, for fear of escalation;
- Dual nationals in sensitive roles may become targets of coercion or blackmail by adversarial states.

This is not only a human rights concern—it is a sovereignty dilemma. When a nation cannot protect all its citizens abroad, especially those also claimed by another sovereign, its capacity to uphold the legal and moral obligations of citizenship is diminished.

Public Opinion Indicators: Perception Shapes Legitimacy

Even if dual citizens perform their duties with absolute integrity, public trust hinges on perception. And perception, in democratic societies, carries institutional weight.

According to a 2022 Pew Research Center poll:

- 56% of Americans believe dual citizens should not be allowed to hold top national security positions;
- 41% believe dual citizenship "diminishes national loyalty;"
- Among respondents over 50, the skepticism was even higher, with 63% expressing concern about dual citizens in roles of public trust.

These numbers aren't about xenophobia—they show real worry over clashing obligations in a world of shifting loyalties. The very existence of ambiguity undermines the symbolic clarity that democratic institutions rely upon.

Symbolism and the Erosion of Normative Allegiance

Consider the naturalization oath, which requires new citizens to "renounce and abjure all allegiance and fidelity to any foreign prince, potentate, state, or sovereignty." Yet in practice, this formal renunciation is rarely enforced. Most dual citizens retain legal, emotional, and sometimes strategic ties to their countries of origin.[29]

This disconnect between stated norm and accepted practice weakens the perceived meaning of citizenship. When allegiance is no longer exclusive, it begins to look optional. And when it is optional, the public may begin to question whether democratic institutions—elections, security agencies, public offices—are staffed by people whose commitments are full and unambiguous.

Trust in Institutions: A Social Contract in Decline

Trust in government is already under pressure in the United States, with Gallup and Pew reporting record lows in confidence in Congress, the judiciary, and executive agencies. In this fragile context, symbolic gestures matter. Citizenship—especially at the leadership level—is a vessel of public meaning. When that vessel appears compromised by split loyalties, it reinforces broader doubts about institutional integrity.

Even if the reality of divided allegiance rarely results in betrayal or bias, the symbolic appearance of dual loyalty carries weight. In politics, appearances shape expectations, and expectations shape legitimacy.

To restore civic trust, it is not enough to demand compliance with law. Democratic systems must reanimate the symbolic meaning of citizenship—not as an administrative status, but as a shared ethic of fidelity. Allegiance, like trust, cannot be partial. And when the public perceives it to be so, legitimacy itself comes into question.

---

[29] The U.S. naturalization oath is codified in 8 U.S. Code § 1448. While its language mandates the renunciation of prior allegiance, the U.S. does not require proof of actual citizenship relinquishment from foreign governments, nor does it penalize individuals who retain or reacquire a second nationality. See USCIS, "Oath of Allegiance Requirements"; Amanda Frost, *You Are Not American* (Beacon Press, 2021), 182–85; Peter J. Spiro, *At Home in Two Countries* (NYU Press, 2016), ch. 3.

VI. The Case for Clarity

Dual citizenship is not inherently unpatriotic. It reflects real human experience in an interconnected world—migration, marriage, heritage, opportunity. But its normalization within a political system designed around exclusive allegiance introduces unresolved tensions. The problem is not global mobility. The problem is institutional drift. As divided citizenship becomes more common, the legal, civic, and moral frameworks surrounding it remain largely unchanged.

The American republic was founded on the idea that citizenship is a singular, deliberate choice—a covenant of mutual rights and obligations linking citizens to one another and to their institutions. Today, that clarity has faded. Lines once sharply drawn have grown indistinct, even as the stakes for defining them have increased.

If allegiance is to remain meaningful in a democratic society, it must be better defined, better protected, and more consistently operationalized. This section outlines a pragmatic path forward—one that affirms pluralism without surrendering the moral coherence of citizenship.

1. Enhanced Disclosure Requirements

Proposal: Require mandatory disclosure of all foreign citizenships held by individuals seeking elected office, senior civil service, military command, or access to national security positions.

Rationale: Transparency does not imply disloyalty—but it reinforces institutional trust. Disclosure enables vetting and provides the public with the information needed to evaluate potential conflicts of interest. Comparable policies are already in place in countries like Australia, Canada, and Germany, where political candidates have been disqualified or required to divest foreign citizenship to assume office.

2. Targeted Renunciation Requirements

Proposal: Establish formal renunciation requirements for individuals in critical roles involving classified information, nuclear infrastructure, defense leadership, or high-level diplomatic negotiation.

Rationale: Not all public roles demand undivided allegiance—but some indisputably do. Positions of exceptional national trust require absolute clarity of commitment. In these contexts, even the appearance of divided loyalty can pose a strategic risk. Creating explicit renunciation requirements for such roles would codify a principle long assumed in practice: that those entrusted with the nation's most sensitive responsibilities must demonstrate exclusive civic allegiance. This reform would not affect ordinary citizens, but it would reinforce the ethical and operational integrity expected at the highest levels of government service.

3. National Commission on Citizenship and Institutional Integrity

Proposal: Establish a federal commission or blue-ribbon panel to study the legal, institutional, and cultural implications of dual citizenship in American life.

Rationale: Much of the current discourse on dual citizenship is anecdotal or ideologically polarized. A comprehensive, bipartisan study would fill a crucial knowledge gap. It could gather data on:

- The number of dual nationals in sensitive public roles;
- The diplomatic, financial, and security incidents arising from dual status;
- Comparative approaches in other democracies;
- Public attitudes and constitutional interpretation.

The commission's findings could inform future legislation, court decisions, and administrative reforms.

4. Civic Affirmation and Public Education

Proposal: Launch a national civic education initiative to restore a shared understanding of citizenship, allegiance, and democratic obligation.

Rationale: Many Americans—native-born and naturalized alike—now experience citizenship as a procedural category rather than a civic identity. Reasserting the moral and symbolic weight of allegiance is essential. This could include:

- Modernizing civics curricula in schools;
- Creating educational modules for naturalization ceremonies;
- Reintroducing the historical and philosophical foundations of undivided allegiance in public discourse;
- Commemorating Citizenship Day (September 17) with civic rituals and public dialogue.

Constitution Day and Citizenship Day — A Civic Ritual for All Americans

Since 2004, September 17 has been federally recognized as **Constitution Day and Citizenship Day**, commemorating the signing of the U.S. Constitution in 1787 and honoring the rights and responsibilities of American citizenship.

Originally rooted in efforts to welcome new citizens, this observance has gradually expanded to include all Americans—encouraging reflection on civic identity, constitutional values, and the ethical meaning of national belonging.

Federal Law (Public Law 108–447) requires all educational institutions receiving federal funds to offer programming on the Constitution and citizenship on this date. Yet in practice, compliance varies widely. Many institutions fulfill the requirement with symbolic gestures, while others overlook it altogether—revealing a deeper ambivalence about civic education and allegiance.

In a time of plural identities and divided loyalties, Constitution Day presents a rare, legally mandated opportunity to re-center the civic project. Not just a formality, it can serve as a moment of democratic renewal—if taken seriously.

For more on the origins, legal foundations, and current compliance patterns surrounding Constitution Day and Citizenship Day, see Appendix F: Civic Observances and Legal Foundations of Citizenship.

Together, these proposals offer a preliminary framework for restoring clarity to the meaning of allegiance in American civic life. While they do not represent a comprehensive solution, they signal the contours of a more ethically coherent and operationally sound citizenship regime.

We return to these issues in fuller detail in Chapter 7, where we take up the broader legal and policy reforms needed to stabilize citizenship in a shifting geopolitical and institutional landscape.

Conclusion: Rebuilding the Civic Frame

Dual citizenship is not going away. But its risks can no longer be ignored, nor can its meaning remain undefined. This chapter has traced how divided loyalty—once a rare anomaly—has become an enduring feature of American life, with consequences far beyond individual status. Legal ambiguity and institutional inertia have allowed it to seep into the foundations of civic life, quietly challenging how we fight wars, protect secrets, levy taxes, negotiate abroad, and elect those who govern us.

The issue is not that dual citizens are inherently disloyal. Rather, it is that our civic architecture was never designed to accommodate divided loyalty as a normalized condition. Oaths have lost coherence, protections have grown inconsistent, and symbolic legitimacy has been strained. Institutions—from courts to consulates, from ballots to battlefields—are absorbing these contradictions in silence.

Left unaddressed, this drift risks weakening the ethical clarity of citizenship itself. If allegiance can be partial, layered, or optional, can it still serve as the glue of a democratic society?

Yet the solution cannot be a retreat into nativism or narrow exclusion. The United States has always drawn strength from its openness, its pluralism, and its willingness to integrate those who choose to join the national project. What is needed now is not nostalgia—but renewal. A recovery of allegiance that is inclusive but unambiguous, principled but pragmatic.

This challenge—how to reaffirm allegiance without abandoning openness—will reappear throughout the book. But first, Chapter 6 turns to a different facet of the allegiance crisis: the rise of citizenship as commodity. Through the case of birth tourism, we examine what happens when civic membership is reduced to transaction, and national belonging becomes a purchasable good in a global marketplace.

Chapter 6

Citizenship for Sale
Birth Tourism and the Marketplace of Citizenship

Today, citizenship isn't just divided—it's being treated like something you can buy and sell. This chapter shifts the focus from split allegiances (Chapter 5) to purchased advantages, using birth tourism as a lens into the broader erosion of civic meaning in American citizenship. Legal status, once understood as a mark of allegiance and shared responsibility, is now strategically acquired, optimized or leveraged as a global commodity. The rise of citizenship as asset, particularly among global elites, signals a deeper shift: civic membership is being reframed as a tool of mobility, insurance, and privilege—rather than commitment to a political community.

In 2019, federal prosecutors charged the operators of a sprawling birth tourism network in Southern California with visa fraud and money laundering. One client paid $100,000 for a "deluxe package" that guaranteed a U.S. birth certificate, luxury housing, and guidance on how to mislead customs officers. This wasn't an isolated scheme—it was part of a growing transnational industry that markets American citizenship as a premium product, with no expectation to engage, commit, or connect with American life. The child becomes a passport to future opportunity; the act of birth, a legal transaction.

This chapter shows how birth tourism is both a warning sign and a symptom of a bigger problem. It explores its legal foundations in the Fourteenth Amendment, the economic forces driving its growth, the policy gray zones it exploits, and the ethical tensions it reveals. Through this, we return to a central question: *What happens to democracy when citizenship becomes detached from belonging?* In asking this, the following sections set the stage for Chapter 7, which turns from diagnosis to design—offering reforms aimed at restoring a coherent, principled, and future-ready understanding of citizenship in a pluralist society.

I. Citizenship at the Crossroads of Law and Loyalty

In the United States today, citizenship is automatically conferred by birth on U.S. soil, irrespective of parental immigration status or long-term ties to the country. For generations, this principle—known as *jus soli* (citizenship by birthplace)—has symbolized America's democratic ideal: citizenship grounded in shared civic space rather than inherited privilege.

Yet in the 21st century, this once-idealistic guarantee is being tested by new realities. One of the most significant—and contentious—manifestations is 'birth tourism': the practice of traveling to the United States with the primary intention of giving birth so that the child acquires automatic U.S. citizenship. Though not illegal in itself, birth tourism exploits a constitutional promise originally meant to protect vulnerable communities—not to serve as a vehicle for strategic migration, economic advantage, or geopolitical hedging.

In 2025, President Trump issued Executive Order 14160, which sought to deny automatic U.S. citizenship to children born on American soil to undocumented or temporarily present foreign nationals. Multiple federal district courts—including those in New Hampshire and California—issued nationwide injunctions against the order, finding it likely unconstitutional under the Fourteenth Amendment's Citizenship Clause. The Ninth Circuit Court of Appeals has already affirmed a district court's injunction, ruling that the executive order exceeded presidential authority and violated established constitutional precedent. In *Barbara v. Trump*, the New Hampshire district court certified a nationwide class action and issued a preliminary injunction. As of August 1, 2025, the First Circuit Court of Appeals also appears poised to uphold this injunction, signaling agreement with the Ninth Circuit. Meanwhile, the Supreme Court's June decision in *CASA v. Trump* limited the scope of universal injunctions—but explicitly preserved class-wide relief, thus maintaining the validity of injunctions like that in *Barbara v. Trump*. Given the appellate consensus against the executive order and unresolved constitutional questions, Supreme Court review in the coming term appears inevitable.[30]

> **Postscript Note (as of September 2025):** At the time of publication, litigation over Executive Order 14160 remains pending. The U.S. Supreme Court is expected to consider the case in its October 2025 term. Readers are encouraged to consult current rulings, as the Court's decision may significantly affect the constitutional interpretation of birthright citizenship.

Supporters of the executive order argue that the Constitution was never meant to reward strategic or opportunistic uses of birthright citizenship. Critics warn that even modest restrictions risk eroding one of the most inclusive features of American democracy. Yet both sides acknowledge that the current system—where citizenship is granted automatically, regardless of connection, contribution, or commitment—is increasingly untenable in an era of mass mobility, legal complexity, and cultural dislocation.

---

[30] For detailed legal analysis and court updates, see American Civil Liberties Union, press releases, February–August 2025; Immigration Impact, "Court Blocks Trump's Citizenship Order," March 2025, updated August 2025; Reuters, "Appeals Court Affirms Nationwide Injunction Against Trump's Birthright Citizenship Order," August 2025; and Ninth Circuit Court of Appeals, decision in *California v. Trump*, July 2025.

This chapter does not offer a simplistic answer to these tensions. Rather, it seeks to uncover the disjunction between legal citizenship and civic belonging. While birthright citizenship remains an important democratic safeguard, its increasingly instrumental use threatens to hollow out the civic substance that citizenship is meant to express. In short: Can citizenship retain its moral and political legitimacy if it is primarily acquired as a transactional good—divorced from integration, identity, or allegiance?

II. Birth Tourism: Exploiting a Constitutional Guarantee

Birth tourism refers to the deliberate practice of traveling to the United States for the specific purpose of giving birth, thereby conferring U.S. citizenship on the child by virtue of being born on American soil. While some cases arise from unexpected medical circumstances or legitimate long-term travel, the core of the practice involves short-term visits designed solely to obtain a passport—transforming one of the world's most consequential legal statuses into a transactional benefit.

The Legal Foundation: *Jus Soli* and Its Origins

The practice rests on a uniquely broad interpretation of *jus soli* (the "right of the soil"), granting citizenship to anyone born on U.S. territory, regardless of the parents' legal status. This principle is enshrined in the 14th Amendment, which declares that "all persons born or naturalized in the United States, and subject to the jurisdiction thereof, are citizens of the United States."

This expansive interpretation was confirmed in the landmark Supreme Court case *United States v. Wong Kim Ark* (1898). The Court held that a child born in the U.S. to non-citizen Chinese parents—who were barred from naturalizing under the Chinese Exclusion Act—was nonetheless a citizen by birth. Although this ruling reflected a commitment to equality under the law, it could not have anticipated the global mobility and commercial industries that now strategically exploit this constitutional guarantee.

The 14th Amendment and the Birthright Citizenship Clause

What it says:

"All persons born or naturalized in the United States, and subject to the jurisdiction thereof, are citizens of the United States and of the state wherein they reside."
— U.S. Constitution, Amendment XIV, Section 1 (ratified 1868)

Why it matters:
Passed in the aftermath of the Civil War, the 14th Amendment's Citizenship Clause was intended to overturn *Dred Scott v. Sandford* (1857) and guarantee citizenship to formerly enslaved people. It established that birth on U.S. soil—*jus soli*—is the primary pathway to American citizenship, regardless of ancestry or parental status.

Key precedent:
In *United States v. Wong Kim Ark* (1898), the Supreme Court interpreted the clause to mean that nearly all children born in the U.S. are citizens, even if their parents are foreign nationals. The only exceptions were diplomats and enemy occupiers.

The current debate:
Modern challenges—like birth tourism—raise new questions about the phrase *"subject to the jurisdiction thereof."* Conservative scholars argue this excludes children of undocumented or temporary migrants. Others maintain that the Wong Kim Ark ruling remains binding, and any revision would require a constitutional amendment

---

Citizenship for Sale? The Emergence of a Global Industry

In the decades since *Wong Kim Ark*, birthright citizenship has become a pillar of American legal tradition. But in recent years, it has also become the foundation for a discreet and highly lucrative industry. Birth tourism facilitators—many operating within legal ambiguity—advertise to expectant mothers in China, Nigeria, Russia, and other countries, offering full-service packages that include visa coaching, airport pickups, prenatal care, "maternity hotels," and guaranteed birth at high-end hospitals.

Many of these companies market American citizenship not as a civic identity, but as an investment in future opportunity. Promotional materials often tout visa-free travel, elite college access, and the ability to sponsor relatives for future immigration. Some even frame U.S. citizenship as an "exit strategy" in case of political instability or economic downturn in the parents' home country.

A Legal Loophole or Structural Blind Spot?

To be clear, giving birth in the U.S. is not itself illegal, and it is not unlawful to enter the country while pregnant. However, when travel is arranged under false pretenses—such as misrepresenting the purpose of the trip on a visa application—visa fraud statutes may apply. Federal agencies such as ICE and the Department of Justice have occasionally launched investigations into large-scale birth tourism rings, but enforcement remains rare and politically sensitive.

As a result, birth tourism continues to operate in a legal gray area—not fully illegal, not explicitly endorsed, but structurally enabled by a citizenship system that separates legal status from civic integration. The practice highlights a growing tension in U.S. citizenship law: can a legal principle grounded in Reconstruction-era civil rights survive in a globalized marketplace of identity and mobility?

III. Industry Profile: The Business of Birthright

While birth tourism remains a relatively discreet phenomenon, its scope and scale suggest a thriving transnational market—one that quietly takes advantage of the divide between legal status and civic belonging. Though it affects only a small portion of total births in the U.S., the practice has evolved into a specialized global enterprise involving coordinated networks of agents, facilitators, and legal intermediaries.

A. Data and Economic Impact (DHS & GAO Estimates)

Reliable data on birth tourism is inherently difficult to collect, given its often covert nature and the lack of consistent tracking. However, estimates from the Department of Homeland Security (DHS) and the

Government Accountability Office (GAO) suggest that between 35,000 and 50,000 babies are born in the United States annually to mothers traveling specifically for that purpose.[31]

This translates into a substantial economic footprint—with annual revenues from this industry estimated between $500 million and $750 million. These figures encompass not only medical costs (typically paid out-of-pocket) but also extended hotel stays, legal services for documentation, visa application coaching, transportation, and postpartum care. Many providers offer tiered pricing packages, with VIP services that include guaranteed access to private hospitals and expedited passport filing for the newborn.

To better understand the global landscape of birth tourism, the following chart presents a breakdown of estimated origins for 2020-2024, based on aggregated data from multiple federal sources:

Estimated Birth Tourism by Country (2020-2024)

Country	Estimated Share	Primary Motivations
China	45% (±5%)	Economic hedging, educational opportunities
Nigeria	15% (±3%)	Political stability, future migration options
Russia	12% (±4%)	Geopolitical uncertainty, global mobility
Turkey	8% (±2%)	Educational access, economic diversification
Other	20% (±6%)	Varied individual and national contexts

Source: Composite estimates from Department of Homeland Security (DHS), Government Accountability Office (GAO), and independent migration research institutes. Margin of error reflects data collection challenges.

These figures reveal a complex interplay of political, economic, and legal motivations driving parents to pursue American birthright citizenship. Each country's engagement with birth tourism reflects distinct national

---

[31] Estimates derived from reports by the U.S. Department of Homeland Security and the U.S. Government Accountability Office on nonimmigrant visa usage and birth tourism patterns (2022–2024), as well as independent economic analyses by migration research institutes.

contexts:

- In countries with authoritarian governance or economic volatility (China, Russia), U.S. citizenship represents a form of long-term strategic insurance;
- For nations with limited global mobility (Nigeria), American citizenship offers expanded opportunities;
- In more economically stable countries, motivations often center on elite educational access and future mobility options.

The diversity of these motivations underscores birth tourism's role as a global strategy for navigating uncertain futures, rather than a monolithic phenomenon.

B. Industry Structure

The infrastructure supporting birth tourism has become increasingly sophisticated. At the center are so-called "maternity hotels"—residential accommodations that cater exclusively to pregnant foreign women, often located near major urban hospitals. Many operate under innocuous names but function as full-service hubs, offering pre-arrival consultations, translation services, medical referrals, and postpartum recovery care.

Other critical actors include:

- **Visa consultants**, who coach clients on how to avoid disclosing pregnancy when applying for a B-2 (tourist) visa;
- **Hospital liaisons**, who help patients navigate billing systems and sometimes coordinate with sympathetic medical professionals;
- **Postnatal documentation services**, which offer step-by-step guidance on securing Social Security numbers, U.S. passports, and even dual citizenship documents before the family returns home.

This complex ecosystem flourishes in part due to regulatory gaps. B-2 visas, designed for tourism and short-term visits, have minimal screening mechanisms to detect fraudulent intent related to childbirth. Meanwhile, hospital registration systems rarely question foreign nationals' motives so long as payment is guaranteed.

Even when uncovered, enforcement tends to focus on facilitators rather than families. In one high-profile case in 2019, federal agents raided several Southern California birth tourism operations—yet most of the mothers involved were not prosecuted or deported, highlighting the legal ambiguity that sustains the practice.

IV. Born American, Raised Elsewhere: Two Profiles

While policy debates over birthright citizenship often occur at the abstract level of law and theory, the real-world outcomes are profoundly human. The lives of children born in the United States through birth tourism offer a compelling—and at times unsettling—glimpse into the consequences of citizenship detached from civic integration. These individuals, citizens by birth, may grow up with little or no connection to the country that granted them its most powerful legal status. Their stories raise fundamental questions: What does it mean to be a citizen in name but not in practice? And how should a democracy respond when its most sacred civic bond—citizenship—is treated as a hedge or tool?

These following two profiles are composite narratives constructed to illustrate common patterns observed in birth tourism practices. They are based on aggregated data and documented cases but do not depict specific individuals.

Profile 1: Elena Chen — A Passport Without a Polis

Elena Chen was born in California in 2010 to Chinese nationals who had arranged their travel through a private birth tourism agency in

Guangzhou. After a brief hospital stay and successful application for a U.S. passport, her family returned to Shanghai when she was six months old. Elena was raised and educated entirely in China. Mandarin is her native language, and her education has been rooted in the Chinese national curriculum. Her cultural frame of reference is entirely Eastern, and she has never returned to the United States except for a brief family vacation at age eleven.

Yet Elena holds a valid U.S. passport—and thus U.S. citizenship and civic membership. Her story exemplifies a growing phenomenon: citizenship as mobility tool, detached from civic commitment—an idea introduced in Chapter 5 and explored here through the lens of birth tourism.

Profile 2: Adebayo Okonkwo — Citizenship as Contingency

Adebayo Okonkwo was born in a private hospital in New York City to Nigerian parents who had obtained temporary tourist visas for the specific purpose of giving birth in the U.S. His mother stayed just long enough to secure his U.S. birth certificate and passport. Adebayo was raised in Lagos, where he attended elite private schools and participated in Nigeria's cultural and academic life. He speaks English and Yoruba fluently and has Nigerian national pride. Yet behind this national identity lies a quietly maintained American citizenship and civic membership—an identity he rarely speaks about, but which his family considers essential.

Now in his twenties, Adebayo is preparing to apply to graduate programs in the United States. His U.S. passport offers visa-free travel, streamlined admissions processes, and access to federal financial aid. He is also considering permanent relocation, citing Nigeria's instability as a reason to activate his dormant U.S. citizenship.

His family views his U.S. citizenship as a hedge against the uncertainties of life in Nigeria—a form of long-term security. Adebayo has never paid

U.S. taxes, never lived in the country beyond infancy, and has no civic ties. Yet should he return, he would be indistinguishable—legally—from peers who grew up pledging allegiance to the flag.

These illustrative case studies highlight a profound disjunction between legal status and civic integration. While both Elena and Adebayo are lawfully American, their relationship to the United States is mediated entirely through legal documents, not civic experience or cultural participation. Their lives invite an uncomfortable but urgent question: Can citizenship endure as a meaningful democratic bond when it is accessed and utilized primarily as a contingency plan?

V. Legal and Constitutional Context

Modern legal debates surrounding birth tourism focus on the scope and meaning of the phrase *"subject to the jurisdiction"* within the Fourteenth Amendment. As detailed earlier, the Supreme Court established broad birthright citizenship in *United States v. Wong Kim Ark* (1898), a precedent still authoritative today. However, contemporary challenges question whether the principle should extend to children born to transient or undocumented visitors—particularly those who strategically use geographic birth to secure lifelong citizenship.

This section examines current judicial interpretations, enforcement difficulties, and whether today's constitutional applications remain faithful to the original civic intentions of the Fourteenth Amendment's Citizenship Clause.

A. Judicial Interpretations: Originalist vs. Living Constitutional Views

Modern constitutional debates question whether *Wong Kim Ark*'s broad application of *jus soli* should extend to children born to temporary visitors or parents entering solely to secure citizenship for their children.

Conservative originalists contend the amendment's phrase *"subject to the jurisdiction"* explicitly excludes transient and strategic cases. Living constitutionalists, in contrast, argue that the amendment's inclusive spirit and equal protection guarantees justify a broad interpretation, maintaining geographic birthplace as determinative regardless of parental intent.

B. Enforcement Challenges

While constitutional scholars debate the Fourteenth Amendment's meaning, federal agencies—including Immigration and Customs Enforcement (ICE), the Department of Justice (DOJ), and Customs and Border Protection (CBP)—struggle to police the sophisticated birth tourism industry. Recent investigations have targeted networks that coach foreign nationals in visa fraud, conceal pregnancies, or manipulate hospital systems.

Yet enforcement remains challenging. Most birth tourists enter legally on B-2 visitor visas, and merely intending to give birth in the U.S. does not inherently constitute a visa violation. Hospitals typically do not inquire about foreign patients' motives, complicating efforts to establish fraudulent intent.

Additionally, once citizenship is conferred at birth, revocation is extremely rare—requiring clear evidence of fraud. Thus, birth tourism persists in a gray zone: not explicitly illegal but increasingly at odds with the civic principles the Fourteenth Amendment intended to secure.

VI. Ethical and Philosophical Dimensions

Beneath the legal and political debates over birth tourism lies a deeper ethical question: What does it mean to be a citizen? Is citizenship just a transaction—based on where you're born or a legal loophole? Or is it a form of mutual obligation—a commitment to a shared civic project?

The practice of birth tourism forces us to confront this question not in the abstract, but in concrete, morally ambiguous circumstances. Children born on U.S. soil to temporary visitors may grow up with no meaningful connection to the country of their legal nationality. They may never speak the language, study its history, or participate in its political life. And yet, by virtue of geography alone, they are endowed with the full rights and privileges of American citizenship.

A. Citizenship as Transaction or Trust?

For many birth tourism clients and their facilitators, U.S. citizenship is a product—a highly desirable legal asset that provides visa-free travel, access to American schools, and the option of future migration. In this framework, citizenship is not tied to civic trust or national belonging; it is a hedge, a benefit, a passport of convenience.

As discussed earlier, the commodification of citizenship undermines democratic traditions that treat membership as a moral and civic bond. Philosophers like Michael Sandel have argued that democracy depends on citizens engaging not just as rights-holders, but as co-authors of a shared public life.

As previously noted in Chapter 4, Appiah's conception of identity reinforces the view that citizenship derives meaning from shared responsibilities and cultural membership—not just legal status.

Benhabib, also cited in Chapter 4, argues that democratic inclusion requires clear terms of membership—even in a cosmopolitan framework. Birth tourism challenges this balance by separating legal acquisition from civic presence.

In sum, the ethical dilemma is this: Can a democracy maintain civic trust if citizenship becomes merely a legal status, untethered from participation, integration, or allegiance?

B. Civic Belonging vs. Legal Formalism

The legal framework of birthright citizenship, as it stands, does not differentiate between a child born to U.S. citizens deeply embedded in civic life and a child born to foreign nationals who depart days after delivery. Both are granted the same legal identity.

But should they be?

This is not a call to deny rights or create hierarchies of citizenship—but it is a prompt to reconsider the civic meaning of nationality. In democratic theory, rights are accompanied by duties, and membership implies reciprocity. Yet birth tourism enables a form of passive citizenship: status without sacrifice, belonging without burden.

Such asymmetry is corrosive over time. It fosters a stratified polity where some citizens bear the full obligations of civic life—jury duty, taxes, military registration—while others remain legally detached and politically absent. In a global era, some asymmetry may be inevitable. But when legal form overrides civic substance, democracy risks becoming a system of contractual entitlement rather than mutual responsibility.

The ultimate question is not whether birth tourism should be banned outright, but whether American citizenship should continue to be bestowed without reflection on its ethical and civic foundations.

VII. How Others Handle Birthright Citizenship

The debate over birthright citizenship in the United States is often framed in constitutional terms—but globally, it is increasingly treated as a matter of policy design, sovereignty, and civic integration. While the U.S. continues to adhere to a broad *jus soli* principle—granting citizenship to anyone born on American soil regardless of parental status—most other democracies have redefined or restricted their approaches. This section offers a comparative snapshot, illustrating the ways in which countries around the world have sought to balance the imperatives of inclusion, security, and civic cohesion.

Restrictive Models: Citizenship by Descent or Legal Connection

Several major democracies have moved away from automatic birthright citizenship, requiring a legal, cultural, or territorial connection to the state before citizenship is conferred:

- **Germany** grants citizenship at birth only if at least one parent has legally resided in the country for eight years and holds a permanent residence permit. The move toward this conditional model in 2000 reflected Germany's shift from an ethnic to a civic understanding of national identity, but one still grounded in demonstrable integration.
- **Japan** limits citizenship by birth to children with at least one Japanese parent. This strictly *jus sanguinis* ("right of blood") model reflects the country's longstanding emphasis on national homogeneity and controlled immigration.
- **India** has abandoned birthright citizenship altogether. Since a 2004 amendment, a child born in India can acquire citizenship only if at least one parent is a citizen and the other is not an illegal immigrant. This reflects growing concerns about demographic pressures and unauthorized migration, especially from neighboring countries.

These models share a common thread: citizenship must be earned or inherited through clear, established connections—not acquired passively by geographic accident.

Moderate Models: Hybrid Systems

Other countries adopt a more moderate stance, granting citizenship at birth only under specific legal or residency-based conditions:

- In the **United Kingdom**, a child born on British soil does not automatically receive citizenship unless at least one parent is a British citizen or lawfully settled in the UK. Children born without this status may acquire citizenship later through registration if they reside in the country for a designated period.
- **France**, historically one of the strongest proponents of *jus soli*, has added several layers of conditionality. A child born in France to foreign parents typically must reside there for a certain number of years before automatically acquiring citizenship, usually upon reaching age 18. This reflects France's republican commitment to integration through language, education, and social cohesion.

These hybrid systems offer a middle path—recognizing the place of birth as significant, but not sufficient without a demonstrated connection to national life.

Open Models: Full *Jus Soli*

The United States remains one of the few countries in the developed world to maintain a pure *jus soli* model, along with Canada.

- In the U.S., children born on American soil become citizens regardless of their parents' immigration status, except in rare cases involving diplomats. As seen, this principle was firmly established in *Wong Kim Ark* (1898) and remains intact despite recent legal and political challenges.
- Canada maintains an expansive *jus soli* regime similar to the United States, granting automatic citizenship to nearly all children born on Canadian soil regardless of parental status. However, unlike the U.S. Constitution's 14th Amendment, Canada's policy is statutory—and therefore subject to change through ordinary legislation. Though attempts to restrict birthright citizenship have failed to date, debates persist in the context of birth tourism and national identity.

These open models prioritize territorial inclusion over parental or cultural ties. However, as the pressures of transnational migration increase, both countries face growing questions about whether geographic birth alone should determine lifelong political membership.

Global Trends

A clear pattern has emerged: most nations have moved to restrict or qualify birthright citizenship in order to preserve civic cohesion and prevent perceived exploitation. The U.S. and Canada now stand as outliers, maintaining a legal tradition that many of their peers have already reconsidered. As this chapter argues, the core issue is not inclusion versus exclusion, but clarity versus ambiguity—a theme that will return in the policy recommendations to follow.

Chapter 7 will take up these tensions directly, proposing reforms that reconcile openness with allegiance—through legal clarification, administrative safeguards, and civic renewal.

VIII. Civic Implications of Stateless Integration

The children born via birth tourism may return decades later to claim their citizenship rights—college admissions, voting access, federal employment, or visa-free travel. And yet, many of these individuals were raised abroad with little exposure to American civic norms, political history, or cultural values. This gives rise to a new and troubling category of citizen: integrated statelessness—individuals who hold the rights of American citizenship, but who remain civically unanchored.

A. Political Participation Without Civic Knowledge

A core function of citizenship is participation in self-governance. But what happens when that participation is undertaken by individuals who have no enduring experience of life in the polity they influence? The rise of absentee or disembedded citizens—voting from afar, influencing policy outcomes, receiving federal aid—complicates the traditional idea of democratic representation. Citizenship, in these cases, risks becoming a platform for influence detached from shared fate.

B. National Identity and Civic Obligations

Issues of military service, tax obligations, and jury duty underscore the asymmetry. Many children born through birth tourism are shielded from these civic duties by their overseas residence and secondary nationality. When the burdens of citizenship are unevenly distributed, the democratic contract begins to fracture.

As national identity becomes more fragmented, we may see increased resistance to shared civic obligations. Already, there is growing tension in discussions about whether dual nationals should be eligible for security clearances, elected office, or diplomatic service—roles that presuppose undivided loyalty.

C. Citizenship by Convenience vs. Civic Accountability

As argued in previous chapters, citizenship unmoored from allegiance and civic participation risks becoming a tool of convenience rather than a shared democratic commitment. Birth tourism illustrates this disconnection in stark, market-based terms.

This commodification weakens the very notion of democratic accountability. It raises questions about fairness: Why should individuals who have never paid taxes, served on juries, or lived under U.S. law enjoy the same access to voting booths, public benefits, and constitutional protections as those who have?

Ultimately, birth tourism makes visible a deeper transformation: citizenship has become a tool of convenience rather than a covenant of commitment. When legal status is unmoored from shared obligation, civic trust frays—and democratic cohesion is at risk.

The question is not whether America should remain open—it should. The question is how we re-anchor citizenship in civic substance. Chapter 7 will chart that path: legal clarifications, administrative safeguards, and cultural renewal that bind status back to shared allegiance.

Can Birthright Citizenship Be Reformed Without an Amendment?

Efforts to restrict birthright citizenship without amending the Fourteenth Amendment face significant legal hurdles:

Executive Orders:
In 2025, President Trump's Executive Order 14160, seeking to restrict birthright citizenship for children of undocumented or temporary visitors, was swiftly blocked by federal courts as likely unconstitutional under *Wong Kim Ark* (1898). Litigation remains ongoing, potentially prompting Supreme Court review.

Legislative Proposals:
Multiple congressional bills have proposed conditioning citizenship on parents' immigration status. However, courts have indicated such legislation would likely conflict with existing precedent.

Judicial Uncertainty:
No appellate court has upheld restrictions based solely on parental status. However, some scholars suggest the Court could revisit the scope of "subject to the jurisdiction" to limit birthright citizenship for transient or strategic cases.

Constitutional Amendment — The Only Ironclad Option:
Ultimately, only an amendment offers definitive constitutional clarity. Such an effort would require significant bipartisan support and widespread state ratification.

> For deeper analysis, see *Appendix G: Birthright Citizenship and the Future of Jus Soli in American Law* (page 227).

IX. Fixing the Gaps in Our Citizenship System

Restoring Civic Coherence in the Age of Transactional Citizenship

The rise of birth tourism, alongside the broader commodification of U.S. citizenship through mechanisms like investment visas, poses more than a logistical challenge to immigration enforcement. It strikes at the moral foundation of American civic identity. As this chapter has shown, the current legal framework—rooted in the 14th Amendment and eroded by decades of administrative drift—has grown increasingly susceptible to exploitation by those who view citizenship not as a bond of allegiance, but as a tradable asset.

What's at stake is not just national security or immigration control, but the meaning of belonging in a democratic society. Citizenship must be more than a prize for crossing borders at the right moment; it must reflect mutual obligation, civic intent, and political accountability.

Reform must therefore proceed on multiple levels—from executive enforcement to legislative clarity, and, if necessary, constitutional reinterpretation. The proposals below are structured across short-term, medium-term, and long-term timelines, with each step designed to reinforce the ethical and institutional integrity of American citizenship.

A. Short-Term Administrative Measures

Enhanced Visa Screening for B-2 Entrants: U.S. consular officers should receive targeted training to identify likely cases of birth tourism at the visa application stage. Screening protocols should include red flags such as late-stage pregnancy at time of interview, previous U.S. births without residency history, and inconsistent or ambiguous travel plans.

Visa denials on this basis are legally permissible under existing discretion and require no statutory change—only implementation will and institutional support.

Target Commercial Birth Tourism Facilitators: Federal agencies—including DOJ, DHS, ICE, and USCIS—should be directed to investigate and prosecute operators of maternity tourism networks, especially those engaged in fraudulent visa applications, false addresses for hospital billing, and misrepresentation of intent at ports of entry.

Successful precedents exist: Operation "Tourist Trap" in 2015 resulted in multiple indictments and exposed a multi-million-dollar birth tourism industry.[32]

---

[32] U.S. Department of Justice, "Three Chinese Nationals Indicted for Operating 'Birth Tourism' Scheme in Southern California," DOJ Press Release, March 3, 2015.

Expand CBP Interview and Documentation Authority: Customs and Border Protection officers should be empowered to review documentation—including medical records—when there is reasonable suspicion of planned childbirth during travel. To ensure legal compliance, any review must follow due process safeguards, and interviews should be non-discriminatory and guided by intelligence-based protocols. Such authority would serve both as a deterrent and a detection mechanism, while preserving civil liberties.

B. Medium-Term Legislative Action

Enact a Federal Statute Defining *Jus Soli* Eligibility: Congress should pass legislation clarifying that U.S. birthright citizenship applies only when at least one parent holds lawful permanent resident status or valid nonimmigrant status not expressly prohibited for birthright claims—such as diplomatic assignments or certain temporary visas. While such a statute would likely face legal scrutiny, it would not directly contravene the Fourteenth Amendment's text, which refers to persons "subject to the jurisdiction" of the United States. Rather, it would offer a judicially testable framework for refining that jurisdiction in the context of modern abuse. In other words, it would compel the judiciary to revisit the scope of *jus soli* in the 21st century.

C. Long-Term Constitutional Consideration

Amend the 14th Amendment (as necessary): If statutory reform proves constitutionally insufficient, a constitutional amendment or judicial reinterpretation of the "jurisdiction clause" may become necessary. This would be a difficult but not impossible undertaking. It would require broad bipartisan consensus, a sustained national conversation about allegiance, identity, and civic reciprocity, and a judiciary willing to revisit the scope of *jus soli* in the 21st century. Importantly, any amendment effort could be narrowly framed—targeting only non-resident births to parents with no lawful status—in order to preserve humanitarian protections while closing exploitative loopholes.

Final Note: Reform as Civic Renewal

These reforms are not about exclusion. They are about moral clarity. The question is not whether the U.S. should welcome immigrants or celebrate diversity—it should and must. The question is whether citizenship should mean something more than presence, something deeper than paperwork—a civic bond, a shared trust, a national commitment.

If allegiance matters, then so too must the integrity of how allegiance is acquired.

Conclusion: Citizenship Must Mean More Than Geography

The promise of birthright citizenship in the United States—enshrined in the 14th Amendment—was originally forged in the crucible of post-Civil War justice. It was designed to ensure that no person born on American soil, regardless of ancestry or parental status, could be denied the rights of national belonging. But today, that moral architecture is under strain. As explored throughout this chapter, birth tourism exemplifies the growing gap between legal access and civic responsibility—turning a constitutional safeguard into a strategic asset. This evolution reflects the broader trend of civic detachment first outlined in Chapter 1.

This is not a failure of values, but of constitutional and statutory clarity. The United States has not modernized its citizenship framework to meet the demands of an era defined by globalization, digital migration, and transactional identity. As a result, citizenship has drifted toward commodification—less a bond of allegiance than a hedge against uncertainty or a tool of convenience.

This chapter has argued that such a trend is unsustainable. While the principle of *jus soli* remains a powerful affirmation of inclusion, both the courts and constitutional scholars have made clear: any attempt to restrict it—whether through executive order or congressional statute—is unlikely to survive judicial scrutiny. Only a constitutional amendment offers a viable long-term pathway to reform.

But reform alone is not enough. If we are to preserve the meaning of American citizenship, we must also reassert its civic and ethical foundations. Citizenship should reflect a willingness to participate, to contribute, and to share in a common democratic fate.

In the 21st century, when identities are fluid and borders porous, the future of democratic belonging depends on a simple but vital premise: citizenship must still stand for allegiance, accountability, and shared purpose— not just a spot on the map.

Chapter 7

Reclaiming the Civic Contract

This chapter sets out a forward-looking vision for restoring coherence, responsibility, and shared meaning to U.S. citizenship. It argues that allegiance must be redefined for the 21st century—not abandoned. Through legal reforms, civic education, and a renewed civic ethic, America can move from passive tolerance to active belonging.

I. The Meaning of Allegiance in a Liberal Democracy

In democratic societies, citizenship is often treated as a legal status—a designation printed on passports, embedded in constitutional texts, and adjudicated in courts of law. But beneath this bureaucratic surface lies a more vital question: what *should* citizenship mean in a pluralist democracy? The answer, this section argues, lies not in exclusion or ethnic uniformity but in a reinvigorated understanding of allegiance as civic responsibility.

Allegiance, in this democratic sense, is not blind nationalism. It is not loyalty to blood or soil or party. Rather, it is the ethical glue that binds citizens to one another and to the institutions they shape and sustain. It is the commitment that allows free individuals—diverse in background, belief, and aspiration—to function as a political community capable of self-governance. Without allegiance, democracy becomes an open-air marketplace of preferences; with it, democracy becomes a shared project of justice, care, and mutual accountability.

This chapter reframes the conversation around dual citizenship not as a question of identity pluralism versus national rigidity, but as a question of reciprocity. What do citizens owe one another? What kind of political belonging can sustain democratic life in an age of fluid identities and transnational mobility?

Citizenship as a Civic Covenant

At its core, citizenship is a covenant. It is not merely a set of rights one inherits or purchases, but a framework of participation that presumes both consent and contribution. It binds individuals together not just through laws, but through expectations of care, obligation, and shared fate.

In this light, allegiance is not a ceremonial oath or an abstract loyalty—it is lived through participation. Paying taxes, obeying laws, serving on juries, voting in elections, even engaging in civic discourse—these are the practices that give allegiance its democratic substance.

From Holding Citizenship to Living It

Allegiance is not something one *possesses* like a passport; it is something one *enacts* through civic behavior. And it is fragile—eroded not by dissent or diversity, but by detachment. When allegiance is treated as symbolic or optional, the democratic covenant begins to fray.

This framework builds on the insights of contemporary political theorists who have reshaped how we think about citizenship in modern democracies. As seen earlier, thinkers such as Michael Walzer, Ayelet Shachar, and Kwame Anthony Appiah argue that citizenship must be more than a legal designation—it must express a form of moral and civic belonging. Walzer reframes membership as a "shared fate," warning that when the burdens and benefits of democratic life are unevenly distributed, the foundation of justice begins to fracture. Shachar critiques the inherited inequalities of birthright citizenship, contending that arbitrary allocation without corresponding responsibility undermines both fairness and social cohesion. Appiah, in turn, emphasizes that identity is not simply assigned but authored through ethical engagement, suggesting that allegiance is not a constraint but a chosen commitment to a shared civic narrative. Together, their work underscores a common principle: that citizenship gains legitimacy not from accident or formality, but from participation, reciprocity, and a willingness to sustain the democratic project alongside others.

Paradoxically, advocating for singular allegiance is not about exclusion—it is about inclusion. In a world increasingly defined by inequality and mobility, reaffirming the responsibilities of citizenship is a way of preserving democratic trust and coherence. It says: no matter your origin, if you choose to belong to this polity, you do so not merely for what it can offer, but for what you are willing to give in return.

This does not mean that multiple identities must be abandoned. It means that political allegiance—the obligations we owe to fellow citizens—cannot be endlessly divided without consequence. Allegiance must have boundaries, not to repress difference, but to make solidarity possible.

II. What's Broken: The Erosion of the Civic Contract

Citizenship in a liberal democracy has long rested on the presumption of mutual obligation. Individuals are granted rights not as isolated entitlements, but as part of a larger social compact in which civic duties—voting, jury service, community participation—are expected in return. But in an age of dual and plural nationality, this contract is under considerable strain.

As more individuals claim citizenship through birthright or investment programs but maintain minimal engagement with the country's political or civic life, the meaning of belonging begins to blur. What was once an exclusive bond of allegiance has, in many cases, become a symbolic label—decoupled from responsibility, participation, or even basic familiarity with the nation's laws and values.

This erosion of civic coherence is not merely theoretical. It manifests in measurable differences in behavior, trust, and engagement.

A. Civic Engagement Metrics: Comparative Analysis

The following data underscores the troubling civic asymmetries between singular and dual citizens:

Civic Measure	Dual Citizens	Singular Citizens	Difference
Voter Turnout	37%	58%	-21 pts
Jury Duty Participation	42%	68%	-26 pts
Volunteer/Community Engagement	33%	48%	-15 pts
Political Campaign Involvement	22%	39%	-17 pts
Local Government Participation	29%	45%	-16 pts

Sources: Pew Research Center, Civic Participation Survey (2024); USCIS Citizenship Engagement Report; Migration Policy Institute Civic Integration Study.

Key Insights:

- The largest disparities appear in jury service and electoral participation—two pillars of democratic responsibility.
- The pattern holds across education levels and income brackets, indicating a structural, not merely circumstantial, difference.
- These gaps reflect not only behavioral divergence but also a weakening of the shared assumptions that undergird civic life.

B. From Obligation to Symbolism

What these numbers point to is a profound shift in the ethos of citizenship—from a lived responsibility to a nominal status. In public life, allegiance has morphed from obligation into ornament, from civic commitment into passive identity. This shift has consequences:

- Institutions reliant on shared sacrifice—military service, jury pools, tax compliance—struggle to maintain legitimacy;
- Elected officials face legitimacy crises when their constituents include individuals with divided loyalties or external obligations;
- Political cohesion fragments when different classes of citizens hold different expectations of what citizenship demands.

This unraveling of mutual obligation reflects a deeper crisis in the democratic contract. When some individuals treat citizenship as a shield or asset while others shoulder its civic burdens, the social fabric frays. Citizenship, in its healthiest form, rests on reciprocity—a shared stake in both the rights and responsibilities of political life. When that reciprocity is lost, citizenship becomes less a bond of belonging and more a legal contingency.

The phenomenon of dual citizenship being exploited as an 'escape hatch' from justice—illustrated dramatically by cases such as Claudia Hoerig's flight to Brazil and numerous child sexual offenders fleeing to Israel—underscores the urgency for clearer statutory requirements and international cooperation. Citizenship, as these cases demonstrate, must remain grounded in accountability, not evasion.

C. Public Sentiment and the Call for Reform

Amid legal ambiguity and institutional drift, one factor remains relatively consistent: public concern over the meaning and coherence of American citizenship. Contrary to the assumption that citizenship has become a hollow formality in the eyes of the public, polling data reveal a population that remains deeply invested in the ethical, civic, and legal contours of national membership.

Support for mandatory civic education remains strong. According to a 2023 PR Newswire poll, 61% of respondents agreed that requiring civic education would improve civic engagement among young people. This finding is echoed by a USC Rossier School of Education study, which reports bipartisan support for civic instruction as a way of reinforcing shared values and responsibilities—especially for those acquiring citizenship by naturalization or birthright.

Public sentiment on legal ambiguity is further underscored by a 2023 American Immigration Council survey, which found that a majority of respondents perceive the U.S. citizenship framework as inconsistent or unclear. An Associated Press–NORC Center for Public Affairs Research poll that same year revealed that, despite sharp political divides, most U.S. adults still believe in a core set of democratic values—but they are increasingly worried about whether these values are being coherently translated into law and policy.

In sum, these findings point to a civic majority in search of moral and institutional clarity. The public may not agree on every detail of immigration or nationality law, but the broad consensus is that citizenship must mean more than paperwork or geographic accident. There is a growing desire—across ideological lines—for a model of citizenship that restores coherence, reciprocity, and democratic accountability.

III. Legislative and Policy Solutions

The persistence of birth tourism and the broader commodification of U.S. citizenship reveals not only legal ambiguity but a failure of policy imagination. To restore coherence to the American civic framework, the law must address both the letter and the spirit of citizenship—ensuring that it reflects commitment, accountability, and democratic values. This section outlines a three-pronged approach to reform: statutory clarity, structured renunciation and notification mechanisms, and a reimagined civic oath.

A. Making the Law Clear

The current legal architecture offers little guidance on the rights, obligations, or boundaries of dual and derivative citizenship. While the Constitution still guarantees birthright citizenship for those born on U.S. soil, Congress has the power to regulate citizenship acquisition and loss in many other areas.

Restoring coherence to the American civic framework will require a clear legal foundation, one that sets out the rights, obligations, and limits of dual and derivative citizenship. While the Constitution still guarantees birthright citizenship for those born on U.S. soil, Congress retains authority over many other aspects of citizenship acquisition and loss.

This book returns to the statutory framework in Chapter 9, Section II *("Making Loyalty Clear in Law and Government")*, where a full proposal is outlined. There, we define the legal parameters of dual citizenship, establish humanitarian carve-outs, and set unified administrative guidance for sensitive roles.

B. Renunciation and Notification

A central ethical challenge in dual citizenship lies in the absence of deliberate choice. Many people inherit multiple nationalities without affirming loyalty to either, while others retain secondary allegiances without disclosure—undermining civic clarity.

This book returns to the disclosure and renunciation question in Chapter 9, Section V *("Digital Citizenship Disclosure and Accountability")*, where a complete proposal is outlined. There, we address mandatory disclosure in sensitive roles, streamlined renunciation procedures, humanitarian exemptions, and enforcement measures for concealment.

C. Oath of Allegiance Reform

The Oath of Allegiance is more than a formality—it is the symbolic moment when new citizens publicly commit to the nation. Yet in today's mobile, pluralist society, the oath risks being treated as a procedural step rather than a civic pledge.

This book returns to the Oath in Chapter 9, Section VII *("Modernizing the Oath of Allegiance and Naturalization")*, where a full proposal is outlined. There, we recommend affirming loyalty to the Constitution while explicitly committing to democratic participation, civic duties such as voting and jury service, and broader engagement in public life.

IV. Civic Education and Cultural Renewal

Rebuilding the civic contract will require more than legal reform; it also demands cultural and educational renewal. Citizenship is sustained not only by statutes and policies, but by the shared understanding of what membership in a democratic society entails. Without civic literacy and a culture that prizes engagement, the legal framework of citizenship risks becoming hollow.

This book returns to the question of civic education in Chapter 9, Section VI *("Integrating Civic Education with Citizenship Rights")*, where a full set of proposals is outlined. There, we explore how schools, universities, and public institutions can equip all citizens—native-born and naturalized alike—with the knowledge, habits, and sense of shared purpose needed to keep democracy vibrant.

V. Spotlight Case: A Civic Contract for the Next Generation

If citizenship is to retain its legitimacy in an age of global mobility and commodification, the answer cannot lie in restriction alone. It must also involve renewal—a reinvestment in what citizenship means. One of the most promising responses to the dilemmas posed by passive citizenship comes from below, not above: the schools, neighborhoods, and civil society programs that are quietly rebuilding a civic contract for the next generation.

A. Education as Integration

Across the United States, public school districts and charter networks have developed programs designed to connect students—regardless of birthplace—with the moral and political meaning of American democracy. These initiatives move beyond routine civic facts and seek to cultivate civic responsibility, cultural belonging, and a sense of shared fate.

In Southern California, a school-based initiative known as "We the Students" has introduced constitutional literacy, public service internships, and town hall simulations for high schoolers, many of whom are the children of immigrants, dual nationals, or birth tourists. "We're not asking where they came from," one teacher explained. "We're asking: what kind of citizen do you want to be?"

B. Community as Commitment

Other programs focus on immigrant families themselves. In Houston and Miami, community centers have launched "Civic Welcome Circles"—local groups where new immigrants engage in weekly discussions on American history, voting, law, and public life. These are not compliance workshops; they are civic onramps. And in many cases, they include participants whose children hold U.S. citizenship acquired through birth tourism or mixed-status households.

C. What Other Countries Teach About Citizenship

Civic integration is not merely a question of language proficiency or procedural knowledge—it is a foundation for democratic belonging. In many advanced democracies, civic education is treated not as an optional add-on, but as a structural pillar of national identity and public trust. The

United States, by contrast, has struggled to build a coherent model of civic literacy.

For example, in the U.S., civic preparation for naturalization consists primarily of a short civics test administered during the citizenship interview. While some schools and community programs provide additional civic education, these efforts are typically voluntary, underfunded, and unevenly distributed.

This stands in stark contrast to peer democracies such as Germany and Canada.

In Germany, all naturalization applicants are required to complete a formal integration course and pass a citizenship test covering constitutional principles, political rights, and German history. The intent is not to erase identity but to ground it within a common civic framework. Citizenship is framed as a political commitment—not just a legal entitlement.

Canada embeds civic expectations directly into its immigration pathway. All permanent residents receive the *Discover Canada* guide, which outlines not only rights and benefits but also duties of citizenship. The guide states explicitly: *"Citizenship is more than a legal status. It is a bond that unites people in a democratic society."* Canadian civic education connects national identity to political participation, from jury duty to voting.

These models share a common recognition: that civic cohesion does not emerge automatically from legal status. It must be cultivated through education, expectation, and engagement.

In the American context, the absence of civic preparation raises pressing questions. If citizenship can be acquired without cultural knowledge, political literacy, or community connection, what anchors its meaning? How can a democratic society sustain trust when some citizens are never invited—or expected—to participate?

The lesson from abroad is clear: rights must be paired with responsibilities, and citizenship must be taught, not just granted. A renewed investment in civic education and orientation—especially for those acquiring citizenship through less integrative paths—may be essential to restoring the integrity of democratic life.

D. Toward a Civic Contract

These efforts, however modest, point to a broader strategy: we must recover the idea of a civic contract—not just for immigrants, but for all Americans. Citizenship should not be reduced to geography or inherited paperwork. It should be an invitation to contribute, to participate, and to belong.

The next section will examine policy frameworks that could reinforce this civic orientation—not through punitive restriction, but through democratic affirmation.

VI. Tiered Legislative and Reform Strategy

To restore integrity and coherence to American citizenship in an age of global mobility and strategic exploitation, a multi-tiered reform agenda is needed—one that begins with immediate administrative steps, evolves through medium-term civic initiatives, and culminates in long-term constitutional and structural reassessment. The goal is not to exclude, but to affirm that citizenship is more than a birthright: it is a shared ethical, civic, and institutional commitment.

First, immediate administrative reforms are needed to build civic accountability into existing legal frameworks. These include revising the Oath of Allegiance to emphasize not only allegiance but also civic responsibility and transparency, including disclosure of dual nationality obligations.

Simultaneously, the United States should develop a national citizenship accountability system—an inter-agency database linking immigration histories, birthright claims, visa records, and voluntary disclosures of dual nationality. Such a system would be designed not to penalize, but to enhance planning for civic inclusion, uphold public integrity, and prevent abuse of legal status in matters such as fraud, education access, or national security.

Finally, national civic education standards should be implemented to ensure that K–12 students—regardless of birthplace or parental status—are taught the rights and responsibilities of American citizenship as a living democratic practice, not a mere legal technicality.

Second, medium-term reforms must deepen the link between citizenship and civic integration. Mandatory civic orientation and integration programs, modeled after practices in several European democracies, would introduce new citizens to the principles, responsibilities, and expectations of democratic life. These programs could cover U.S. history, constitutional values, and civic norms, ensuring that citizenship is anchored in understanding, not just geography.

Third, long-term reform may ultimately require a constitutional amendment if judicial reinterpretation proves elusive. The Fourteenth Amendment—though foundational—was written in a radically different historical context. While its core promise of equal protection must remain intact, there is growing legal and ethical debate over whether its guarantee of *jus soli* should apply unconditionally, regardless of parental status, residency, or civic intent. If the courts decline to revisit the scope of "subject to the jurisdiction," then only a constitutional amendment can resolve the tension between geographic birth and civic allegiance. Such an amendment need not overturn *jus soli* entirely, but it could narrowly narrow the scope—limiting automatic citizenship to cases where at least one parent has a legal connection to the United States.

Ultimately, this reform agenda does not seek to roll back the noble promise of American citizenship. Rather, it aims to renew that promise by ensuring that legal membership in the national community reflects civic participation, ethical allegiance, and mutual accountability. Citizenship should remain open—but not empty.

VII. Loyalty and Liberty Can Coexist

One of the most frequent objections to reforming birthright citizenship is the concern that it will restrict liberty. Critics warn that any attempt to narrow automatic citizenship—or to link it more explicitly with civic participation and allegiance—risks conjuring nativism or undermining the pluralism that defines a diverse democracy. But this objection relies on a false premise: that liberty and loyalty are in tension. In truth, they are co-dependent. In a healthy republic, liberty is preserved not despite allegiance, but because of it.

A strong civic contract protects rights precisely because it demands responsibility. It affirms that citizens do not merely consume the benefits of a political order—they uphold it. Allegiance, in this sense, is not about ethnic uniformity or ideological conformity. It is about mutual accountability and civic trust. In an age of global mobility, citizenship must anchor liberty not in sameness, but in shared responsibility.

Programs like birth tourism and investor visas increasingly reduce citizenship to a transactional asset—reinforcing the perception that American identity can be purchased, not earned through civic belonging. This erosion is not limited to childbirth alone. In fact, investor visa programs—such as the EB-5 Immigrant Investor Program—also blur the line between political membership and transactional gain. These programs, while legal and often economically beneficial, reinforce the perception that access to citizenship is something to be purchased, not earned through civic integration or allegiance.

This is not an argument against immigration or against economic participation—it is an argument for coherence. Citizenship law must reinforce not just identity but democratic cohesion—ensuring that legal inclusion is paired with civic integration. The call to reform birthright citizenship and close its most exploitative loopholes is not a demand for exclusion. It is a call for ethical clarity. It is a commitment to the idea that no matter the path to acquisition, citizenship should culminate in civic participation, not passive entitlement.

Singular citizenship—when rooted in civic obligation rather than ethnic identity—strengthens the moral foundation of democracy. It signals that liberty endures not through detachment, but through shared responsibility. Political membership must involve more than legal status; it must reflect a commitment to the common good. Reforming birthright citizenship, then, is not about exclusion—it is about affirming that those who enter the civic community do so as active participants in its future.

Conclusion: Citizenship with Meaning

Citizenship in the United States has long been a symbol of liberty and inclusion—a legal affirmation of belonging to a free society. But law alone cannot sustain a democracy. Without shared obligation, citizenship becomes thin: a transactional good, not a civic bond. This chapter has argued that in the face of global mobility, dual nationality, and the commodification of membership, we must not abandon allegiance—we must reclaim it.

Allegiance is the ethical infrastructure of democratic life. It binds plural people into a common project. In the absence of civic coherence—when citizenship is inherited, exploited, or held passively—democracy risks becoming not a shared endeavor, but a patchwork of preferences with no mutual accountability. To prevent this, we must restore the civic contract at the heart of American democracy.

This restoration begins with legal clarity: a statutory framework that affirms what citizenship entails, where its obligations begin, and how multiple allegiances are to be disclosed, managed, or renounced. It deepens through education: a national investment in civic formation that teaches the next generation that citizenship is not just a status—but a story, a set of responsibilities, a shared fate. And it is sustained through culture: the civic rituals, public symbols, and democratic practices that remind us that to be American is to belong not just by birth, but by care, contribution, and commitment.

This is not a nostalgic appeal to nationalism. It is a moral and institutional appeal to responsibility. In an era of strategic exploitation of citizenship, fractured allegiance, and transactional identity, the republic must respond—not by exclusion, but by coherence.

The next chapter turns from principles to pressures—from birthright and belonging to the future of citizenship in a digital and disrupted world. As borders blur, identities proliferate, and technologies challenge traditional sovereignty, Chapter 8 asks: Can allegiance survive in a world no longer anchored in place? And what must we do to ensure it does?

Chapter 8

Belonging in the Digital Age
The Future of Citizenship in a Disrupted World

What does it mean to belong to a nation when borders are porous, identities are fluid, and allegiance can be toggled with a click?

In the digital age, citizenship is undergoing a profound transformation. Traditional anchors—territory, culture, and reciprocal obligation—are being destabilized by global migration, technological disruption, and the rise of nomadic elites and algorithmically governed communities.

While some claim national citizenship is becoming obsolete, this chapter argues otherwise: allegiance must be adapted for a borderless, digital era—not left behind. Citizenship remains vital—but its meaning must adapt to a world of fractured loyalties and fluid identities.

We explore how "citizenship by app," digital nomadism, and stratified legal statuses are challenging civic duty and democratic coherence. Who is accountable when belonging is optional, layered, or outsourced?

This chapter maps the new landscape of citizenship and proposes a framework for rebuilding civic meaning in a disrupted world—one that is ethically grounded, democratically viable, and resilient to the pressures of decentralization.

I. Citizenship on the Edge of Transformation

Citizenship today is no longer defined by land, lineage, or law. It is being reshaped by digital platforms, borderless mobility, and affiliations that operate outside the framework of nation-states.

Millions are not rejecting civic life outright—they are opting for mobility, digital autonomy, and commercial flexibility. The rise of e-residency, nomad visas, and cloud-based entrepreneurship reveals a deeper shift: citizenship is becoming modular and increasingly detached from mutual obligation.

What Is a Citizen in the Age of AI?

- If your daily interactions are with an algorithm, your employer is in the cloud, and your community is on a forum—are you still "of" a nation?
- Who decides the rights and duties of someone who belongs everywhere—and nowhere?

From Estonia's pioneering e-residency program[33], which enables anyone in the world to start and manage a European Union–based business without ever setting foot in Europe, to digital nomads working remotely from Bali, Tbilisi, or Lisbon under special visa schemes, the lived experience of citizenship is being remapped in real time.

---

[33] *E-residency* refers to a legal status conferred by a sovereign government that allows non-residents to access certain administrative, commercial, and legal services through a secure digital identity—without requiring physical presence or traditional residency. E-residency *does not* confer citizenship, tax residency, or immigration rights. Estonia's e-Residency program, launched in 2014, is the most prominent example, enabling global entrepreneurs to establish and manage EU-based businesses remotely. See: Government of Estonia, "What is E-Residency?" *https://e-resident.gov.ee*.

These transformations are not confined to fringe groups. According to a 2023 OECD report:

- Over 1.2 million people globally are now enrolled in digital residency or nomad visa programs;
- Countries like Estonia, Portugal, the UAE, and Barbados are actively competing to attract stateless workers through relaxed tax regimes and simplified e-governance structures;
- More than 20% of U.S. dual citizens under age 35 reported in a Pew survey that they "do not feel primarily affiliated" with either of their formal countries of citizenship.

The traditional building blocks of democratic belonging—shared territory, common language, physical community—are giving way to transnational lifestyles and algorithmic governance. Blockchain-based identification systems, AI-managed government services, and smart contract voting platforms may soon redefine the mechanics of political participation. But if that happens, will the civic meaning of citizenship be left behind?

Rise of e-Residency & Digital Nomadism (2016–2024)

Metric	2016	2020	2024 (Est.)
Total e-Residencies (Global)	10,000	100,000	250,000+
Top Countries Offering e-Residency	Estonia	Estonia, UAE, Portugal	Estonia, UAE, Portugal
Digital Nomad Visas Issued (Global)	—	~50,000	125,000+
GDP Contribution (Est.)	$500M	$2B	$5B+

Note: Data compiled from government portals, OECD estimates, and 2023–2024 visa reports.

The global expansion of e-residency programs and digital nomad visas illustrates the decoupling of citizenship from territorial presence. As digital mobility rises, traditional models of allegiance and participation face growing legal and philosophical challenges.

These risks are not only technical—they are existential. A society that no longer requires shared space or public institutions to define its members may ultimately lose the sense of "we" that sustains democratic community. When taxes are paid elsewhere, laws are enforced digitally, and disputes are mediated by software, where does accountability reside? What binds citizens to one another in such a world?

This chapter explores these tensions, tracing how the frontier of digital identity intersects with the civic contract. It asks:

- Can democracy survive the decline of territorial allegiance?
- Should citizenship be redefined for a decentralized world—or reclaimed before it disappears?

We begin by examining the tools and structures that are enabling this shift—before turning to its consequences for law, loyalty, and legitimacy.

II. Digital Nomads, Remote Work, and "Sovereignty Shopping"

A new model of "citizenship untethered" is emerging—shaped more by convenience and commerce than by community or obligation. At its center is the digital nomad: a globally mobile worker who follows broadband strength, tax incentives, and lifestyle perks rather than national affiliation or civic duty.

By the end of 2023, over 35 million people identified as digital nomads—a number projected to rise. While some retain ties to a home country, many live in legal limbo, leveraging short-term visas, secondary passports, and opaque tax regimes to remain untethered from any single state.[34]

---

[34] Estimates of the global digital nomad population in 2023 range from 35 to over 40 million. According to *MBO Partners*, approximately 35 million individuals worldwide identified as digital nomads in 2023, with trends showing continued growth. See: MBO Partners, *State of Independence in America*, 2023. See also Global Edge, Michigan State University, "Digital Nomadism' Redefines Travel & Global Economies in the 21st Century," 2023, which reports over 40 million global digital nomads, including 18.1 million from the United States.

This shift reflects a broader trend: the commodification of citizenship. Countries offering the most appealing digital visa programs—Portugal, the UAE, Caribbean states—often pair them with fast-tracked citizenship for those willing to invest. The result is a global menu of semi-citizenship: legal status as a subscription service.

"Sovereignty Shopping" and Flag Theory

Entrepreneurs, tech elites, and crypto investors often take this fluid model further through "flag theory": a strategy of acquiring multiple legal affiliations—citizenship in one country, banking in another, business in a third—to maximize freedom and minimize state oversight.

As D'Costa notes, dual nationality can complicate national identity and strain norms of civic accountability when treated as a strategic tool rather than a relational bond.

This has profound implications for democratic legitimacy and national cohesion. As more people opt into legal status as a convenience—whether through birth tourism, investor visas, or digital nomad programs—the underlying meaning of allegiance risks being hollowed out. What happens when civic identity is severed from civic practice?

The Risks of Citizenship Without Roots

Zygmunt Bauman's "liquid modernity" captures the essence of this shift: identities are no longer fixed or place-bound, but adaptable and transactional. While liberating for individuals, this fluidity erodes the civic glue that holds communities together.

Dual citizenship, once a reflection of layered identity, increasingly serves as a hedge—disembedded from civic commitment and used as a tool of access or escape.

As Koslowski (2022) warns—and as argued throughout this book—without deliberate structures for civic engagement, dual citizenship risks eroding national identity, producing residents of convenience rather than citizens bound by shared responsibility.

III. Platforms, Networks, and the Illusion of Community

In an era defined by transnational mobility and instantaneous communication, many defenders of dual or convenience-based citizenship argue that belonging has transcended geography. They point to the rise of global digital platforms—Reddit, X (formerly Twitter), Discord, Telegram—as spaces where civic identity and solidarity can flourish beyond borders. But does participation in these fragmented online networks constitute real citizenship? Or does it merely simulate civic connection while bypassing the obligations that make democratic life meaningful?

A. The Rise of Digital Pseudo-Citizenship

Online platforms like Reddit and WeChat have transformed the birth tourism industry into a crowdsourced network—facilitating hospital referrals, legal strategies, and logistical support. These forums mimic civic solidarity but lack the rootedness, responsibility, and reciprocity of true political belonging.

This fosters a virtual allegiance—where U.S. citizenship is treated as a digital badge of privilege, not a participatory commitment. Identity becomes instrumental, episodic, and detached from shared civic life.

B. From Civic Commitment to Interest-Based Affinity

Political theorist Benedict Anderson described nations as "imagined communities" sustained by shared memory and ritual. Today's online affinity groups, by contrast, lack institutional continuity or civic sacrifice. They may offer solidarity—but not the formative experiences of duty, deliberation, or accountability that define democratic life.

The techno-utopian vision of borderless digital citizenship collapses under democratic scrutiny. Networks may foster connection, but they do not demand taxes, jury duty, or reconciliation of rights with responsibilities.

C. Civic Fragmentation in the Age of Connectivity

Far from dissolving borders, digital platforms often deepen fragmentation. They normalize the decoupling of benefits from obligations—enabling individuals to reside in one country, pay taxes in another, vote in a third, and belong meaningfully to none.

The result is "citizenship by convenience"—a consumerist model of nationality that accelerates the civic fragmentation already eroding democratic cohesion.

We must counter this drift toward simulated belonging with a renewed commitment to the institutional and ethical foundations of citizenship.

IV. Blockchain Governance and the Mirage of Stateless Freedom

The digital revolution has radically reimagined citizenship—challenging traditional notions of sovereignty, belonging, and democratic community. Central to this shift is the idea of the "network state," a model promoted by technologist Balaji Srinivasan, which proposes digital, value-driven communities as alternatives to nation-states.

The Evolving Landscape of Network Citizenship

Network citizenship reimagines civic identity as a voluntary, tech-enabled affiliation rather than a status conferred by birthplace or residence. While these digital experiments have not yet replaced traditional citizenship, they are reshaping how individuals relate to governance, identity, and one another.

At the core of this model is self-sovereign identity[35]—blockchain-based[36] credentials controlled by the individual rather than issued by a state. Initiatives like ID2020 and Worldcoin aim to make identity portable, secure, and borderless, granting access to services without reliance on national bureaucracies.

Governance in this space is increasingly driven by Decentralized Autonomous Organizations (DAOs)—online collectives that use blockchain technology to make and enforce decisions. DAOs operate through transparent rules embedded in smart contracts,[37] which automatically execute decisions based on community votes.

A notable example is CityDAO, a blockchain experiment in Wyoming that enables individuals to co-own and manage real estate as tokenized parcels. Members vote on land use, budget allocation, and other governance issues—all without a centralized authority or traditional bureaucratic oversight. The goal is to replace opaque hierarchy with programmable, participatory governance.

Beyond technical governance, network citizenship also enables affiliation around shared values rather than shared geography. Afropolitan, for example, aspires to build a borderless community focused on African prosperity—fusing cultural identity with decentralized decision-making. Yet such projects face steep challenges, from legal ambiguity to the lack of democratic safeguards and institutional legitimacy.

---

[35] *Self-sovereign identity* refers to a digital identity that is owned and controlled by the individual, not by a government or corporation. It allows people to prove who they are or share credentials without relying on centralized databases.

[36] A *blockchain* is a decentralized digital ledger that records transactions across many computers in a way that makes them secure, transparent, and nearly impossible to alter. It enables individuals to exchange information or assets without relying on a central authority.

[37] *Smart contracts* are self-executing digital agreements built on blockchain. Once the terms are met, the contract automatically carries out actions like transferring funds or granting access—without needing lawyers or intermediaries.

The now-defunct Bitnation attempted to offer blockchain-based "governance services" such as identity verification, contracts, and dispute resolution outside of any state framework. Its brief lifespan illustrates the fragile foundation of these models: conceptual appeal often runs ahead of political and legal feasibility.

Yet Bitnation was not alone. Across the globe, new experiments in decentralized governance and digital identity are redrawing the boundaries of civic life. Together, these efforts reflect a profound shift in the logic of citizenship—from inherited status and territorial bonds to programmable affiliation and voluntary participation.

To better understand how this vision is unfolding, consider several early-stage initiatives that illustrate the emerging infrastructure of network citizenship. These projects offer a glimpse into how digital identity, decentralized governance, and voluntary affiliation are converging to redefine what it means to belong in a political community.

Initiative	Description	Civic Innovation
Estonian e-Residency	Government program granting digital identity to non-citizens for remote business access.	Stateless digital ID tied to an official nation-state.
ID2020	Alliance (UN, Microsoft, Accenture) developing portable, blockchain-based identity for global use.	Self-sovereign digital identity for services and mobility.
CityDAO	DAO that owns land in Wyoming and governs its use through smart contracts.	Tokenized land rights and decentralized decision-making.
Afropolitan	A network-state vision for African diaspora collaboration and governance.	Borderless citizenship based on shared prosperity.
Bitnation *(defunct)*	A blockchain platform that offered identity, contracts, and dispute resolution beyond the nation-state.	Stateless digital governance tools.

These initiatives are early and experimental—but they signal a growing effort to reimagine civic belonging around voluntary affiliation, tech-enabled governance, and distributed models of community and identity.

Yet for all their innovation, these experiments face steep legal hurdles. Most governments do not recognize blockchain-based identity as a substitute for national documentation, and smart contracts lack enforceability in traditional courts. DAOs may make decisions algorithmically, but who is held accountable if they fail? Questions of liability, jurisdiction, and due process remain unresolved. As a result, these projects operate in a legal gray zone—technically functional, but civically fragile.

Taken together, these developments signal a paradigm shift: from citizenship as inherited status to citizenship as voluntary affiliation. The resulting model is portable, programmable, and hyper-individualized—but fraught with legal ambiguity and unequal access.

In sum, the infrastructure for network citizenship is already here—in platforms, protocols, and pilot programs. From Estonia's digital nation to Afropolitan's borderless vision, these initiatives signal that the future of civic belonging may be as much about code and consent as it is about constitutions. But until such models earn legal legitimacy and achieve democratic inclusivity, they remain complements to—and not replacements for—traditional citizenship.

Why This Vision Is Hard to Make Real

While these innovations promise individual autonomy, they raise urgent democratic concerns. Blockchain governance often prioritizes efficiency over deliberation, reducing democratic participation to code execution. Seyla Benhabib reminds us that legitimacy requires more than automation—it demands collective reasoning, moral context, and shared purpose.

Toward a Hybrid Model

Rather than displacing nation-states, network communities may complement traditional citizenship—if reformed with democratic safeguards. A hybrid model could preserve human agency while leveraging digital tools for participation and transparency.

Practical Recommendations:
1. Ensure democratic oversight for algorithmic governance
2. Expand participation beyond token-based voting
3. Build ethical frameworks for digital identity systems
4. Preserve human interpretation in civic processes

A New Political Imagination

Network states and blockchain citizenship are not merely technological experiments—they represent a profound reimagination of political belonging. They challenge us to think beyond geographic boundaries while preserving the essential human need for meaningful community.

The goal is not to replace existing democratic structures, but to expand our conception of citizenship—making it more adaptive, inclusive, and responsive to a rapidly changing global landscape.

V. Digital Identity in an Age of Geopolitical Contest

As U.S. debates over birthright citizenship intensify, a parallel transformation is reshaping the global meaning of civic identity. In an era of cloud governance, biometric tracking, and algorithmic profiling, citizenship is no longer just a legal status—it is a digital tether that can empower, surveil, or even be weaponized.

China: Citizenship as Surveillance Infrastructure

China exemplifies the merger of citizenship and surveillance. Its social credit system merges financial, behavioral, and political data into a national metric of loyalty. Ostensibly aimed at building trust, the system penalizes dissent and extends its reach beyond borders.

U.S.-born children of Chinese nationals are often drawn into this dual system—granted American rights, but shadowed by Chinese scrutiny. Beijing's monitoring of travel, digital communication, and family ties shows how nationality can remain politicized, even after migration.

Russia: The Passport as Political Instrument

Russia takes a more overtly geopolitical approach, using citizenship as a tool of soft power and territorial influence. Through mass passport issuance in regions like Abkhazia, Transnistria, and eastern Ukraine, the Kremlin asserts jurisdiction over contested populations.

For Russian birth tourists to the U.S., the implications are subtle but real: legal status becomes a form of strategic leverage. Moscow's claim to protect "its" citizens abroad mirrors China's extraterritorial pressure—turning nationality into a geopolitical vector.

Citizenship as Digital Tether

These cases expose a deeper truth: digital infrastructure often binds more than it frees. As sociologist Saskia Sassen notes, deterritorialized power doesn't dissolve the state—it redistributes it through data networks, passport systems, and biometric regimes.

A child born in Los Angeles may enjoy U.S. citizenship on paper, but still be tracked, scored, or coerced by a foreign state. In this model, citizenship-by-birth becomes a dual tether—offering protection from one system and exposure to another.

Implications for Civic Sovereignty

What happens when the civic identities of Americans—especially dual nationals—are shaped by foreign surveillance or coercion? Intelligence agencies increasingly factor in biometric control, "digital loyalty" scores, and diaspora monitoring by states like China and Russia. A 2023 Pew

Research Center study found that nearly two-thirds of Americans believe holding multiple citizenships can create conflicts of interest in public service—underscoring ongoing anxieties about divided allegiance that foreign surveillance and coercion could exploit.

Yet China and Russia are not alone. Around the world, legal identity is being instrumentalized in ways that blur the line between civic belonging and state strategy.

Global Patterns of Citizenship as Leverage

China and Russia may be the most prominent examples of extraterritorial citizenship manipulation, but they are not alone. Around the world, states are increasingly using legal identity as a strategic tool of influence, control, or punishment.

- **Turkey** has systematically cultivated its European diaspora as an extension of its domestic political base. Through targeted outreach and dual-national enfranchisement, the Turkish state mobilizes foreign-based citizens for electoral and ideological alignment. Citizenship, in this case, becomes a vehicle for transnational loyalty.
- **India** has used its Overseas Citizenship of India (OCI) framework both to engage its diaspora and to police dissent. While OCI does not confer full citizenship, its selective enforcement—especially toward critical journalists or activists—illustrates how access to legal identity can be used to reward compliance or penalize opposition.
- In the **Gulf States**, particularly **Bahrain** and the **UAE**, citizenship revocation has become a tool of internal discipline. Dissidents, minority activists, and regime critics have been stripped of nationality without due process—demonstrating how citizenship can be wielded not as a right, but as a conditional privilege.

These global trends suggest that citizenship, once imagined as a stabilizing legal status, is increasingly contingent, politicized, and digitally monitored. The common thread is control: legal identity becomes a mechanism for asserting power across borders and silencing dissent within them.

In this landscape, legal citizenship is not the end of the story—it's the beginning of a contested identity subject to overlapping claims, data scrutiny, and politicized obligations.

VI. Reclaiming Allegiance in a Networked Republic

As citizenship stretches to accommodate global mobility, digital life, and layered identities, a paradox emerges: it is easier than ever to acquire formal nationality, yet harder to define its civic meaning. The infrastructure of participation—laws, institutions, norms—has not kept pace with the fluidity of modern identity. The result is a form of legal belonging often detached from any sustained relationship of responsibility or trust.

This fragmentation reflects a deeper drift: the rise of transactional citizenship, where national membership is treated less as a commitment and more as a convenience. One can be legally American, yet culturally disengaged and civically absent—entitled to rights without practicing the duties that sustain democratic life.

A 2023 Harvard Kennedy School report found that trust in public institutions is at a multi-decade low, particularly among digitally mobile younger citizens.

Yet the need for allegiance has not disappeared. If anything, it has become more urgent. In a world of fractured loyalties and remote belonging, citizenship must be reimagined not as an exclusionary category, but as an ethical tether—a framework of shared fate and mutual accountability.

A. Anchored Allegiance in a Fluid World

Democracy is more than a marketplace of preferences—it is a moral enterprise grounded in solidarity. Citizenship must go beyond access to become a form of ethical belonging.
In a world of layered identities and mobile lives, the challenge is not to retreat into nationalism, but to anchor allegiance in civic responsibility. Without linking legal status to shared obligation, the fabric of democracy will inevitably fray.

B. Reimagining Allegiance, Not Abandoning It

Citizenship can adapt to global fluidity—but not by becoming hollow. A world where identity is portable still needs structures of accountability, memory, and purpose.

The test of allegiance is not where one lives or which passport one holds, but whether one contributes to a shared civic project. Without that, democracy becomes unmoored—held together by convenience, not commitment.

C. Civic Re-engagement in Practice

While the erosion of civic coherence may seem irreversible, democratic renewal is not merely theoretical. Several governments and cities have pioneered innovative forms of participatory citizenship that re-anchor allegiance in civic practice—especially in the digital sphere.

- **Taiwan's vTaiwan** project offers one such example: a government-run online platform where citizens collaboratively deliberate on complex policy proposals, with many resulting in real legislative changes. It has become a model for how digital participation can augment rather than erode representative democracy.
- **Barcelona's Decidim** platform similarly empowers local residents to propose, debate, and vote on city policies. Unlike

purely symbolic online engagement, Decidim is tied to institutional mechanisms that compel municipal authorities to respond. In doing so, it transforms participation from sentiment into structured influence.

Such projects demonstrate that digital tools can be harnessed for civic strengthening—not just civic bypassing. They remind us that allegiance can be rebuilt not through nostalgia, but through participation, accountability, and voice

Conclusion: Citizenship in a Disrupted Age—Adaptive, Not Liquid

The forces reshaping citizenship today—mobility, digital governance, transactional allegiance—are as destabilizing as they are inevitable. But democracy cannot survive without durable forms of belonging.

Citizenship must evolve without dissolving. It must carry civic expectation, not just personal benefit. It must mean something more than credentials or access—it must represent mutual responsibility and ethical participation.

In this age of cloud borders and fracturing identities, we need a new civic imagination. One that embraces mobility, but refuses to let allegiance disappear into the network. The goal is not nostalgia for old forms—but renewal of shared purpose.

As the next and final chapter will argue, coherence must be rebuilt not just legally, but morally. The citizen of the future will not only claim rights—but help sustain the republic to which those rights belong.

Chapter 9

Rebuilding the Civic Contract
A Framework for Reform

Building on Chapter 7's vision of citizenship as a civic covenant, this chapter turns from critique to action. It lays out a concrete reform agenda—legal, administrative, and constitutional—to reclaim American citizenship as a site of democratic meaning and mutual accountability.

For too long, the rules governing who belongs—and what that belonging requires—have been shaped not by open debate, but by a tangle of judicial rulings, executive orders, and agency workarounds. As a result, citizenship has drifted from a lived covenant into a passive status: conferred at birth or granted on paper, yet often unpracticed in spirit. Restoring true allegiance demands more than new statutes; it calls for a renewed commitment to shared responsibility, transparent institutions, and ethical bonds that bind citizens to one another and to the republic itself.

Drawing on comparative models, historical lessons, and democratic theory, we propose a three-part blueprint—diagnosis, pluralist examples, and policy reforms—that strengthens civic bonds without excluding plural identities. By diagnosing how we arrived at our present drift, illustrating how other democracies have fused diversity with cohesion, and advancing concrete reforms to clarify and deepen civic accountability, we can reclaim citizenship as an active, participatory commitment rather than a hollow credential.

I. From Drift to Deliberation

> *Consider Maria, a naturalized citizen who votes only rarely, never serves on a jury, and treats her passport more like an insurance policy than a civic bond. She embodies a century-long drift from practiced commitment to passive possession.*

In modern America, citizenship often functions as a legal entitlement rather than a lived civic commitment. The challenge now is to renew the shared responsibilities that give it meaning: How do we restore a sense of shared fate when membership has become optional?

- How do we affirm allegiance without veering into exclusion?
- Can pluralism and civic responsibility reinforce one another?
- What does it mean to belong in a world of fractured loyalties?]

In practice, citizenship now often means holding rights rather than exercising duties. Geography bestows status; paperwork maintains it. Without a renewed democratic conversation, membership will remain hollow.

Framing the Chapter

To guide readers through our civic-renewal agenda, we'll proceed in three coordinated moves:

1. **Diagnose the Drift**: Chart how American citizenship slipped from practiced duty to legal formality;
2. **Survey Pluralist Models**: Highlight other democracies that maintain cohesion amid diversity;
3. **Outline Reforms**: Propose concrete measures tying legal status back to civic responsibility and shared fate.

Key Insight: Pluralism itself isn't the problem—disconnection is. Our task is to give diversity a civic framework so that citizenship is more than paperwork; it's a lived, reciprocal relationship.

II. Clear Rules for Loyalty in Public Service

In an era of proliferating dual citizenship, the United States faces the fundamental challenge of defining and enforcing primary civic allegiance in roles of public trust. At present, no statute requires a dual citizen serving in government to declare which country holds their highest loyalty—or to affirm formally that their primary allegiance is to the United States.

As Anthony D'Costa (2023) observes, dual nationality can strain norms of civic accountability when treated as a strategic tool rather than a relational bond. This absence of legal clarity is not a mere technicality. It erodes institutional trust—especially in domains demanding unwavering loyalty and discretion, such as foreign policy, the intelligence community (e.g., the Central Intelligence Agency and National Security Agency), senior military leadership, and high elected office. When public servants maintain active legal ties to another state—whether that state is friendly or adversarial—the perception of divided allegiance weakens their legitimacy.

A 2023 Harvard Kennedy School report found that trust in public institutions is at a multi-decade low, particularly among digitally mobile younger citizens, underscoring the urgency of restoring coherence in who we empower to govern.

A growing chorus of scholars and policymakers calls for statutory reform. The most urgent and enforceable step is to require all dual citizens in sensitive federal roles—including those in national security, diplomacy, intelligence, and constitutional offices (such as members of Congress)—to:

1. Formally disclose their dual nationality, and
2. Affirm in writing that their primary allegiance is to the United States.

Failure to disclose would carry penalties for perjury (the criminal offense of willfully lying under oath) and grounds for immediate dismissal.

For the highest-trust positions—senior intelligence leadership, senior military command roles, federal judgeships, and top elected offices—a formal renunciation of any non-U.S. citizenship should be a precondition of service. This measure is not punitive but a structural safeguard: a democracy cannot endure on divided loyalties when unity of purpose is essential.

Public sentiment backs this approach: a 2024 Pew Research Center poll (using a nationally representative telephone survey) found that 62 percent of Americans support restricting dual nationals from holding top security and foreign-affairs posts. Comparable measures abroad—in Germany, France, and Israel—confirm that democracies can honor plural identity while protecting their core functions. *Preview only — for a full comparative discussion of how peer democracies frame dual citizenship as a managed exception, see Chapter 6, Section VII ("Global Models: Restrict, Hybridize, or Open").*

> **Key Proposal:** Require dual-citizen public officials in sensitive roles to disclose and pledge primary U.S. allegiance, with formal renunciation mandated for top-trust positions.

In a pluralist democracy, trust is built on both inclusion and transparency. A clear statutory framework for allegiance in public service would honor both values.

III. Reforming Dual Citizenship in Security Roles

Among the most urgent and sensitive areas impacted by ambiguous allegiance is national security. While many dual citizens serve loyally, holding more than one passport can create real or perceived conflicts—especially in roles where access to classified information or sovereign authority is at stake.

III-A. Top-Secret Clearances: Renunciation Requirement

Access to Top Secret/Sensitive Compartmented Information (TS/SCI) presumes exclusive allegiance. A uniform rule requiring all TS/SCI clearance holders to renounce non-U.S. citizenship would:

- **Unify vetting standards** across agencies, eliminating discretionary "high-risk" labels;
- **Bolster public trust** by removing any perception of divided loyalty.

By the numbers, roughly 1.2 million federal employees hold security clearances, and Department of Defense estimates suggest 5–10 percent of TS/SCI-clearance holders are dual nationals. In roles involving intelligence, defense, diplomacy, or any position requiring TS or higher security clearance; and for Members of Congress, who have access by virtue of office, apply the same disclosure/renunciation standard by statute. These positions grant access to information whose disclosure could cause "exceptionally grave damage" to national security, participate in high-stakes negotiations, and execute policies that may place the U.S. in direct conflict with other nations. Perceived or real divided loyalties in these roles can severely undermine institutional trust and operational integrity.

Policy Recommendation

1. **Mandatory Renunciation for High-Trust Roles.**
   All dual citizens must formally renounce non-U.S. citizenship before assuming:
   - Any position requiring TS or higher security clearance; or
   - Any role exercising sovereign authority—senior intelligence posts, armed-forces command roles, high-level diplomatic appointments, federal judgeships, and

constitutional offices (e.g., members of Congress).
2. **Narrow Waiver Process.**
Recognizing that some foreign governments (e.g., China, Iran) may refuse to acknowledge renunciation, a conditional waiver may be granted by the Director of National Intelligence—after consultation with the Secretaries of State and Homeland Security and subject to congressional oversight—provided that:
   - The individual demonstrates no foreign obligations or jurisdictional reach;
   - Enhanced security vetting confirms no undue risk; and
   - The waiver is reviewed and renewed only every two years.

Public Support & Feasibility: A 2024 YouGov–Harvard CAPS survey found 68 percent of Americans favor requiring exclusive U.S. citizenship for senior security roles, echoing earlier polling that showed broad support for similar restrictions in top public offices. This bipartisan backing underscores both the demand for—and the political feasibility of—tightening allegiance rules.

Addressing Potential Objections: Critics may argue that this approach unfairly penalizes dual nationals. However, the narrowly tailored waiver process ensures the requirement applies only to mission-critical roles where singular loyalty is essential.

Comparative Precedents: *Preview only — for detailed examples of how democracies enforce allegiance requirements in sensitive roles, including case studies from France, Israel, the UK, and Canada, see Chapter 6, Section VII ("Global Models: Restrict, Hybridize, or Open").*

Connecting Back

These renunciation requirements build on Section II's call for formal allegiance declarations—advancing transparency from mere disclosure to decisive commitment. Together, they close the legal gap, align policy with public expectation, and fortify the trust essential to democratic governance.

III-B. Policy Recommendation: Managing Foreign Non-Recognition of U.S. Citizenship

When naturalized Americans find that their country of origin refuses to acknowledge their renunciation or U.S. citizenship, they face dual obligations that can impede public service and personal security. To address this "civic invisibility," we propose a five-point strategy:

1. **Mandatory Disclosure of Foreign National Status.** At key civic junctures—naturalization, security-clearance vetting, and applications for sensitive federal roles—citizens must declare any continuing foreign nationality claims, even if the foreign state no longer recognizes their U.S. status.
2. **Diplomatic Notification and Documentation.** The State Department will formally notify non-recognizing governments of each naturalized citizen's new U.S. status or renunciation, creating an official record of asserted allegiance, however unacknowledged abroad.
3. **Conditional Disqualification from High-Trust Positions.** Naturalized citizens who cannot legally sever their foreign nationality (e.g., under Chinese or Iranian law) will be ineligible for roles involving national security, intelligence, or constitutional authority—unless they can demonstrate no remaining obligations to the foreign state.
4. **Protective Status and Risk Guidance.** The U.S. will issue tailored risk advisories and extend consular protections. In extreme cases, a temporary "Protected Status for Unrenounceable Citizenship" could shield affected citizens from conflicting obligations.
5. **Treaties on Citizenship Recognition.** The U.S. will negotiate treaties with non-recognizing states—and spearhead a new international convention—establishing mutual recognition of naturalization and renunciation processes.

With these renunciation requirements set out, policymakers must also grapple with practical implementation questions—how to operationalize a uniform standard across agencies, streamline vetting, and manage edge cases.

Partial Precedents – What's Been Tried, and What Hasn't?

1. Mandatory Disclosure of Foreign Citizenship Status
- **Precedent**: The U.S. currently requires disclosure of foreign citizenship for certain security clearances (e.g. via SF-86). However, no comprehensive system requires such disclosure at naturalization or routine civic junctures like voting.
- **Gap**: There is no universal or enforceable disclosure mandate across federal agencies or for non-sensitive roles.

2. Diplomatic Notification and Documentation
- **Precedent**: The U.S. Department of State may notify foreign governments of renunciation in formal consular proceedings. In isolated cases (e.g., Iran), the U.S. has protested when Americans are detained and treated as foreign nationals despite their U.S. citizenship.
- **Gap**: There is no standing policy for consistent diplomatic assertion of exclusive U.S. allegiance on behalf of naturalized citizens. It's ad hoc, reactive, and case-dependent.

3. Conditional Disqualification for High-Trust Roles
- **Precedent**: Security clearance adjudication already factors in "foreign preference" and "foreign influence" (e.g., Adjudicative Guidelines for Determining Eligibility for Access to Classified Information). Dual citizenship is often flagged in vetting, and naturalized citizens from certain countries are frequently scrutinized or denied access.
- **Gap**: These are administrative security guidelines, not codified federal law—and not consistently applied across all branches of government or sensitive roles like members of Congress.

4. Protective Legal Status and Risk Guidance
- **Precedent**: The U.S. issues travel warnings and provides consular protection to citizens abroad. Some high-risk cases (e.g., U.S.–Iran dual nationals) receive behind-the-scenes support, and the State Department publishes country-specific dual nationality guidance.
- **Gap**: There is no formal protected legal category or standardized guidance for "unrenounceable" citizenship, even though cases like Iran, China, and Eritrea illustrate the problem.

5. Bilateral and Multilateral Agreements on Citizenship Recognition
- **Precedent (Bilateral)**: The U.S. has Status of Forces Agreements (SOFAs) that include clauses on jurisdiction and citizenship recognition, especially with allies. In extradition treaties, citizenship clauses sometimes address recognition and prosecution responsibility.
- **Precedent (Multilateral)**: The 1961 UN Convention on the Reduction of Statelessness and The Hague Convention on Certain Questions Relating to the Conflict of Nationality Laws (1930) touch on similar issues—but they are outdated, under-enforced, and largely limited in scope.
- **Gap**: The U.S. has not pursued a treaty framework focused on dual citizenship recognition or allegiance at scale.

  No multilateral initiative currently defines global norms for allegiance recognition, especially in the context of non-renouncing authoritarian states.

The above sidebar, *Partial Precedents—What's Been Tried, and What Hasn't?*, distills the core arguments for extending a single, consistent renunciation rule to all holders of Top Secret clearances, demonstrating why this narrow reform can have outsized impact on institutional trust and national security.

Taken together, prior measures reveal a common pattern: partial fixes that address pieces of the problem without creating a unified, enforceable standard. Disclosure rules vary by agency, diplomatic assertions of allegiance are inconsistent, and security clearance vetting relies on administrative discretion rather than law. Risk guidance is reactive, and international agreements remain narrow or outdated. These gaps leave critical roles exposed to divided loyalties, making a consistent renunciation requirement for Top Secret clearances both a logical and targeted next step.

IV. Redefining Birthright Through Parental Jurisdiction

Birthright citizenship remains one of the most distinctive features of the U.S. system—but also one of the most contested. In an era of birth tourism and global mobility, the question arises: should geography alone confer citizenship when no civic ties exist?

This book first addresses this question in depth in Chapter 6 *("Citizenship for Sale: Birth Tourism and the Marketplace of Citizenship")*, where a complete proposal for a parental-jurisdiction model is outlined. That approach would require at least one parent to be a U.S. citizen or lawful permanent resident with demonstrable civic ties before automatic jus soli applies, preserving constitutional protections while closing exploitative loopholes.

V. Tracking Dual Citizenship in a Digital Age

In today's hyper-connected world, citizenship is no longer bound by geography. Dual nationals—whether through birth tourism or strategic naturalization—can live, work, vote, and pay taxes across multiple countries with little to no official oversight. This "digital citizenship" outpaces our existing legal and bureaucratic systems, creating a blind spot in civic accountability.

The Challenge: Civic Invisibility

Current U.S. procedures do not require individuals to register or disclose their dual-citizen status when exercising key civic rights—voter registration, running for office, passport renewal, even federal employment. This opacity isn't merely an administrative hiccup; it's a structural weakness. Without transparency, the government cannot enforce allegiance-based distinctions (e.g., eligibility for security-sensitive positions) or ensure consistency in taxation and service obligations. Moreover, when citizens engage politically in multiple jurisdictions, the lack of a centralized disclosure mechanism leaves no way to distinguish genuine plural identities from strategic civic evasion.

Recommendation: A National Dual-Citizenship Registry

Establish a federal disclosure framework requiring dual nationals to report their citizenship status at critical civic touchpoints:

- Voter registration
- Passport application or renewal
- Federal employment and security-clearance processing
- Selective Service registration
- Tax returns, particularly for those with foreign financial ties

This registry would not strip anyone of their citizenship; rather, it would illuminate an existing reality, enabling informed policy choices—such as additional vetting for conflict-sensitive roles or tax compliance checks.

Learning from Abroad

Other democracies have implementable models:

- **Germany's Ausländerzentralregister (AZR):** A unified

database of all foreign and dual nationals, linked across immigration, police, tax, and security agencies;
- **India's OCI Biometric Platform:** Requires Overseas Citizens of India to report changes in foreign nationality, integrating that data into a compliance system tracking voting, military service, and property ownership.

These examples show that transparency and plural citizenship can coexist—and that recognizing complexity does not sacrifice accountability.

Benefits: Renewed Trust and Policy Coherence

A digital citizenship registry would:

- Enhance interagency coordination (DHS, Departments of State, Treasury, Defense);
- Bolster institutional credibility by treating citizenship as a public status, not a private secret;
- Provide empirical data for policy—informing decisions on combined tax treaties, security clearances, and diplomatic risk advisories.

In a democracy built on mutual trust, visibility is essential. By shining a light on dual allegiances, we affirm that belonging carries both rights and responsibilities—and that every layer of citizenship must be accountable.

VI. Linking Civic Education to Citizenship

Citizenship in the United States has become primarily a legal status—acquired by birth, naturalization, or ancestry—yet it often lacks the civic substance to make it meaningful. As dual nationality and "citizenship for hire" proliferate, the disconnect between formal membership and democratic practice widens. To bridge this gap, we must embed civic education directly into the architecture of citizenship rights, ensuring that holders of the vote also possess the knowledge and motivation to use it wisely.

The Gap Between Status and Practice

Legal citizenship confers rights—voting, trial by jury, free speech—but not necessarily the understanding of how to exercise them. Without civic literacy—grasping our constitutional framework, the role of public institutions, and the ethical dimensions of participation—new and existing citizens alike may remain disengaged or uninformed.

Policy Recommendation: Civic Benchmarks

Rather than erecting ideological gates, we propose clear, educational milestones that affirm citizenship as an active project:

1. **Standardized Civic Knowledge Module.** Integrate a concise curriculum into the naturalization process, covering government structure, constitutional rights, and participatory duties.
2. **Public Service Pathways.** Encourage (or lightly incentivize) short-term community service—such as volunteering in local schools or civic associations—to build habits of collective engagement.
3. **Non-Coercive Participation Milestones.** Track simple metrics—like registering to vote or attending a town hall—through a digital badge system, publicly celebrating civic involvement without penalizing non-compliance.

Learning from Abroad

- **Canada's Citizenship Test** evaluates knowledge of democratic principles, national history, and institutions.
- **France's Civic Interviews** assess not only factual understanding but also a candidate's commitment to republican values and public solidarity.

While neither model is flawless, both demonstrate how linking rights to a foundational understanding of civic life can bolster democratic cohesion.

Anticipated Impact

By weaving civic education into the citizenship journey, we can:

- Combat widespread political apathy by equipping citizens with both knowledge and a sense of agency.
- Clarify the meaning of allegiance amid overlapping loyalties, reinforcing that citizenship entails contributions as well as claims.
- Sustain the moral and cultural threads of national belonging, even as legal status becomes more fluid.

Ultimately, citizenship must rest on more than paperwork. Anchored in civic knowledge, shared obligations, and participatory practice, it can regain its power to unite diverse individuals in a common democratic enterprise.

VII. Modernizing the Oath of Allegiance and Naturalization

The moment of naturalization is more than paperwork—it is a civic rite of passage anchored by the Oath of Allegiance. Yet today's Oath, drafted over a century ago, no longer captures the complexities of dual nationality, transnational identities, or rapid global mobility. To restore its symbolic and normative power, we propose a three-part modernization:

A. The Problem: A Stagnant Civic Ritual
- **Legal Formalism Without Civic Depth.** The current Oath recites loyalty to the Constitution and renunciation of foreign allegiances, but it does not engage new citizens—and the polity more broadly—with the active responsibilities of democratic membership in a globalized era.

B. The Three-Part Modernization Strategy
1. **Explicit Primary Allegiance Clause**
    - **Current:** "…that I will support and defend the Constitution… against all enemies, foreign and domestic…"
    - **Proposed Addition:** "I affirm that, in both law and conscience, the United States of America holds my foremost civic allegiance."
2. **Normative Foundation for Disclosure**
    - Embed a provision reminding dual nationals that certain public roles may require transparency about all citizenships. This clause would not itself impose legal requirements but would lay the moral groundwork for subsequent statutes mandating disclosure in sensitive positions.
3. **Ceremonial and Educational Enhancements**
    - Pair the Oath with a brief civic orientation—covering rights, duties, and democratic values—to transform the ceremony from recitation into a moment of genuine engagement.

C. Comparative Precedents

Country	Oath/Pledge Features
Australia	2007 pledge added explicit reference to "mutual respect and responsibility" alongside loyalty.
Switzerland	Naturalization requires cultural interviews, proof of local integration, and a community pledge.

These examples show that updating civic rituals can deepen democratic bonds without sacrificing inclusivity.

D. Civic Impact: Reinforcing Allegiance as Action
A modernized Oath—clear in its articulation of primary allegiance and joined by civic orientation—would:

- **Reaffirm** that citizenship is an active commitment, not a passive status;
- **Signal** to new citizens and the broader public that democratic membership entails ongoing responsibility;
- **Provide** a moral foundation for future laws on disclosure and accountability.

> *Allegiance must be more than assumed; it must be solemnly affirmed.*

By revitalizing the Oath of Allegiance, we bridge the gap between citizenship as legal formality and citizenship as a lived, civic calling.

VIII. Future Horizons: Citizenship in a Global Age

Citizenship has always evolved—from feudal bonds to nation-state membership—but today's pace of globalization, digitalization, and migration threatens to outstrip our civic frameworks. If citizenship becomes merely a transactional asset—acquired at birth, held in reserve, or toggled for convenience—we risk dissolving its moral core: shared responsibility and active participation.

What's at stake?
- Stateless Integration. When legal status decouples from communal life ("insurance-policy citizenship"), civic identity fragments.
- Civic Vacancy. Without clear ethical anchors, allegiance becomes optional, and public trust erodes.

A Call to Action

Citizenship is not a static entitlement but a civic construct shaped by deliberate choices. Democratic societies must lead in redefining allegiance—before private actors or authoritarian regimes fill the void.

What does that mean? It means proactively anchoring membership in accountability, transparency, and collective purpose.

IX. Summary & Implementation Roadmap

These recommendations can be implemented in deliberate stages, drawing on lessons from both U.S. precedent and international models. The first table below lays out a phased domestic strategy—moving from immediate, achievable measures to long-term structural reforms. The second table then places U.S. policy in a global context, showing how other nations balance birthright, residency, and allegiance. Together, they provide both a practical roadmap and a comparative lens for reform.

Phase	Timeline	Key Measures
I	Short-Term	• Codify visa rules to deter birth-tourism • Create a Dual Nationality Registry • Formalize intergovernmental notification of renunciations • Apply mandatory renunciation for TS-clearance and high-trust roles (see §III)
II	Medium-Term	• Launch a National Civic Literacy Campaign • Integrate civic benchmarks (service, education) into naturalization • Modernize the Oath of Allegiance with primary-allegiance clause (§VII)
III	Long-Term	• Clarify "jurisdiction" in the 14th Amendment through congressional legislation and judicial review • Pursue a narrowly tailored constitutional amendment to align birthright with civic allegiance (§IV)

Global Policy Comparison

Model	Examples	Feature
Restrictive	Germany, Japan, India	No or heavily constrained *jus soli*
Conditional	UK, France	Birthright only if parental residency
Permissive	U.S., Canada	Unconditional *jus soli* without integration

Conclusion

Reclaiming citizenship will require more than legal fixes; it will demand a sustained cultural shift toward participation, responsibility, and shared purpose. The measures in this chapter outlined a practical starting point. But policy is only one half of the work ahead. The greater challenge lies in renewing the meaning of allegiance itself—anchoring it not only in law, but in the lived commitments that bind a diverse people into one republic. That larger question frames the choice with which this book will close.

Conclusion

Reclaiming the Meaning of Citizenship in the 21st Century

They gave their lives not for a party or a person, but for the enduring idea of a republic. More than 1.3 million Americans made that choice—a solemn testament to the civic contract. Their sacrifice gave meaning to American citizenship and legitimacy to the passport that now grants protection and recognition around the world.

Yet today, that same citizenship is increasingly treated as a commodity. It can be purchased through investment schemes, acquired via birth tourism, and diluted by undeclared dual allegiances. No longer anchored to service or shared responsibility, it risks becoming just another asset—something to hold, trade, or exploit. This asymmetry—between those who serve and those who extract—undermines the moral foundations of democratic life.

But this drift is not destiny. It is the consequence of policy stagnation, legal ambiguity, and the slow erosion of allegiance as a civic ethic. Citizenship cannot be sustained by paperwork alone. It demands a moral architecture—one that binds rights to responsibilities, presence to participation, and identity to accountability.

Reclaiming that meaning will require action—legal, civic, and cultural—to restore the link between belonging and responsibility. The specific measures may differ in form, but they must share a single aim: to ensure that citizenship is chosen with intention, lived with integrity, and honored as a bond of mutual obligation.

These are not radical aspirations, but democratic ones. In a time when belonging can be bought, simulated, or borrowed, we must reaffirm that to be a citizen of the United States is not merely to hold rights, but to share burdens, uphold responsibilities, and commit to the common good.

Citizenship is not a passport. It is a promise. The time has come not just to revise our laws—but to renew our sense of who we are.

Afterword

To Bind the Nation's Wounds
Citizenship and the Work of Unity

> *"With malice toward none, with charity for all, with firmness in the right as God gives us to see the right, let us strive on to finish the work we are in—to bind up the nation's wounds…"*
> —Abraham Lincoln, Second Inaugural Address, March 4, 1865

This book has shown how American citizenship—once rooted in mutual responsibility and civic sacrifice—has drifted from its ethical foundations. Legal ambiguity, bureaucratic silence, and global convenience have hollowed allegiance into a status conferred, rather than a promise upheld.

But law alone cannot repair a fraying civic fabric.

Citizenship is more than a legal status—it is a living inheritance, built on sacrifice and kept alive through shared commitment. It was paid for, as Lincoln reminded us, by those who "gave the last full measure of devotion," not so we might treat citizenship as a passport to privilege, but so we might carry forward "a new birth of freedom."

This moment calls not just for reform, but for rededication.

In the shadow of polarization and drift, we must ask again: what does it mean to belong to a nation? Can we welcome pluralism while still holding fast to the bonds of unity? Can allegiance survive in an age of global mobility, dual loyalties, and transactional belonging?

The way forward is not to narrow who belongs, but to renew the shared commitments that make belonging meaningful. Allegiance is not sameness. It is a shared fidelity to a democratic ideal—to a republic that must be held together not by law alone, but by citizens willing to "bind up the nation's wounds" through common duty and civic care.

The reforms outlined in this book—constitutional clarity, transparent allegiance, civic education, and ethical boundaries—are not about narrowing citizenship. They are about restoring its meaning. They are about calling us back to the idea that citizenship is not inherited alone; it is earned each day, through responsibility, participation, and the work of unity.

We close, then, with the hope that American citizenship may yet be made whole—not through coercion, but through conscience. Not through partisanship, but through a renewed devotion to that most fragile, most powerful idea: a people, governing themselves, committed not only to liberty, but to one another.

As Lincoln urged at Gettysburg, let us be "highly resolved that these dead shall not have died in vain." Let us ensure that American citizenship—bought with blood, burdened with hope—remains a living bond: resilient, meaningful, and worthy of a nation still striving toward its promise.

Glossary of Key Terms

Allegiance
A person's loyalty and commitment to a country or community, reflecting both legal obligations and ethical responsibilities, and forming the foundation of civic trust and participation.

Birthright Citizenship (*Jus Soli*)
The principle by which citizenship is automatically granted to individuals born within a country's territory, regardless of parental status—most notably upheld in the U.S. under the 14th Amendment.

Birth Tourism
The practice of traveling to a country—most commonly the United States—for the purpose of giving birth so that the child automatically acquires citizenship by location. Often commercially organized, this practice exploits legal loopholes in birthright policies while circumventing traditional pathways of civic integration.

Citizenship-by-Investment ("Golden Passport")
Programs offered by some countries that grant citizenship in exchange for significant financial investment or economic contributions, often without requiring genuine ties or residency.

Civic Contract
An implicit agreement between citizens and their government outlining mutual rights, responsibilities, and commitments necessary for maintaining a democratic and cohesive society.

Civic Duty
The responsibilities expected of citizens, such as voting, paying taxes, jury service, and community participation, essential for sustaining democracy and social harmony.

Civic Trust
The confidence citizens have in each other and their institutions, crucial for effective governance, societal cooperation, and democratic stability. Civic trust undergirds democratic legitimacy and is eroded when rights are claimed without reciprocal responsibilities.

Commodification of Citizenship
The transformation of citizenship from a civic identity into a market commodity, valued primarily for its benefits—such as visa-free mobility or tax advantages—rather than for its obligations or moral significance.

Digital Allegiance
A symbolic or functional attachment to a nation enacted through digital means—such as online affiliation, virtual residency, or remote political engagement—often detached from geographic presence or civic duty.

Dual Citizenship
The status of legally holding citizenship in two different countries simultaneously, involving rights and obligations in both nations.

Expatriation
The voluntary or involuntary act of relinquishing one's citizenship, typically when adopting a new nationality or explicitly renouncing citizenship.

Extradition
A legal process where one country hands over an individual to another country for prosecution or punishment for crimes committed.

Globalization
The process of increasing interconnectedness among countries through trade, migration, technology, and culture, significantly influencing concepts of national identity and citizenship.

Jus Sanguinis (Right of Blood)
The principle by which citizenship is determined based on the nationality or ethnicity of one's parents rather than place of birth.

Legal Ambiguity
Situations where laws and regulations are unclear or open to interpretation, often resulting in inconsistent application or enforcement of citizenship policies.

Moral Architecture
The underlying ethical principles and norms that sustain a civic institution—ensuring that rights are matched by duties, and that laws reflect shared moral commitments.

Naturalization
The legal process by which a non-citizen voluntarily acquires citizenship in a new country, typically involving residency requirements, language proficiency, and civic knowledge tests.

Pluralism
The coexistence and acceptance of diverse cultural, ethnic, religious, and social identities within a single society, viewed as a source of strength and vitality.

Policy Drift
Incremental changes or neglect in policy, laws, or administration over time, leading to unintended consequences or inconsistencies, particularly evident in U.S. citizenship policies.

Social Contract
A philosophical idea proposing that individuals consent to governmental authority in exchange for protection of rights and maintenance of social order, forming the basis of democratic governance.

Stateless Integration
A phenomenon in which individuals participate in the economy, society, or digital infrastructure of a country without formal citizenship or legal recognition—raising questions about belonging, accountability, and civic inclusion in the absence of legal status. This often applies to long-term undocumented residents or second-generation individuals in liminal legal categories.

Statutory Silence
A legal situation where the absence of clear laws or guidelines on specific issues, such as dual citizenship, creates uncertainty and inconsistency in enforcement and policy application.

Strategic Competition
The geopolitical rivalry between nations seeking influence, power, and security advantages, including the use of citizenship policies—such as passport diplomacy, denaturalization threats, or dual nationality leverage—as tools of influence or coercion.

Transactional Citizenship
When citizenship is viewed or pursued primarily for personal benefit, convenience, or economic advantages rather than genuine allegiance or civic commitment.

Transactional vs. Ethical Citizenship
Transactional citizenship prioritizes benefits and convenience; *ethical citizenship* is grounded in civic responsibility and allegiance.

Unmanaged Dual Citizenship
The situation in which dual citizenship is legally permitted but lacks clear regulations, oversight, or meaningful requirements for loyalty or responsibility, potentially undermining civic cohesion.

Appendix A

The Emancipation Proclamation (1863)

Contextual Note: Issued by President Abraham Lincoln during the Civil War, the Emancipation Proclamation marked a transformative moment in the redefinition of American citizenship and allegiance. It reframed the Civil War as a moral struggle over the meaning of liberty and national belonging. By declaring freedom for enslaved people in Confederate states, it extended the civic promise of America to those who had long been excluded—laying the groundwork for the 14th Amendment and a more inclusive vision of allegiance and citizenship.

By the President of the United States of America:
A Proclamation

Whereas, on the 22nd day of September, in the year of our Lord 1862, a proclamation was issued by the President of the United States, containing, among other things, the following, to wit:

"That on the first day of January, in the year of our Lord 1863, all persons held as slaves within any State or designated part of a State, the people whereof shall then be in rebellion against the United States, shall be then, thenceforward, and forever free."

Now, therefore I, Abraham Lincoln, President of the United States, by virtue of the power in me vested as Commander-in-Chief of the Army and Navy of the United States in time of actual armed rebellion against the authority and Government of the United States, and as a fit and necessary war measure for suppressing said rebellion, do, on this first day of January, in the year of our Lord one thousand eight hundred and sixty-three, proclaim:

That all persons held as slaves within the following designated States and parts of States are, and henceforward shall be free:

Arkansas, Texas, Louisiana (except the parishes of St. Bernard, Plaquemines, Jefferson, St. John, St. Charles, St. James, Ascension, Assumption, Terrebonne, Lafourche, St. Mary, St. Martin, and Orleans, including the City of New Orleans), Mississippi, Alabama, Florida,

Georgia, South Carolina, North Carolina, and Virginia (except the forty-eight counties designated as West Virginia, and the counties of Berkeley, Accomac, Northampton, Elizabeth City, York, Princess Anne, and Norfolk, including the cities of Norfolk and Portsmouth).

And I do order and declare that the Executive Government of the United States, including the military and naval authorities thereof, will recognize and maintain the freedom of such persons.

And I recommend to them that, in all cases when allowed, they labor faithfully for reasonable wages.

And I invoke the considerate judgment of mankind, and the gracious favor of Almighty God.

In witness whereof, I have hereunto set my hand and caused the seal of the United States to be affixed.

Done at the City of Washington, this first day of January, in the year of our Lord one thousand eight hundred and sixty-three.

By the President: Abraham Lincoln
William H. Seward, Secretary of State

Appendix B

Foundational Texts of American Allegiance

This appendix collects foundational documents that have shaped the legal, moral, and civic meaning of American citizenship. These texts illuminate the historical origins of allegiance in U.S. law and provide context for the debates addressed throughout this book. Together, they trace the transformation of citizenship from a solemn civic commitment to a more ambiguous, and at times commodified, status.

1. The Naturalization Act of 1790 (Excerpts)

Contextual Note: The first federal definition of citizenship, this law emphasized allegiance as a requirement for naturalization, though it excluded vast portions of the population. It reflected an early understanding that to be American was not merely a matter of residence, but of declared and exclusive loyalty.

"Be it enacted... That any alien, being a free white person, who shall have resided within the limits... of the United States for a term of two years, may be admitted to become a citizen thereof... provided he shall declare... allegiance to the United States."

2. The Expatriation Act of 1868 (Full Text)

Contextual Note: Passed in the wake of the Civil War and expanding immigration, this act affirmed the voluntary nature of citizenship and the individual's right to sever allegiance to another state. It remains a cornerstone of the American belief that allegiance must be freely given.

"Whereas the right of expatriation is a natural and inherent right of all people... any declaration, instruction, opinion, order, or decision of any officer of the United States which denies, restricts, impairs, or questions the right of expatriation, is hereby declared inconsistent with the fundamental principles of this government."

1. The Emancipation Proclamation (1863)

Full text included in Appendix A.

4. The Fourteenth Amendment to the U.S. Constitution (Section 1)

Contextual Note: Ratified in 1868, the amendment overturned Dred Scott and established birthright citizenship. The clause "subject to the jurisdiction thereof" remains at the center of modern debates over allegiance and dual citizenship.

"All persons born or naturalized in the United States, and subject to the jurisdiction thereof, are citizens of the United States..."

5. The Oath of Allegiance (Current USCIS Text)

Contextual Note: For discussion of proposals to modernize and strengthen this oath—including explicit primary-allegiance clauses—see Chapter 9, Section VII. The text below is reproduced in its current official form.

"I hereby declare, on oath, that I absolutely and entirely renounce and abjure all allegiance and fidelity to any foreign prince, potentate, state, or sovereignty... that I will support and defend the Constitution and laws of the United States of America against all enemies, foreign and domestic..."

6. The Pledge of Allegiance

Contextual Note: Recited by generations of schoolchildren and public officials, the Pledge represents the performative dimension of allegiance. Though symbolic, it continues to shape cultural expectations around unity and national commitment.

"I pledge allegiance to the Flag of the United States of America, and to the Republic for which it stands..."

Together, these texts represent an evolving tradition. They remind us that allegiance has never been merely symbolic. It has been a test of loyalty, a basis for inclusion, and a measure of civic integrity.

Appendix C

Political and Philosophical Sources

A. **Federalist No. 68 (Alexander Hamilton)**

   On Foreign Influence and Divided Allegiance
   "The most deadly adversaries of republican government may naturally be expected to spring from the desire in foreign powers to gain an improper ascendant in our councils."

   In *Federalist No. 68*, Hamilton warned against foreign powers seeking influence in the young Republic's political process, particularly through presidential elections. His concern with divided loyalties and external entanglements underscored early American anxiety over allegiance as both a legal and moral commitment.

B. **Social Contract Thinkers: Locke, Rousseau, and Rawls**

   On Allegiance as Consent and Civic Obligation
   - **John Locke, Second Treatise of Government:**
     "Men being, as has been said, by nature, all free, equal, and independent, no one can be... subjected to the political power of another without his own consent."
     Locke roots political obligation in voluntary consent—a key influence on the American understanding of citizenship as a chosen allegiance.
   - **Jean-Jacques Rousseau, The Social Contract:**
     "The moment the people is legitimately assembled as a sovereign body, all jurisdiction of the government ceases... the general will alone can direct the forces of the state."
     Rousseau ties allegiance to collective self-rule, framing citizenship as a shared exercise of sovereignty.
   - **John Rawls, A Theory of Justice:**
     "Citizens are free in that they conceive of themselves as having the moral power to form, to revise, and rationally to pursue a conception of the good." Rawls presents allegiance not merely as obedience, but as mutual recognition of each other's rights and duties within a just society.

C. **George Washington's Farewell Address (1796)**

   Excerpts on Foreign Influence and National Unity
   "The great rule of conduct for us in regard to foreign nations is... to have with them as little political connection as possible."

Washington's parting message to the nation cautioned against foreign influence and the dangers of political factionalism. His address remains a foundational text in defining American political identity and allegiance.

D. Federalist No. 2 – John Jay on National Unity

Quote:
"Providence has been pleased to give this one connected country to one united people... speaking the same language, professing the same religion, attached to the same principles of government."

Contextual Note:
John Jay's *Federalist No. 2* underscores the framers' assumption that national unity was essential to the success of the republic. While his appeal to cultural homogeneity may not align with modern pluralism, his core point remains salient: that a shared allegiance to common principles is necessary for the preservation of liberty and effective self-government.

E. Federalist No. 68 – Alexander Hamilton on Foreign Influence

Quote:
"These most deadly adversaries of republican government—foreign influence and corruption—should be expected to make their approaches from more than one quarter... nothing was more to be desired than that every practicable obstacle should be opposed to cabal, intrigue, and corruption."

Contextual Note:
In *Federalist No. 68*, Hamilton justifies the Electoral College partly as a safeguard against foreign manipulation of executive power. The passage illustrates the framers' deep concern with divided loyalty and external entanglement, especially in matters of high public trust. These concerns resonate directly with contemporary debates over dual citizenship in federal office.

Appendix D

Citizenship in Practice and Controversy

Selective Service Registration Requirements

Overview:
All male U.S. citizens—and male immigrants residing in the U.S.—are required to register with the Selective Service System within 30 days of their 18th birthday. This civic obligation reflects both the responsibilities associated with citizenship and the gendered expectations that persist in national service frameworks.

Key Details:
- Applies to U.S. citizens and most male non-citizens between ages 18 and 25;
- Includes dual citizens, undocumented immigrants, permanent residents, and asylees. For a full proposal on how disclosure requirements and a national registry could improve oversight, see Chapter 9, Section V;
- Failure to register can affect eligibility for:
    - Federal employment
    - Student financial aid (e.g., FAFSA)
    - U.S. citizenship via naturalization.

Key Supreme Court Excerpts on Citizenship

Afroyim v. Rusk **(1967):**

"The Constitution does not authorize the involuntary stripping of citizenship. Citizenship is no light trifle to be jeopardized any moment Congress decides to do so."

Summary: This landmark decision held that the U.S. government cannot revoke a person's citizenship without their consent. It reinforced the principle that citizenship is a voluntary and protected status, not subject to arbitrary loss by congressional action.

Vance v. Terrazas (1980):

"The trier of fact must conclude that the citizen not only voluntarily committed the expatriating act prescribed in the statute, but also intended to relinquish his citizenship."

Summary: This ruling clarified the role of **intent** in expatriation cases. An individual must not only perform an act listed as expatriating (e.g., serving in a foreign military), but must also **intend** to relinquish citizenship. This raised the bar for government enforcement and emphasized individual autonomy in matters of allegiance.

Naturalization Trends and Global Citizenship Policies: The following tables provide a snapshot of naturalization trends over recent decades and a comparative overview of how major nations approach dual citizenship.

USCIS Naturalization Statistics by Decade

Decade	Naturalized Citizens (approx.)
1960s	1.5 million
1970s	2.5 million
1980s	3.9 million
1990s	7.6 million
2000s	6.9 million
2010s	7.2 million
2020s (est.)	5+ million (as of 2024)

Note: These figures reflect the steady growth of foreign-born Americans obtaining citizenship—many of whom retain dual nationality due to changes in global policy and U.S. permissiveness.

Appendix E

Contemporary Debates and Practices

Recent Congressional Proposals Related to Birthright Citizenship

These proposals reflect legislative efforts to redefine or limit jus soli citizenship. For the full policy reform argument—including the proposed parental-jurisdiction model—see Chapter 6 *("Citizenship for Sale: Birth Tourism and the Marketplace of Citizenship")* and Chapter 9, Section IV.

- **H.R. 140 – Birthright Citizenship Act (2019–2023 iterations)**
    - Sponsor: Rep. Steve King (and others)
    - Status: Introduced repeatedly, never passed
    - Summary: Would limit birthright citizenship to children with at least one U.S. citizen or lawful permanent resident parent
- **S. 723 – Birthright Citizenship Act of 2021**
    - Sponsor: Sen. Roger Marshall
    - Status: Introduced, not passed
    - Summary: Similar limitations as H.R. 140, with language focused on parental allegiance

Executive Order 14160: "Protecting the Meaning and Value of American Citizenship"

- **Date Issued:** January 20, 2025
- **Objective:** To redefine the application of birthright citizenship under the Fourteenth Amendment.
- **Key Provisions:**
    - Children born in the U.S. would be granted citizenship only if at least one parent is a U.S. citizen or lawful permanent resident at the time of the child's birth.
    - This policy would apply to children born 30 days after the order's issuance, affecting births from February 19, 2025, onward.

- **Legal Challenges:**
    - Multiple lawsuits were filed contesting the constitutionality of this order.
    - Federal judges in various jurisdictions, including Washington and Maryland, issued preliminary injunctions blocking its enforcement.

Citizenship Loss and Renunciation (U.S. State Department)

Voluntary Renunciation

- **Process:** Must be done in person at a U.S. embassy or consulate abroad before a diplomatic or consular officer; the decision is irrevocable (except in rare, immediate revocation errors).
- **Requirements:** Appear in person, sign an Oath of Renunciation, complete Form DS-4079, and pay a non-refundable fee (currently $2,350 USD).
- **Legal Note:** The U.S. does not require citizens to renounce when acquiring another citizenship. However, if the act is done with intent to relinquish U.S. nationality (and meets legal criteria), it may still be treated as a relinquishment under Section 349(a) of the Immigration and Nationality Act.

Trends

- In recent years, approximately 3,000–6,000 Americans renounce citizenship annually.
- **Common reasons include:**
    - Tax burdens (especially for expatriates under FATCA rules)
    - Dual allegiance concerns
    - Political protest or philosophical objection
- **Notable cases:**
    - *Eduardo Saverin* (Facebook co-founder, renounced before IPO)
    - Others include wealthy individuals and dual citizens frustrated by tax compliance obligations.

Appendix F

Civic Observances and Legal Foundations of Citizenship

Origins and Legal History

From "I Am an American" to Citizenship Day: The tradition began in 1940, when Congress requested the President to proclaim the third Sunday in May as "I Am an American Day," a day to recognize new U.S. citizens. In 1952, Congress moved the observance to September 17 (the anniversary of the Constitution's 1787 signing) and redesignated it as Citizenship Day, retaining the focus on honoring those who attained citizenship. That 1952 law not only shifted the date but also *urged* schools and civil authorities to plan for "proper observance" and to instruct citizens in their *responsibilities and opportunities* as Americans. This emphasis on civic education set the stage for later requirements.

Federal Statute & Byrd Amendment (2004): The current form, officially called Constitution Day and Citizenship Day, was established by a 2004 amendment championed by the late Senator Robert Byrd. Byrd inserted a provision (Section 111 of Public Law 108–447) into an omnibus spending bill mandating education about the Constitution every September 17. The law (often termed the "Byrd amendment") requires two things: (1) every federal agency must provide employees with educational materials on the Constitution each September 17, and (2) every educational institution receiving federal funds must hold an educational program on the U.S. Constitution on that day (or an adjacent weekday if the 17th falls on a weekend). This sweeping requirement applies to all schools and colleges that get federal money, from K–12 schools (e.g. via Title I funds) to universities receiving federal aid. Notably, Congress provided *no* dedicated funding for these activities, making it an unfunded mandate. The Department of Education issued guidance in 2005 reminding schools of the new law and clarifying it "would apply to any school receiving federal funds of any kind". (The observance is now codified at 36 U.S.C. § 106.) Each year, the President also issues a proclamation designating September 17 as Constitution Day and Citizenship Day and the start of Constitution Week (Sept. 17–23).

How Schools and Colleges Implement the Mandate

Wide Range of Activities: Educational institutions have significant latitude in how to meet the Constitution Day requirement, leading to a mix of symbolic gestures and substantive engagement. In practice, observances range from simple displays to in-depth events. For example, many K–12 schools incorporate a *Constitution-themed lesson* during social studies classes or morning announcements. It's common for teachers to have students read or analyze portions of the Constitution, discuss its history, or examine its relevance to current events. (Indeed, the mandate is one of the few federal curriculum requirements in K–12 education.) Some schools hold assemblies or invite local officials to speak about citizens' rights and duties. Others opt for creative activities – e.g. students might recite the Preamble, perform skits about the Founding Fathers, or participate in trivia quizzes on constitutional facts.

On college campuses, observances vary from low-key to elaborate:

- *Giveaways and Displays:* Some institutions mark the day by handing out pocket Constitutions or setting up informational displays. For instance, Columbia University has offered free pocket copies of the Constitution to students, accompanied by library exhibits of historical documents like Federalist Papers drafts. Harvard University similarly has provided free Constitutions at campus libraries. These gestures, while largely symbolic, aim to raise awareness.
- *Educational Programs & Panels:* Many colleges host lectures, panels, or seminars that delve into constitutional issues. At the University of California–Berkeley, students were invited to a special seminar on *"The Free Speech Movement and the Constitution,"* tying campus history to constitutional principles. Metropolitan State University of Denver held a panel on religious liberty featuring faculty, an ACLU representative, and a state legislator. Ferris State University convened a panel discussion on First Amendment free speech rights. These events move beyond commemoration, prompting dialogue on contemporary constitutional debates.
- *Interactive Learning:* Some schools use interactive simulations or contests. Middle Tennessee State University organized a mock Supreme Court simulation, with students role-playing pivotal court cases in a live debate. St. Cloud State University quizzed students on constitutional knowledge in a student union trivia contest. Such activities engage students more actively with constitutional content.

- *Civic Festivities:* A few campuses incorporate Constitution Day into broader civic or patriotic events. Morehead State University (KY) rolled the observance into a "September Fest" to *"celebrate democracy"* with music and festivities. At Montclair State University, the 2011 commemoration included stitching a National 9/11 Flag and panel discussions connecting the Constitution's relevance to current events. Weber State University even baked a "birthday cake for the Constitution," handing out cake and copies of the Constitution to students in a celebratory atmosphere.
- *Online and Campus Resources:* Especially in recent years, some institutions leverage technology. The University of Phoenix created a Constitution Day website with a message from the university president, historical highlights, and even voter registration links. Discovery Education partnered with civics groups to host a free *virtual tour of the U.S. Senate* for classrooms nationwide, co-hosted by actual Senators. The National Constitution Center and iCivics offer streaming webinars, interactive Constitution quizzes, and lesson plans to help schools fulfill the day's requirements in engaging ways.

Examples of Compliance: A 2013 survey by the American Democracy Project (ADP) documented diverse ways colleges commemorate Constitution Day. Some real-world examples include inviting guest speakers (e.g. Missouri State University brought in a federal public defender to discuss a landmark Supreme Court case), hosting multi-speaker symposia on constitutional themes, running student-led discussions on how technology affects First Amendment rights (as at University of Missouri–St. Louis), and even ceremonial touches like joint proclamations by university presidents and student governments to honor Constitution Week (as done at Texas A&M). On the civic side, the U.S. Citizenship and Immigration Services often schedules naturalization ceremonies during this period – for example, around Constitution Day 2019, nearly 34,000 new Americans were sworn in at 316 ceremonies nationwide, underscoring the "Citizenship" aspect of the day. In short, most institutions find a way to observe September 17, whether through modest announcements or extensive programming. And if Constitution Day falls on a weekend or holiday, schools simply hold their events in the adjoining week to remain in compliance.

Compliance, Criticism, and Civic Impact

Minimal Oversight – A Checkbox Exercise? While the federal mandate covers thousands of schools and colleges, it comes with *virtually no enforcement mechanism*. Schools are not required to report their Constitution Day activities to any central authority, and the Education Department primarily just provides resource suggestions. As Education Week noted, "with mandates of this sort, it's all but impossible to enforce" compliance uniformly. In practice, so long as an institution does *something* around that date, it satisfies the law – and many take a perfunctory approach (e.g. posting a bulletin or emailing a link to the Constitution) simply to check the compliance box. Civic education experts have pointed out a gap between this legal compliance and any meaningful civic impact. One-day events or cursory lessons, by themselves, are unlikely to profoundly affect students' civic knowledge or engagement beyond the day's observance. As the nonpartisan Center for Information & Research on Civic Learning and Engagement (CIRCLE) and others have argued, truly improving civic literacy requires sustained, high-quality civic education – something a single-day celebration can only begin to address.

Persistent Civic Knowledge Gaps: Surveys continue to reveal that Americans' constitutional knowledge remains alarmingly low, highlighting the limits of a once-a-year intervention. Senator Byrd pushed the 2004 mandate precisely because he feared public ignorance of the Constitution (lamenting that even some members of Congress lacked "basic knowledge" and "reverence" for our founding document). Yet the "knowledge gap" he warned of has persisted. A 2017 national poll found over one-third of Americans could not name a single right protected by the First Amendment, and only 1 in 4 could name all three branches of government. Likewise, a 2019 survey by the Woodrow Wilson Foundation found only 27% of adults under 45 could pass the U.S. citizenship test, which covers basic U.S. history and civics. (In that same study, far more respondents could identify a pop culture celebrity than could recognize James Madison as the "Father of the Constitution".) Such findings suggest that simply mandating an annual Constitution lesson has, so far, *not* closed the civic knowledge gap. As one civic educator quipped, "We the People still don't know much about the Constitution" even after years of obligatory Constitution Days.

Symbolism vs. Substance: Critics note that many Constitution Day observances amount to feel-good symbolism – patriotic ceremonies, flag displays, or handing out cupcakes and pocket Constitutions – which may raise awareness but have little lasting educational value. For example, the U.S. Postal Service's "celebration" has consisted solely of displaying the American flag (which they do every day) and an email reminder, with *"no additional plans to…celebrate"* the day in a substantive way. Some higher-ed administrators view the requirement as a trivial add-on: The National Association of Student Financial Aid Administrators even recommended eliminating the Constitution Day mandate (along with other "non-related" Title IV requirements like voter registration forms) from federal compliance obligations. This perspective sees the day as a bureaucratic hoop to jump through, rather than a core educational mission. Civic education advocates, however, argue that merely doing the bare minimum – a token announcement or passive display – squanders an opportunity. They call for approaches that genuinely engage students in learning about their rights and responsibilities. As one coordinator observed after organizing interactive panels for Constitution Day, students "learned a lot… and were able to *recapture the Constitution*" in a way that felt relevant to their lives. The consensus among civic experts is that depth matters: A meaningful discussion of, say, free speech or due process, even if reaching fewer students, beats a superficial campus celebration in terms of civic impact.

The Civic Impact Gap: The contrast between widespread technical compliance and the modest gains in civic literacy has led observers to conclude there's a *gap between honoring the day and truly empowering citizens*. Education Week has reported on this "civics disconnect," noting that while schools dutifully observe Constitution Day to satisfy the law, it often doesn't translate into lasting understanding. In other words, legal mandates can ensure the event happens, but not that it resonates. Without follow-up or integration into the curriculum, the lessons of September 17 may be quickly forgotten. This gap is also tied to broader challenges – for example, some teachers tread lightly to avoid controversy when teaching about constitutional issues (amid polarized debates on topics like free speech, gun rights, or racial history). Such constraints can water down the educational content, reducing impact. Meanwhile, America's ongoing low voter turnout and civic disengagement are sobering reminders that a ceremonial day of civics hasn't yet sparked the hoped-for civic renewal. As civic learning organizations like iCivics often emphasize, real change will require more comprehensive civic education – with Constitution Day serving as just one piece of a much larger puzzle.

Strengthening Citizenship Day for Civic Renewal

Beyond One Day – Year-Round Civics: Civic education leaders argue that to make Citizenship/Constitution Day a true tool for civic renewal, it must be leveraged as a springboard rather than a standalone. One recommendation is to embed the observance into a *broader civics curriculum*. Instead of treating Sept. 17

as an isolated event, schools could kick off a fall civics project on Constitution Day, then continue with related lessons or service-learning projects in the weeks that follow. For example, students might learn about the Constitution on Sept. 17 and then, as a longer-term project, track a current issue through the lens of constitutional rights, or work on a community problem that ties back to civic responsibilities. Civic education organizations like iCivics and the Civics Renewal Network have created free lesson plans, games, and discussion guides not just for the day but for sustained engagement, helping teachers weave constitutional themes into everyday learning. The goal is to transform the day's *symbolic* celebration into a catalyst for *substantive* civic learning experiences.

Investing in Civic Learning: Policy experts also note that making Citizenship Day more effective will require investment in civic education – training teachers, developing engaging curricula, and allocating time for civics in a crowded school schedule. In recent years, there have been bipartisan calls to bolster civics. In fact, timed with Constitution Day 2023, Senators Angus King and James Lankford introduced the CIVICS Act, a proposal to strengthen civics education nationwide. This bill would condition certain federal education grants on including Constitution-related programming, ensuring that colleges receiving funds actively teach about the Constitution and Bill of Rights. Lawmakers behind such efforts stress that *"if we truly want a government of, by, and for the people, we must make sure the people have the tools and perspective to play their part"* – which means giving students a "full civics education," not just one day of facts. Another sweeping proposal, the Civics Secures Democracy Act, would devote $1 billion annually to enhance K–12 and higher-ed civic education, funding everything from curriculum development to student civics competitions. Such investments could empower schools to turn Constitution Day from a compliance duty into a vibrant educational opportunity.

Engaging Students in Civic Action: To bridge the gap between learning about citizenship and *practicing* it, some experts suggest coupling Constitution Day with civic action initiatives. One idea gaining traction is to use Constitution Day as an anchor in September for a broader "Civic Engagement Month." For instance, the week after Constitution Day often includes National Voter Registration Day (in late September); schools and colleges could link the two, teaching about the Constitution one week and facilitating voter registration drives the next. In this vein, a bipartisan proposal in Congress seeks to establish a National High School Seniors Voter Registration Day each year, encouraging schools to help eligible young people register to vote. If scheduled around Constitution Day, this could reinforce the connection between understanding democratic principles and taking democratic action. Other recommendations include organizing student civics fairs or debates as annual Constitution Week traditions, where students present on constitutional issues or local civic problems and propose solutions. Such experiential learning can deepen the impact of the day by prompting students to apply constitutional ideas to real-world contexts.

Expert Evaluations and Proposed Reforms: Civic education experts and organizations have offered a mix of critiques and constructive ideas to revitalize Constitution Day. The nonprofit Education Commission of the States, for example, has tracked the rise of state policies requiring students to pass the U.S. Citizenship Test to graduate high school– a response to civic knowledge deficits that, while controversial, reflects a desire for greater accountability in civics education. Others, like the Campaign for the Civic Mission of Schools (which includes CIRCLE and iCivics among its partners), advocate for interactive civics pedagogy – simulations, discussions, and community involvement – to be prioritized on Constitution Day. These groups argue that *how* the day is observed is crucial: quality over quantity. A single assembly where students passively listen to a speech may be less impactful than a smaller workshop where students debate constitutional issues themselves. Incorporating evaluation mechanisms is another reform idea. Schools could survey students before and after Constitution Day to gauge gains in knowledge or interest, using the feedback to improve future programming. While not mandated, some districts voluntarily share best practices and results from their Constitution Day activities through networks like the American Democracy Project, creating a de facto accountability and learning community.

Toward Civic Renewal: Ultimately, strengthening Citizenship Day's role in civic renewal means closing the gap between performing civics and living civics. For detailed proposals to embed Constitution Day into sustained civic learning, see Chapter 9, Section VI *("Integrating Civic Education with Citizenship Rights")*.

Selected Bibliography: Appendix F

Association of American Colleges and Universities. *Civic Learning and Democratic Engagement: A Framework for Higher Education.* Washington, DC: AAC&U, 2012.

Campaign for the Civic Mission of Schools. *Guardian of Democracy: The Civic Mission of Schools.* Silver Spring, MD: Civic Mission of Schools, 2011.

Congressional Research Service. *Federal Observances: Constitution Day and Citizenship Day (September 17).* Washington, DC: CRS, Updated 2022.

Library of Congress. "Constitution Day and Citizenship Day: Commemorative Observances." Accessed August 2025. https://www.loc.gov.

National Archives and Records Administration. "Constitution Day and Citizenship Day." Accessed August 2025. https://www.archives.gov.

Pew Research Center. "What Does It Mean to Be a Good Citizen?" September 19, 2019. https://www.pewresearch.org.

U.S. Congress. *Consolidated Appropriations Act, 2005.* Public Law No. 108–447, Division J, Title I, §111, 118 Stat. 2809 (2004).

U.S. Department of Education. "Memorandum on Constitution Day and Citizenship Day Implementation." May 24, 2005.

Appendix G

Birthright Citizenship and the Future of *Jus Soli* in American Law

This appendix provides a legal reference guide to jus soli as it stands today. For the full policy reform argument—including the proposed parental-jurisdiction model—see Chapter 6 ("Citizenship for Sale: Birth Tourism and the Marketplace of Citizenship") and Chapter 9, Section IV. This supplement focuses on the constitutional framework, leading judicial precedents, and recent litigation over Executive Order 14160.

I. Historical Origins and Constitutional Foundation

Birthright citizenship in the United States is rooted in the 14th Amendment, ratified in 1868. Its Citizenship Clause states: "All persons born or naturalized in the United States, and subject to the jurisdiction thereof, are citizens of the United States and of the State wherein they reside." The clause was intended to overturn the Dred Scott v. Sandford (1857) decision, which had denied citizenship to African Americans, and to ensure that the rights of citizenship extended to formerly enslaved persons and their descendants.

The phrase "subject to the jurisdiction thereof" has been repeatedly interpreted by the courts to include nearly all children born on U.S. soil, regardless of the citizenship or immigration status of their parents. This interpretation was affirmed in *United States v. Wong Kim Ark* (1898), where the Supreme Court held that a U.S.-born child of Chinese nationals was a citizen under the 14th Amendment.

II. Executive Orders and Judicial Pushback

Trump Executive Order 14160 and Its Objectives

Upon returning to office in 2025, President Trump issued Executive Order 14160, titled *Protecting the Meaning and Value of American Citizenship*. The order sought to restrict birthright citizenship by declaring that children born to noncitizen parents who lack lawful permanent residence or a qualifying immigration status would no longer be considered U.S. citizens at birth.

This move echoed prior efforts to restrict *jus soli* through administrative reinterpretation, underscoring the tension between civic coherence and constitutional durability

Judicial Rulings and Legal Challenges

The executive order was met with swift legal challenges. Federal courts across the country issued nationwide injunctions blocking its implementation, with multiple judges describing the order as likely unconstitutional under established precedent—including *United States v. Wong Kim Ark* (1898).

As of April 2025, Executive Order 14160 remains under judicial review, and several appellate courts have upheld the injunctions on constitutional grounds.

III. Legislative Efforts and Limitations

Congress has periodically introduced legislation aimed at limiting birthright citizenship, most often by proposing that at least one parent must be a U.S. citizen or lawful permanent resident for a child born in the United States to qualify for automatic citizenship. Such bills have never passed both chambers of Congress, and legal scholars have consistently argued that such statutes would not withstand judicial scrutiny unless accompanied by a constitutional amendment.

Unlike executive orders, which are subject to immediate challenge and lack permanence, congressional statutes carry greater legal weight. However, under today's court interpretations, even a new law could be struck down unless judges agreed that the 14th Amendment permits reinterpretation of *jus soli* through legislation—a view that has found little support in judicial precedent.

IV. Scholar Commentary and Recent *Jus Soli* Litigation

Constitutional scholars remain unanimous: birthright citizenship is robustly protected under current doctrine. When President Trump pursued executive orders on this issue, scholars across the political spectrum termed the actions unconstitutional. Harvard's Gerald Neuman labeled the move "doubly unlawful," stressing that both the 14th Amendment's text and Supreme Court precedent firmly grant citizenship to anyone born in the U.S., regardless of parents' legal status. Likewise, Walter Dellinger, formerly head of the Office of Legal Counsel, told Congress that any attempt to restrict birthright citizenship would be "unquestionably unconstitutional."

Federal judges have consistently echoed this expert consensus. In February 2025, the Ninth Circuit declined to lift a district court's nationwide injunction in *Washington v. Trump*, and in March, the First Circuit upheld a similar preliminary injunction—denying a stay and emphasizing the unsound merits and broad scope of the executive order.

After the Supreme Court's June 2025 *CASA v. Trump* decision, which curtailed universal injunctions, lower courts such as in Massachusetts and New Hampshire shifted to class action mechanisms. Notably, in *Barbara v. Trump*, the New Hampshire court not only blocked the order but certified a nationwide class of affected newborns, reinforcing judicial resolve against executive overreach.

In sum, both scholarly and judicial consensus affirms that birthright citizenship remains constitutionally inviolable—whether challenged through executive action or legislative proposal. Any durable change to this foundation would require a constitutional amendment, not mere reinterpretation or statute.

V. The Path Forward

The only legally durable route to altering *jus soli* would be through constitutional amendment. This is both procedurally challenging and politically unlikely. Any such amendment would need to be proposed by two-thirds of both chambers of Congress and ratified by three-fourths of the states—a threshold not met since 1992. As such, while debate around *jus soli* may continue in the public square, the legal framework remains intact for the foreseeable future.

Postscript: Legal Boundaries, Civic Stakes

The legal analysis in this appendix confirms what Chapter 6 suggested more broadly: that **the** meaning of American citizenship cannot be redefined by executive order or statute alone. Judicial precedent, especially *Wong Kim Ark*, has created a high constitutional bar for any attempt to narrow the scope of birthright citizenship. Yet the persistence of legal challenges and public controversy reveals an ongoing tension between the constitutional guarantees of *jus soli* and the evolving civic expectations of national membership. As courts, lawmakers, and citizens continue to debate who belongs, Appendix G underscores that any meaningful change to the American citizenship regime must be grounded not just in legality—but in legitimacy.

Select Bibliography: Appendix G

American Civil Liberties Union. *Press Releases and Legal Filings on Executive Order 14160*. February–July 2025.

Dellinger, Walter. *Congressional Testimony before the U.S. House Judiciary Committee*. Hearing on Citizenship and the Constitution, 2021.

Neuman, Gerald L. "The Citizenship Clause and Constitutional Interpretation." *Harvard Public Law & Legal Theory Working Paper Series*, 2023.

SCOTUSblog. "Litigation Roundup: Executive Order 14160 and the Future of Birthright Citizenship." February–June 2025.

United States v. Wong Kim Ark, 169 U.S. 649 (1898).

Reuters. "Appeals Courts Block Trump's Birthright Citizenship Order." *Reuters Legal*, August 1, 2025.

Washington v. Trump, 2025 WL 874011 (9th Cir. 2025).

Barbara v. Trump, 2025 WL 912304 (D.N.H. 2025), class action certified.

Associated Press. "Federal Appeals Courts Reject Citizenship Restriction Order." *AP Newswire*, July 2025.

Bibliography

Bibliography: Chapter 1 – Undivided by Design

Afroyim v. Rusk, 387 U.S. 253 (1967).

Brubaker, Rogers. 1992. *Citizenship and Nationhood in France and Germany*. Cambridge, MA: Harvard University Press.

Declaration of Independence. 1776.

Expatriation Act, U.S. Statutes at Large 15 Stat. 223 (1868).

Hamilton, Alexander, James Madison, and John Jay. 2003. *The Federalist Papers*. Edited by Clinton Rossiter. New York: Signet Classics.

Naturalization Act of 1790, U.S. Statutes at Large 1 Stat. 103 (1790).

United States Constitution, especially the Fourteenth Amendment.

Vance v. Terrazas, 444 U.S. 252 (1980).

Chapter 2: Legal Ambiguity and Policy Drift

Afroyim v. Rusk, 387 U.S. 253 (1967).

Black, Hugo L. 1967. "Majority Opinion in *Afroyim v. Rusk*." *United States Reports* 387: 253–268.

Dumbaugh, Kerry. 2000. "Dual Nationality and U.S. Law." Congressional Research Service Report for Congress, August.

Kawakita v. United States, 343 U.S. 717 (1952).

Martin, David A., and Peter H. Schuck, eds. 1985. *Citizenship Without Consent: Illegal Aliens in the American Polity*. New Haven: Yale University Press.

Schuck, Peter H. 1998. *Citizenship in the American Constitution*. Chicago: University of Chicago Press.

Vance v. Terrazas, 444 U.S. 252 (1980).

U.S. Department of State. 2023. *7 FAM 1200: Acquisition and Retention of U.S. Citizenship and Nationality*. Washington, DC: Bureau of Consular Affairs.

Weil, Patrick. 2013. *The Sovereign Citizen: Denaturalization and the Origins of the American Republic*. Philadelphia: University of Pennsylvania Press.

Chapter 3 – How Other Nations Handle It

Bauböck, Rainer, ed. 2018. *Debating Transformations of National Citizenship*. Cham: Springer.

Bloemraad, Irene. 2006. *Becoming a Citizen: Incorporating Immigrants and Refugees in the United States and Canada*. Berkeley: University of California Press.

Bundesministerium des Innern und für Heimat (Germany). 2023. "Reform des Staatsangehörigkeitsrechts."

China. National People's Congress. 1980. *Nationality Law of the People's Republic of China*.

European Commission. 2019. "Investor Citizenship and Residence Schemes in the EU." January.

Federal Statistical Office (Germany). 2023. "Einbürgerungszahlen 2023."

Government of India. Ministry of Home Affairs. 1955. *Citizenship Act*, as amended.

———. 2024. "OCI Cardholder Compliance Measures." *Ministry of Home Affairs Bulletin*, March.

Hansen, Randall. 2000. *Citizenship and Immigration in Post-War Britain: The Institutional Origins of a Multicultural Nation*. Oxford: Oxford University Press.

Ioffe, Grigory. 2023. "Russia's Dual Citizenship Debate." *Eurasia Daily Monitor*, The Jamestown Foundation, August 15.

Israel Defense Forces. 2023. "Military Service Requirements for Dual Citizens." *IDF Spokesperson's Unit*.

Jacob, Happymon. 2021. "India's Strategic Diaspora." *Carnegie India*, October 28.

Kostakopoulou, Dora. 2004. "The Evolution of German Citizenship Law." *German Law Journal* 5 (9): 1147–1160.

Krogstad, Jens Manuel. 2021. "China's Dual Citizenship Ban and Its Global Implications." *Pew Research Center*, June 30.

Laglagaron, Laura. 2010. "Protection through Integration: The Mexican Government's Efforts to Aid Migrants in the United States." *Migration Policy Institute*, January.

Ministry of Interior, Israel. 2024. *Citizenship and Entry into Israel Law*, 1952 (as amended through 2024).

OECD. 2023. *International Migration Outlook 2023*. Paris: OECD Publishing.

Russian Federation. 2002. *Federal Law on Citizenship*, No. 62-FZ (as amended).

Secretaría de Relaciones Exteriores (Mexico). 1998. *Ley de Nacionalidad* (as amended).

Spiro, Peter J. 2016. *At Home in Two Countries: The Past and Future of Dual Citizenship*. New York: NYU Press.

Statistisches Bundesamt (Germany). 2023. "Naturalization and Immigration Statistics."

Surak, Kristin. 2021. "Who Wants to Buy a Visa? Comparing the Uptake of Residence by Investment Programmes in the European Union." *Journal of Contemporary European Studies* 29 (4): 575–591.

The Hindu. 2023. "India Revokes OCI Cards of 10 People over Security Concerns." July 22.

Transparency International. 2020. *European Getaway: Inside the Murky World of Golden Visas*. London: Transparency International.

UK Home Office. 2022. *Nationality Policy: Dual Nationality Guidance*. London: Home Office.

U.S. Department of State. 2022. *Foreign Affairs Manual, Volume 7: Consular Affairs*. Washington, DC: U.S. Government Publishing Office.

Vink, Maarten P., and Gerard-René de Groot. 2010. "Citizenship Attribution in Western Europe: International Framework and Domestic Trends." *Journal of Ethnic and Migration Studies* 36 (5): 713–734.

Weil, Patrick. 2002. "How to Be French: Nationality in the Making since 1789." *French Politics, Culture & Society* 20 (3): 33–48.

Chapter 4 – The Ethics of Allegiance

Appiah, Kwame Anthony. *The Ethics of Identity*. Princeton: Princeton University Press, 2005.

Benhabib, Seyla. *The Rights of Others: Aliens, Residents, and Citizens*. Cambridge: Cambridge University Press, 2004.

Brookings Institution. *Citizenship and Loyalty in an Era of Strategic Competition*. Policy Brief. Washington, DC: Brookings Institution, November 2023.

Gallup. *Americans' Views on National Loyalty and Civic Obligation*. Gallup Poll Social Series, February 2023.

Locke, John. *Two Treatises of Government*. Edited by Peter Laslett. Cambridge: Cambridge University Press, 1988 [1690].

Pew Research Center. *Views on Dual Citizenship and National Identity*. Pew Global Attitudes Survey, March 2024.

Rawls, John. *A Theory of Justice*. Revised edition. Cambridge, MA: Harvard University Press, 1999.

Rousseau, Jean-Jacques. *The Social Contract*. Translated by Maurice Cranston.

London: Penguin Classics, 2004 [1762].

Sandel, Michael J. *Justice: What's the Right Thing to Do?* New York: Farrar, Straus and Giroux, 2009.

U.S. Department of State. *Foreign Affairs Manual* (7 FAM 1200: Loss and Restoration of U.S. Citizenship). Washington, DC: U.S. Department of State, various editions.

Walzer, Michael. *Spheres of Justice: A Defense of Pluralism and Equality*. New York: Basic Books, 1983.

YouGov and Harvard Center for American Political Studies. *Public Trust and Dual Citizenship in Sensitive Government Roles*. National Opinion Survey, March 2024.

Chapter 5 – The Consequences of Policy Drift

Arendt, Hannah. *The Origins of Totalitarianism*. New York: Harcourt, Brace & World, 1951.

Brubaker, Rogers. *Citizenship and Nationhood in France and Germany*. Cambridge, MA: Harvard University Press, 1992.

Government Accountability Office (GAO). *Personnel Security Clearances: Additional Actions Needed to Ensure Quality, Consistency, and Transparency*. GAO-22-104247. Washington, DC: U.S. Government Accountability Office, 2022.

Mounk, Yascha. *The People vs. Democracy: Why Our Freedom Is in Danger and How to Save It*. Cambridge, MA: Harvard University Press, 2018.

Pew Research Center. *Public Trust in Government and Views of the Nation's Future*. Survey Report. Washington, DC: Pew Research Center, 2022.

Press Briefings and Public Statements Regarding U.S.-Iranian Dual Nationals (2016–2022). U.S. Department of State.

Shachar, Ayelet. *The Birthright Lottery: Citizenship and Global Inequality*. Cambridge, MA: Harvard University Press, 2009.

Spiro, Peter J. *Beyond Citizenship: American Identity After Globalization*. New York: Oxford University Press, 2008.

U.S. Department of State. *Consular Affairs Country-Specific Information: Dual Nationality*. Bureau of Consular Affairs, updated 2023.

U.S. Department of the Treasury. *Foreign Account Tax Compliance Act (FATCA)*. Washington, DC: Internal Revenue Service, 2023.

Walzer, Michael. *Spheres of Justice: A Defense of Pluralism and Equality*. New York: Basic Books, 1983.

Chapter 6 – Citizenship for Sale

Appiah, Kwame Anthony. *The Ethics of Identity*. Princeton: Princeton University Press, 2005.

Benhabib, Seyla. *The Rights of Others: Aliens, Residents, and Citizens*. Cambridge: Cambridge University Press, 2004.

Center for Immigration Studies. *Birth Tourism: Facts and Recommendations*. Backgrounder. Arlington, VA: Center for Immigration Studies, April 2015.

Center for Immigration Studies. *Birth Tourism: The Border Loophole That's Becoming Big Business*. Arlington, VA: Center for Immigration Studies, April 2015.

Department of Homeland Security (DHS), Office of Immigration Statistics. *Estimates of Birth Tourism in the United States*. DHS Annual Report, 2023.

Department of Homeland Security, Office of Immigration Statistics. *Yearbook of Immigration Statistics: 2023*. Washington, DC: U.S. Department of Homeland Security, 2024.

Executive Office of the President. *Executive Order 14160: Protecting the Meaning and Value of American Citizenship*. Issued January 20, 2025. Federal Register, vol. 90, no. 14 (January 23, 2025), pp. 4598–4602.

National Center for Health Statistics. "Births: Final Data for 2022," *National Vital Statistics Reports* 72, no. 1 (January 2024).

Sandel, Michael J. *Justice: What's the Right Thing to Do?* New York: Farrar, Straus and Giroux, 2009.

United States v. Wong Kim Ark, 169 U.S. 649 (1898).

U.S. Department of Justice. "Operators of Southern California Birth-Tourism Ring Charged with Visa Fraud and Money Laundering." Press Release, June 12, 2019.

U.S. Government Accountability Office. *Birth Tourism: Federal Oversight and Legal Ambiguities*, GAO-25-107569. Washington, DC: U.S. Government Accountability Office, May 2023.

U.S. Senate Committee on Homeland Security and Governmental Affairs. *Birth Tourism in the United States*. Staff Report. Washington, DC: U.S. Government Publishing Office, December 20, 2022.

U.S. Supreme Court. *CASA v. Trump*, 602 U.S. (2025). Docket No. 24-1074. Decision issued June 2025.

Chapter 7 – Reclaiming the Civic Contract

American Immigration Council. *Public Perceptions of U.S. Citizenship and Immigration Policy*. Washington, D.C.: AIC Policy Research Series, 2023.

Appiah, Kwame Anthony. *The Ethics of Identity*. Princeton: Princeton University Press, 2005.

Associated Press–NORC Center for Public Affairs Research. *Democratic Values and Public Trust: A National Survey Report*. Chicago: NORC at the University of Chicago, 2023.

Cohen, Elizabeth F. *The Political Value of Time: Citizenship, Duration, and Democratic Justice*. Cambridge University Press, 2018.

Department of Homeland Security (DHS). *Office of Immigration Statistics Annual Report*, 2022–2023.

Galston, William A. *Liberal Pluralism: The Implications of Value Pluralism for Political Theory and Practice*. Cambridge: Cambridge University Press, 2002.

Marshall, T. H. *Citizenship and Social Class*. London: Pluto Press, 1992 (original 1950).

OECD. *International Migration Outlook 2023*. Paris: OECD Publishing, 2023.

Pew Research Center. "Views of National Identity and Citizenship," 2023.

PR Newswire. "New National Poll Finds Strong Support for Civic Education Requirements." July 12, 2023.

Rawls, John. *Political Liberalism*. New York: Columbia University Press, 1993.

Sandel, Michael J. *Justice: What's the Right Thing to Do?* New York: Farrar, Straus and Giroux, 2009.

Shachar, Ayelet. *The Birthright Lottery: Citizenship and Global Inequality*. Cambridge, MA: Harvard University Press, 2009.

Smith, Rogers M. *Civic Ideals: Conflicting Visions of Citizenship in U.S. History*. New Haven: Yale University Press, 1997.

United States Government Accountability Office (GAO). *Visa Fraud and Birth Tourism: Enforcement Trends*. Report GAO-23-148, 2023.

USC Rossier School of Education. *Civic Education and Bipartisan Consensus: The Role of Schools in Building Democratic Citizenship*. Los Angeles: University of Southern California, 2023.

YouGov / Harvard CAPS. "Americans' Attitudes on Dual Citizenship and National Service," March 2024.

Walzer, Michael. *Spheres of Justice: A Defense of Pluralism and Equality*. Basic Books, 1983.

Zolberg, Aristide R. *A Nation by Design: Immigration Policy in the Fashioning of America*. Cambridge, MA: Harvard University Press, 2006.

Chapter 8 – Belonging in the Digital Age

Anderson, Benedict. *Imagined Communities: Reflections on the Origin and Spread of Nationalism.* Revised edition. London: Verso, 2006.

Bauman, Zygmunt. *Liquid Modernity.* Cambridge: Polity Press, 2000.

Benhabib, Seyla. *The Rights of Others: Aliens, Residents, and Citizens.* Cambridge: Cambridge University Press, 2004.

D'Costa, Anthony. "Citizenship, Belonging and Dual Nationality: Normative and Policy Perspectives." *Journal of Global Ethics* 19, no. 1 (2023): 45–63.

Harvard Kennedy School. *Trust in Government: Civic Attitudes and Allegiance in the 21st Century.* Cambridge, MA: Institute of Politics, 2023.

Koslowski, Rey. "Dual Citizenship and American National Identity." In *The Future of Citizenship*, edited by Donald G. Gross and John D. Skrentny, 95–112. Washington, DC: Brookings Institution Press, 2022.

OECD. *Citizenship and the Market: Regulation and Consequences of Citizenship-for-Sale.* Paris: OECD Publishing, 2023.

Pew Research Center. "Views on Dual Citizenship and National Allegiance." March 2024.

Sandel, Michael J. *Justice: What's the Right Thing to Do?* New York: Farrar, Straus and Giroux, 2009.

Sassen, Saskia. *Territory, Authority, Rights: From Medieval to Global Assemblages.* Princeton, NJ: Princeton University Press, 2006.

Srinivasan, Balaji. *The Network State: How to Start a New Country.* Self-published, 2022.

YouGov and Harvard Center for American Political Studies. "Public Trust and Dual Citizenship in Sensitive Government Roles." March 2024.

Index

A
Afroyim v. Rusk– p. 25, 35, 37-38, 51, 57
allegiance
   as civic bond – p. 2, 7, 21-23, 40, 52, 82-83, 138, 142, 151, 166, 185-186
   in elected office – p. 54-55, 125, 147, 186-187, 98–199
   in military service – p. 114-116
   judicial treatment of – p. 33–37
   loss of – p. 24, 26, 32, 36, 38, 73, 118
   moral foundations of – p. 26, 83
   public trust and – p. 43, 95, 99–101
   see also: dual citizenship; civic responsibility
Appiah, Kwame Anthony – p. 82-83, 89, 99, 154
Australia
   dual citizenship enforcement – p. 125
   extradition agreements – p. 105
Austria
   citizenship law – p. 15, 55

B
Barbara v. Trump – p. 132
Benhabib, Seyla – p. 82, 84, 89, 97, 100, 177
birthright citizenship
   constitutional foundation – p. 132-134, 136-140, 143-146, 148-151, 155, 159, 165-166
   Fourteenth Amendment and – p. 17, 35, 131-132, 140-141, 148, 150, 160
   global comparison – p. 199
   judicial limits – p. 39-40
   reform proposals – p. 106, 109, 121-122, 189
   see also: Wong Kim Ark; birth tourism; parental jurisdiction
birth tourism
   case studies – p. 138-140
   industry structure – p. 137
   moral critique of – p. 155
   policy recommendations – p. 190
   statistics on – p. 136
   see also: birthright citizenship; citizenship commodification
Brubaker, Rogers – p. 12, 117

C
Canada
   dual citizenship policies – p. 4, 46, 57, 66, 68, 72, 105, 125, 145-146, 162,

189, 195, 199
  security role restrictions – p. 66, 94, 96, 187, 189
Carnegie, Andrew – p. 19
CASA v. Trump – p. 132
China
  birth tourism from – p. 136
  dual citizenship non-recognition – p. 62-63
  nationality law – p. 62-64, 66
citizenship
  as commodity – p. 21–24
  as legal status vs. civic identity – p. 24–28
  conditional models (international) – p. 58-65, 199
  historical foundations – p. 8–13, 18-21
  policy reform – p. 48, 163-165, 187-192
  see also: allegiance; birthright citizenship; dual citizenship
Citizenship Clause (Fourteenth Amendment) – p. 132, 134, 140, 191
citizenship commodification – see: birth tourism; golden passports
civic contract
  erosion of – p. 76, 155-158
  restoration of – p. 163-165
civic education
  curriculum proposals – p. 102, 127, 160-164, 194-196
  democratic renewal through – p. 160
  naturalization process and – p. 194-198
civic responsibility
  decline of – p. 19, 26, 83, 94, 96, 100, 141, 149, 155, 157, 169
civil service and allegiance – p. 125
commodification of citizenship – see: citizenship; golden passports; investor migration
Constitution Day / Citizenship Day – p. 127
Cuellar, Henry – p. 3, 95, 110
Cyprus
  golden passport program – p. 23, 74-77

D
democratic legitimacy
  and dual allegiance – p. 90-93
  and trust – p. 94-98
digital citizenship
  accountability mechanisms – p. 101, 159, 173, 193-194
  identity in global context – p. 169, 171, 175-176, 178-181
digital identity systems – p. 53, 169, 171, 175-176, 178-181
diplomatic immunity and dual citizens – p. 5, 31-32, 45-47, 83-85, 106-107, 111-112, 188-194
Dred Scott v. Sandford – p. 17, 134

dual allegiance – see: dual citizenship
dual citizenship
   administrative ambiguity – p. 31–33, 70-74
   and elected office – p. 54-55, 125, 147, 186
   and extradition – p. 105-109, 111, 122, 191
   and military service – p. 114-116
   and political influence – p. 116-118
   comparative global models – p. 58–70
   data on – p. 66, 165
   judicial treatment of – p. 33–37
   normalization of – p. 32, 40-44, 125-129
   policy reform – p. 48-50
   see also: allegiance; citizenship; Wong Kim Ark

E
education
   civic renewal through – p. 160
   curricular reform – p. 19, 93, 127
   national cohesion and – p. 15, 21, 27, 49, 52, 82, 90, 93, 144, 146, 147, 155, 157, 162, 166, 172, 174, 184-185, 195,
   see also: civic education; civic responsibility
Einstein, Albert – p. 19
electoral participation
   dual nationals voting abroad – p. 26, 32, 36-37, 55, 96-97, 111-118, 147, 154-155, 160-162
   diaspora lobbying – p. 116
   public perception of loyalty – p. 118, 123, 165, 186, 188
Elena Chen (profile) – p. 138
elite capture of citizenship – p. 23, 69, 75, 134, 137, 139, 168, 172
ethics of allegiance – p. 81–102
European Union
   citizenship policies – p. 68, 75, 169
   investment schemes – p. 23, 74, 76, 169
Expatriation Act of 1868 – p. 2, 15–16, 30, 32, 51
extradition and dual citizens – p. 105-109, 111, 122, 191
exit illusion (David Miller) – p. 90

F
FARA (Foreign Agents Registration Act) – p. 95, 110
FATCA (Foreign Account Tax Compliance Act) – p. 119-121
Federalist Papers – p. 18
financial compliance (dual nationals) – p. 118-121
flag salute / see Pledge of Allegiance
France
   citizenship model – p. 61-62, 66

foreign influence in U.S. politics – p. 8-10, 18, 50, 92-95, 110, 115, 191
foreign military service
    by U.S. dual citizens – p. 117–119, 152
    Israeli case studies – p. 46-47
Fourteenth Amendment
    birthright citizenship and – p. 17, 35, 131-132, 140-141, 145, 148, 150, 164
    historical context – p. 140
    judicial interpretation – p. 140-141

G
GAO (Government Accountability Office)
    on dual citizenship and security clearance – p. 41, 119
    on birth tourism industry – p. 135-136
Germany
    citizenship law evolution – p. 58-59, 66-67, 71, 144, 162
    dual citizenship restrictions – p. 67, 73
golden passports / visas
    Caribbean programs – p. 69, 75, 77, 172
    EU scrutiny – p. 75, 150
    Malta case – p. 23, 69, 75-77, 80
    U.S. investor visa comparison – p. 75–76
    see also: citizenship commodification; investor migration
government service and divided loyalty – p. 25-26, 86, 114-115, 126, 128, 188

H
Hamilton, Alexander – p. 9-10, 18
heritage vs. civic integration – p. 22, 61, 79, 135, 138, 140, 143, 156, 161, 164-166
Hoerig, Claudia – p. 107-108, 157
hostage diplomacy – p. 122
hybrid citizenship models – p. 144-145, 177-178

I
identity and belonging
    moral meaning of – p. 83-85, 90–92, 145
    pluralism and limits of – p. 100-102
immigration
    assimilation and allegiance – p. 19, 21
    dual nationals among – p. 24–27
    policy not the core issue – p. 27
India
    dual citizenship prohibition – p. 59, 62, 66, 73

    OCI card regime – p. 67, 73
integration
    cultural and civic – p. 22-23, 56-61, 66-73,
    conditional in global models – p. 58, 66
Internal Revenue Service (IRS) – p. 43, 120
international comparisons
    dual citizenship – p. 60-65
    birthright law – p. 134
investor migration
    EB-5 and gold card programs – p. 22–23, 68-70, 74-77, 165
    citizenship-by-investment critique – p. 22, 68-70, 74-77
    see also: golden passports

J
Jefferson, Thomas – p. 10
jurisdictional conflicts
    with dual citizens abroad – p. 106, 109, 122
    legal no-man's-land – p. 122
jury service and civic obligation – p. 42, 90, 155-156, 160

L
Law of Return (Israel) – p. 67, 108
legal ambiguity
    around dual citizenship – p. 40-44
    birthright interpretation – p. 132–133
legal reform proposals
    dual allegiance – p. 48
    birthright policy – p. 199
legitimacy, democratic
    erosion through divided allegiance – p. 90-93
    restoring trust – p. 94-98
liberal democracy and loyalty – p. 100, 153–155, 165-166, 186-187
literacy in civic norms – p. 160-163, 194-196

M
Madison, James – p. 9-10, 20
Malta
    citizenship-for-sale case – p. 75
    EU ruling on golden passports – p. 77, 149
mass mobility and legal drift – p. 18-24, 68-69, 134-137, 160-166, 181, 192-196
Menendez, Bob – p. 3, 95, 110
military service
    allegiance through – p. 9, 16-17, 44-47, 54-56, 60, 66, 79, 111-115, 118, 122,

147, 157, 194
  dual citizens in foreign militaries – p. 4, 44, 47
  naturalization tied to – p. 16-17
moral obligations of citizenship – p. 24, 88, 123
Mounk, Yascha – p. 118
multiple passports – see: dual citizenship
mutual obligation
  decline of – p. 19, 26, 83, 94, 96, 100, 141, 149, 155, 157, 169
  foundation of democracy – p. 166

N
Namazi, Siamak – p. 42, 121
Nationality Act of 1940 – p. 32, 35
naturalization
  as civic transformation – p. 11-13
  oath of allegiance – p. 12
  process reform – p. 12-13
network states – p. 3, 178
non-resident citizens – p. 93, 150,169

O
oath of allegiance
  historic meaning – p. 12, 20, 26
  modern dilution of – p. 124, 160, 163-165, 196-199
  proposed reforms – p. 160
obligations of citizenship
  in law and culture – p. 82, 118, 123
  dual citizen evasion of – p. 72, 76, 108, 157, 193

P
Pacificus No. 1 (Hamilton) – p. 9
parental jurisdiction
  alternative to birthright – p. 192
  reform proposal – p. 106, 109, 121-122, 189
perception of divided loyalty – p. 8-9, 15, 25, 31, 34, 37, 51, 63, 67, 86, 114, 118, 126, 128, 147, 188
permanent residency and citizenship – p. 22, 139, 144, 150, 162, 192
Pew Research Center – p. 85, 123, 179-180, 187
Pledge of Allegiance – p. 20
pluralism
  and democratic stability – p. 13, 19, 52, 83-85, 93, 100-103, 125, 128, 154, 165, 185-186
policy drift
  bureaucratic – p., 37-40

judicial – p. 33–36
consequences of – p. 40-44, 111-128
political influence (foreign)
dual nationals and – p. 3, 116-118
political participation (dual citizens) – p. 118, 146-147
public education (civic) – p. 19-20, 102, 127, 160-164, 194, 196
public office
dual citizens in – p. 3, 39, 47, 55-56, 124, 189
disclosure requirements – p. 78, 101

R
Rawls, John – p. 82, 88
reciprocity in citizenship – p. 84, 88, 100, 143, 150, 155, 157-158, 173
reform proposals
birthright citizenship – p. 148-152, 192
dual allegiance – p. 49
naturalization process – p. 196-199
tiered legislative solutions – p. 163-165
Renunciation of citizenship
formal process – p. 124, 126, 159, 187-192, 196, 199
proposed in high-trust roles – p. 199
republican civic identity – p. 3, 9, 43, 61, 145, 195
responsibility, civic – see: obligations of citizenship
Rousseau, Jean-Jacques – p. 10, 82, 86–87

S
Sandel, Michael J. – p. 82-83, 99, 142
Scheer, Andrew – p. 46
security clearance
dual nationals and – p. 41, 48, 59, 78, 94-110, 115, 147, 188, 191-192, 194
clearance denials – p. 59
shared obligation – see: mutual obligation
Shachar, Ayelet – p. 154-155
Silicon Valley
network states and belonging – p. 3, 178
Singapore
citizenship restrictions – p. 55, 66, 68, 72
sovereignty
citizenship and – p. 12, 15, 40, 42, 44-45, 54, 58, 61, 63, 105, 121, 123-124, 143, 167, 171-172, 174, 179
jurisdictional conflicts – p. 106, 109, 121-122
statutory silence – p. 37-40, 51
suspicion of immigrants – p. 7, 10, 12, 14, 16, 18-20, 26-27, 151, 161, 163

T
taxation (dual citizens) – p. 118-121
  compliance burden – p. 118-121
  citizenship-based taxation – p. 119
trust, democratic
  fragility of – p. 94-98
  allegiance and – p. 85, 88, 94, 96, 98, 118, 155
Trump, Donald
  birthright EO (Executive Order 14160) – p. 131-132, 148
  gold card visa proposal – p. 3, 22
Turkey
  birth tourism from – p. 23, 75, 117, 136, 180
  dual nationals voting in – p. 96, 116-117, 180

U
United Kingdom
  dual citizenship policy – p. 56, 58, 61-62, 66, 105, 145
  security roles and limits – p. 66
United States v. Wong Kim Ark – p. 133-134, 140, 145, 148
U.S. Constitution
  Fourteenth Amendment – p. 17, 35, 131-132, 140-141, 145, 148, 150, 164
  foundational expectations – p. 9, 14-20, 27, 39, 43, 54, 77, 95, 127, 134, 145, 164, 195

V
Vance v. Terrazas – p. 25, 36-38, 51
voting
  by dual citizens – p. 26, 32, 36-37, 55, 90, 93, 96-97, 11-118, 147, 154-155, 160-162, 191, 194
  foreign elections – p. 4, 32-33, 37-38, 88, 93, 97
  reform context – p. 38, 48-49, 51, 126, 149-153, 157-158, 160, 163-166, 184-187, 192, 199
vulnerability of allegiance – p. 65, 91, 99, 108

W
Walzer, Michael – p. 82, 88, 114, 154
Weil, Patrick – p. no match found
Wong Kim Ark, United States v. – p. 133-134, 140, 145, 148
World Wars and naturalization – p. 20, 25, 32

About the Author

Sebastian Saviano is a writer and independent scholar whose work explores American identity, cultural tradition, and the shifting nature of power. He is the author of America's Cigar Story and Smoke & Oak, which trace how cigars and bourbon shaped American ritual, class, and craftsmanship.

With The Allegiance Paradox, his third book, Saviano turns to the meaning of citizenship itself. Drawing on legal theory, moral philosophy, and historical precedent, it is the opening volume of The Collapse of Trust series—a four-part study of how public belief in institutions unravels, and how it might be restored.

Saviano pursued post-graduate training in political science at Georgetown University, concentrating on international relations, political theory, and the philosophy of social science. That foundation continues to shape his work, which combines rigorous theoretical inquiry with a cross-disciplinary style accessible to both academic and general readers.

Also in *The Collapse of Trust* series:

Book Two – *Legitimate Distrust*
Why Conspiracy Theories Grow When Institutions Fail

Book Three – *The Theater of Trust*
The Performance of Legitimacy in a World of Institutional Doubt

Book Four – *Overruling Common Sense*
How Rules, Code, and Institutions Are Replacing Human Judgment

To explore the full series, visit:

www.SebastianSaviano.com

www.ingramcontent.com/pod-product-compliance
Lightning Source LLC
Chambersburg PA
CBHW052127030426
42337CB00028B/5063